GW01281313

TRANSPORT IN TRANSITION

Transport in Transition

Aspects of British and European experience

Edited by
JAMES McCONVILLE
JOHN SHELDRAKE

Avebury

Aldershot · Brookfield USA · Hong Kong · Singapore · Sydney

© James McConville and John Sheldrake 1995

All rights reserved. No part of this publication may be reproduced, stored in a retrieval system, or transmitted in any form or by any means, electronic, mechanical, photocopying, recording or otherwise without the prior permission of the publisher.

Published by
Avebury
Ashgate Publishing Limited
Gower House
Croft Road
Aldershot
Hants GU11 3HR
England

Ashgate Publishing Company
Old Post Road
Brookfield
Vermont 05036
USA

British Library Cataloguing in Publication Data

Transport in Transition: Aspects of
British and European Experience
I. McConville, James II. Sheldrake, John
388.094

ISBN 1 85628 664 9

Library of Congress Catalog Card Number: 94-73136

Printed and bound by Athenæum Press Ltd.,
Gateshead, Tyne & Wear.

Contents

The contributors vii

Acknowledgments viii

1 Introduction 1
  James McConville

2 Collectivism and UK transport: the challenge 11
  of liberalization
  John Sheldrake

3 The context of choice and competition in transport: 24
  an overview of privatization in Western Europe
  Paul Webb

4 Travel and the assertive consumer 40
  Stephen Shaw

5 Local government and road passenger transport 60
  Kevin Hey

6 Planning in an unplanned environment: the Transport 77
  Act 1985 and municipal bus operators
  Alan Whitehead

7	Urban transport: recent European experience *Martin Higginson*	96
8	Problems of market mechanisms in the development of EU combined transport networks *Mike Garratt*	130
9	The development of road freight distribution depots *Frank Worsford*	140
10	Ownership and productive efficiency: the experience of British ports *Zinan Liu*	163
	Index	183

The contributors

Mike Garratt is a Partner in MDS Transmodal, shipping and freight transport consultants.

Kevin Hey is Senior Lecturer in the Department of Business studies, University College, Salford.

Dr. Martin Higginson is Economic Adviser to the Confederation of Passenger Transport UK.

Dr. Zinan Liu is Lecturer in the Department of Economics, London Guildhall University.

Dr. James McConville is London School of Foreign Trade Professor and Director of the Centre for International Transport at London Guildhall University.

Stephen Shaw is Senior Lecturer in Transport and Tourism in the Business School at the University of North London.

Dr. John Sheldrake is Reader in Modern History in the Department of Politics and Modern History at London Guildhall University.

Dr. Paul Webb is Lecturer in the Department of Politics at Brunel University.

Dr. Alan Whitehead is Professor of Public Policy at Southampton Institute at Higher Education.

Frank Worsford is Senior Research Fellow in the Transport Studies Group at the University of Westminster.

Acknowledgments

The Editors would like to thank Pat Mullarkey of London Guildhall University and Gloria Phyall of the LSFT Secretariat at the Institute of Chartered Shipbrokers for their help in the production of this book.

J.McC. and J.S.
Moorgate and Whitechapel,
September 1994

1 Introduction
James McConville

Introduction

The last two decades have witnessed the widespread deconstruction of state regulation and intervention within the UK and Europe. Even where state intervention has been retained its purpose has largely been to encourage competition rather than for reasons of social/economic welfare. At the same time there has been increasing public acceptance of the central role which transport plays in socio-economic development and cost effective commercial management. On the one hand this has resulted in calls for greater privatization and on the other stressed the importance of an integrated transport system. Consideration of these two phenomena and their interaction formed the basis of a colloquium, *Choice and Competition in National and International Transport*, held at London Guildhall University in 1993. This volume is a distillation of the papers given at that colloquium and the discussion which took place. Chapters 1 to 3 are concerned with the changing political attitudes and environment surrounding state intervention against which the developments in transport must be viewed. The remaining chapters examine various transport modes and sections of the transport infrastructure to assess the extent to which the changing political environment has impacted upon them.

While transport has always had a significant political profile the growing recognition of its socio/economic importance in recent years has raised it to a matter of passionate private and public concern. In the small, affluent, densely populated countries of Northern Europe, and in particular the UK, social and economic prosperity is perceived to be dependent on the movement of ever increasing amounts of freight and passengers, over longer and longer distances. Within this perception is an acceptance of a dynamic element inherent in the whole spectrum of transport technology bringing rapid disturbances and occasionally violent changes; a perception combined with the high value placed on the social presumption of personal mobility, a presumption inconceivable to poorer and earlier societies. Thus both society and its individual members spend larger and larger amounts of their economic resources on transport while simultaneously becoming more exercised by the social and environmental impact of such resource allocation. Transport is a pre-eminent industrial sector in all advanced economies. In the industrial rich countries; i.e. members of the Organization for Economic Co-operation and Development (OECD), consumer expenditure on transport represents between 4-9% of gross national product. It accounts for approximately 17% of the UK's total consumer expenditure, and some 2-5% of employment. An industry of this magnitude will be involved in a constant process of modification and change. In recent years these developments, both in organization and technology, have been fundamental and rapid, particularly in the UK and Northern Europe.

A late 19th century economist observed that "The dominant economic fact of our own age is the development not of manufacturing but of the transport industries. It is these which are growing most rapidly in aggregate volume and in individual power, and which are giving rise to most anxious questions as to the tendencies of large capitals to turn the forces of economic freedom to the destruction of that freedom" (Marshall, 1889, p.331). In many respects this statement could have been made in the 1990s, the only difference being the greater general public awareness of, and need for, transport which exists now as compared to a hundred years ago. Furthermore, transport now embodies a much more diverse variety of modes than could have been envisaged by even the most informed individual at the end of the 19th century.

Transport is not a single entity, it is a complex of associated industries each satisfying different demands within different market structures and performing different transport functions. When analysing the elements in transport policy it is important to take note of the variety of situations each policy is designed to regulate or influence.

The economic features of the transport sector have an important influence upon the parameters of government policy. Broadly, this has created a situation where demand is virtually ignored and there is an almost total concern with the supply of transport. The most obvious reason for this is that there are no substitutes for transport and its tendency towards "natural" monopoly. However, within supply, governments concentrate much more on the infrastructure than the mobile unit. The transport infrastructure is an extremely expensive, long-lasting and specific asset, which has no alternative use but which enjoys economies of scale. Such characteristics mean that investment is out of the question except for extremely large conglomerates and the state. The latter, therefore, has always invested heavily in transport infrastructure. In addition the state is concerned with transport's contribution to economic efficiency and its strategic importance. This massive specific capital investment can be juxtaposed with the comparatively inexpensive mobile unit. With few exceptions vehicles are cheap, flexible, have short life spans and can only enjoy very limited economies of scale. Such limited capital requirements encourage medium and small sized companies and individual entrepreneurs to participate heavily in the transport sector - road haulage being the prime example. State interest here is primarily directed at regulation to secure revenue as a means of contributing to the infrastructure and for wider purposes. It also secures certain standards of safety. The economic and operational structure of the industry therefore means the state becomes deeply enmeshed in the infrastructure component at all levels, and yet it takes only a comparatively limited interest in the actual unit of production. Such a generalised argument does not ignore the relative ease of substitution of public for private ownership within the industry as well as particular modes.

As an advanced economy's income rises, the share of consumption expenditure devoted to purchasing and operating cars grows disproportionately, a movement to which government responds by investing ever increasing amounts in the road infrastructure. The massive expansion in the road network throughout the period since the Second World War in the U.K. can be illustrated from two points of view. Firstly, freight movement. There was an increase in freight between 1952 and 1991 of approximately 250% in terms of billion ton kilometres. The central feature was the replacement of rail by road; with rail comprising 42% of movement in 1952 and no more than 7% by 1991. Pipelines have also increased in importance; a form of transport in direct competition with railways, with its commitment to bulk commodities over long distances. Secondly, while the impact of freight movement on road usage has been profound, it pales when compared with that of cars; a situation highlighted by the triumphant statement of Margaret Thatcher that the UK had attained the position of being a "great car economy", referring presumably not only to the importance of car production within the economy but also to the level of car ownership. An earlier comment of more perception was made by Sir Geoffrey Crowther in the Preface to the *Buchanan Report*. We are nourishing a monster of great potential distructiveness. And yet we love him dearly. Regarded as "the traffic problem", the motor car is clearly a menace that could spoil our civilization, but translated into terms of the particular vehicle, it stands outside our door, regarded as one of our most treasured possessions, or dearest ambition, an immense convenience, and expander of the dimensions of life, a symbol of the modern age. The extent of the impact of this symbol of the modern age is indicated by the expansion in passenger movement between 1951 and 1961 of approximately 250%, in terms of billion passenger kilometers. The car and van, in percentage terms, have increased 300% to become the most prominant modes.

The rise of the private individual form of road transport can be seen against the decline and the use of publicly provided transport. Railways and road passenger transport provided 60% of passenger kilometers in 1951. This has declined in percentage terms to a mere 12% of the total. In the late 1950's and during the 1960's only one third of households could claim regular car usage. There was a sharp increase in this during the 1960's and there was a strong increase, decade on decade, to create a position by 1991 where only one third of households were without any regular car use. In fact, by 1991, 25% of households had the use of two or more cars, a percentage which can be compared with the early 1960's of 2%. Bus services have since their peak in the late 1950's steadily declined, and in an attempt to halt this there has been the introduction of one-person operated bus services, park and ride, expresses and limited stop buses. All of little avail, particularly in rural and suburban areas where there has often been partial or total withdrawl of such services.

The most important organizational fact about transport is not merely its enormous size and scale, but its social visibility. It is a social and economic activity which essentially takes place within the wider environment and impacts upon it. "Transport is an engineering industry carried on, not privately within the walls of a factory, but in public places where people are living, working, shopping and going about their daily business. The noise, smell, danger and other unplesant features of large, fast-moving machinery are brought close to people, with potentially devastating consequences for the human environment" (Thomson, 1974, p46).

Consciousness of the impact of transport on the environment has been present since the establishment of railways in the UK but with the emergence of the private car such concerns have increased. The car turned personal transport from an extremely scarce commodity into one that exists in abundance bringing with it a similar abundance of pollution and congestion creating costs for the wider society. Costs not reflected in the market price of the individual consumer's transport but ones that are born by the community at large. Such externalities have, it has been argued, ensured the state's increased involvement in transport's activities. In addition it has made transport an industry of which the general public are more politically aware than any other. The problem is that transport policy has to cope both with different modes which function in discrete markets and the interaction of modes and markets. Policies may be mode specific, integrated or a combination of the two. The principal policy approaches can be generalised down to three distinct perspectives, or perhaps at their extremities, ideologies. The first is to intervene directly in the industry, with some mixture of public ownership and planning. At one extreme of this policy continuum there is complete state control. However, in the present context it refers to some interventory mix, dealing with both industry development and what has been termed the "natural" monopolies which are a central element of the transport industry. This policy is achieved by instructing companies to act in ways which are consistent with some overall plan for the industry and perhaps the whole economy. There is usually some continuing discussion on the substance of these instructions to relate them to the dynamic of the industry. This is evidenced in the set of criteria for nationalized transport industries and the regulatory system influencing and monitoring their progress and operation.

The second approach is to see each policy problem as an individual one, a modification of intervention; what can be termed a piecemeal approach or perspective. Here an analysis of welfare gains and losses of each individual situation is attempted to prioritise the activities or outcomes aiming at maximising welfare goals. Such policies are pragmatic, having at their core a cost benefit analysis, which is particularly prevalent in the consideration procedures of transport infrastructure investment.

The final approach is that of laissez-faire; the principle of non-intervention of the state into economic affairs, in particular the determination of price. Here the individual is encouraged to pursue self interest, untrammelled by government restraint. This would be the opposite extreme on the policy continuum from that of complete state control. Out of this classical stance has grown a neo-classical Austrian school of economics which lays stress on the concept of marginal utility to promote a competitive market with the dominant element in the analysis being the wants of the individual and market freedom. This school of thought can be split into two wings. Firstly, the liberal wing, which sees the market mechanism as dispenser of all virtues and resource allocation and the state as made up of inefficent bureaucracies serving to corrupt the market premise. Obviously this is closely akin to a laissez-faire position. Secondly, what can be termed the neo-conservative position which, rather than perceiving the state as a corrupting influence, sees it as a structure that can be used to achieve some wider agenda than simply confirming the market mechanism. Thus, it can be manipulated to remove all collective tendencies within the economy and once this is achieved, it can serve to secure an authoritarian government. Often, however, this becomes the primary aim, subsuming other market aims to some degree. There is of course often considerable tension, if not disagreement, between the two methods or aims of these wings of the same central ideology.

These three ideologies, or approaches or perspectives take up different positions in a spectrum of policies, the latter for obvious reasons being located on the extreme right. The inital one is on the extreme left, with its state ownership and control. The piecemeal pragmatic approach is in the central position. To oversimplify the model put forward, the situation is one where economic efficiency and public welfare can be satisfied either by some form of regulation or control, or by some element of market mechanism.

The latter solution overcomes the criticism that controls and protects large units with "natural" monopoly power such as the nationalized transport utilities from the discipline of the market. The remedy is said to lie in the creation of a structure which makes such transport entities open to the threat of potential competitive entry. This is the central tenet of the theory of contestable or perfectly contestable markets which are constructed on the assumptions of no barrier to entry or exit, no sunk costs and technological transferability. This market structure means that competitive entry would occur during periods of excess profitability and once such surpluses were competed away firms would exit, at no cost, to other more fruitful areas. An analysis which means that companies will be unable to make any form of monopoly profit. It also changes the emphasis away from the number of firms and other factors to barriers to entry and exit. An example of the influence of contestable market theory on transport policy may be illustrated by the recent legislation affecting airlines in the United States and the European Commission's recommendation regarding liner shipping in the European Union.

> Any analysis of the costs and benefits of deregulation must take into account these factors: the market for transportation services is not perfectly competitive; economies of scale and scope do exist; economic barriers to new entry in several of the modes are significant; oligopolies and monopolies have resulted; and the theory of contestable markets has not been sustained by the empirical evidence. (Dempsey, 1989, pp 252-3).

A socio-political model has been formulated for the transport industry which predicts a three stage metamorphosis of privatization, perhaps the ultimate freedom from control and deregulation.[1] The duration of these changes being influenced by the levels of underlying economic activity. The initial phase covers the expectation and formulative period. New innovative firms enter the industry or sector creating service and price competition. Established companies reorganize, invest and expand their operations. To cut costs, labour is shed, causing an increase in productivity. Usually these are below the levels forecasted. There is a movement towards concentrating on primary, high capacity routes for both freight and passenger services. The second phase is one of stable or decreasing prices. Increased service concentration on primary routes with price differentiation on the lesser routes. There is also an overall increase in usage, regular bus services in the UK being an exception to this. Despite this increase, both established and new firms invariably find the enthusiam of the initial period has left them with substantial over-capacity. This, and rising costs, means the life of capital equipment is extended and there is a lack of new capital investment, innovative or otherwise. A number of firms find themselves in increasing difficulty. Circumstances which change their central function from one of supplying a service or product to one of devising an overriding strategy for survival.

The third phase is the crucial one in the whole process, that of eliminating the firms that lack a substantial capital base, not necessarily the uncompetitive firms. This is a period of survival, for companies seriously weakened in the second phase. These companies begin to fail, bankruptcies increase, as do takeovers, amalgamations and other forms of transference of control. Out of such turmoil emerge monopolies, oiligopolies or other collusive forms of market structure. The services begin to increase in price and decline in quantity. There is, by this time, an almost total concentration on primary routes. Any remaining small competitors are confronted by predatory pricing and general anti-competitive practices. At such times, any regulatory institutions established often with limited powers to ensure "fair play" become active. In the UK the Office of Fair Trading, for example, finds itself acutely embarrassed in such circumstances and attempts some limited action in the short term to alleviate such practices. This does little to inhibit the underlying trend towards industrial concentration.

The above generalised model was in some cases in the UK avoided, as there was a simple process of the transference of public into private monopoly. This was done with minimal gestures towards competition but substantial contributions to the public purse.

To examine in more detail the extremely long legacy of state intervention and regulation in the transport industry in the UK. In modern times its central aim was to modify and control railways, initially to ensure safety standards, particularly in relation to passengers. This was quickly followed by intervention focussing on the potential exploitative monopoly powers possessed by the railways. State apprehension of this latent power remained long after its potential had vanished, and this anxiety had a strong influence in legislation enacted during the inter-war period to control and regulate the supply of passenger transport and haulage on roads.

While it can be argued that for a considerable period following the Second World War UK governments held broadly to a consensus policy on the main issues, such a proposition does not hold in relation to transport. As Savage pointed out as early as 1959 "Changes in political complexion of successive governments were far from being incidental matters in the post war history of British transport. Deep differences in political and economic philosophy between the two main parties profoundly influenced the organisation and successive re-organisation of transport in the two post-war decades" (Savage, 1959, p176). During this period the philosophical core of the differences lay in the attitudes to private and public ownership, characterised by the two main political parties. All governments aspire to the productive sector of the economy being "efficient" however defined. So far as transport is concerned there was an emphasis on modifying structures on reorganization while there were claims of policies of surgery without diagnosis. The policy of the two parties during this period can be described briefly. The Labour Government after 1945 attempted to a lesser or greater degree to construct a transport system with integration as its central aim as a method of modifying the scale and frequency of market failures within the industry.

This integrated approach can be seen as one constructed on a combination of private, public or state enterprise. Here there is a direct interventon in the market. The central part of this policy was the nationalized sector of the industry which was heavily state regulated. The private sector was seen as playing a minor role interacting with these large "natural"' monopolies. The Conservatives after 1951 concentrated on "competition" as a method of achieving some form of co-ordination. In this the underlying aim was dropped as facilitating the operation of a price mechanism became predominant. The philosophy justification for this form is, as has already been argued, in the Austrian economic school as highlighted by Margaret Thatcher's famous comment "there is no such thing as society; there are individual men and women and their families" (Bell and Cloke, 1990, p7). This comment is of major significance because it demonstrates the extent to which the acceptance across all political divides of the concept of "society" had been fundamentally challenged. Encouragement of the "communal spirit" had been essential to achieving social and economic recovery in the post-war years. The economic security of the 1960s and the hedonistic individualism to which it gave rise in both the United States and Europe undermined the idea that the state was an ally posessing the capability to secure and retain increasing levels of social and economic welfare.

At the same time governments were coming to recognise that the involvement of the state was likely to grow rather than diminish if the accepted expectations of the welfare state were to be met. A situation which was becoming less politically and economically viable in a mixed democratic economy. It was perhaps fortunate for the politicians that the need to "distance the state" coincided with a growth in individualism. The state was seen as having a detrimental role in the development of society and its attempts to meet the insatiable appetite of the "generated wants" of the consumer society of the 1970s were greeted with cynicism. This enabled goverments to distance themselves from anything that could be seen as strategic planning on either a short or long run basis. Since it was here that mistakes could be easily identified and blame placed firmly on the government.

The first indication of this new policy came with the Conservative Government of 1970-1974. There was a low key approach with some minor de-nationalizations and a stricter approach to public sector deficits. A trend continued by the Labour Government of the late 1970s when, under conditions set by the International Monetary Fund, it began gradually to retreat from previous policy assumptions. The sacrosanct aim of full employment was quietly dropped and spending on welfare curtailed. Not surprisingly the Conservative Government's return to power did little to radically change this trend. However, its election in 1979 and re-election in 1983, did not actively place privatization or deregulation on the political agenda. In the early 1980s it was almost totally preoccupied with monetarism as a solution to inflation, in particular the strict control of money supply. During the mid-1980s privatization gradually emerged as part of the government's underlying belief that the private sector should be encouraged to play a larger role in the creation of national wealth.

Privatization is underpinned by a presumption of ownership being of fundamental importance and private ownership having the unique ability to create economic and social efficiency. It is interesting to note that members of the public were still encouraged to be owners in privatization launches, but as individual shareholders and not as a communal group as previously.

Privatization has no simple definition, it has a multiplicity of forms and objectives which can be distilled into three basic categories. Firstly, it can be defined, most narrowly, as the sale of publicly owned assets, mainly public utilities, to private firms; the transfer of public enterprise to the private sector, often termed de-nationalization. Secondly, there is deregulation or liberalization. This does not necessarily involve any change in the ownership structure, it simply means the removal or modification of restrictions on the provision or production of certain goods or service. Such modifications usually include relaxation of controls over entry and exit to any industry or sector. Thirdly, privatizing may merely be the contracting out or franchising of the provision of certain goods or services to public bodies by private companies. This function having been undertaken previously by the public bodies themselves. The scale of public asset sales can, perhaps, be used as a gauge of the level of active privatization. It rose rapidly to a peak of £7.5bn in 1988/89 since when it has declined steadily, public assets are, after all, a finite commodity.

Throughout the short history of privatization, initially developed in the

United States and latterly in the UK and Europe, it has undergone numerous changes in both its form and objectives. In the case of the UK it has been argued that

> the fact that a policy has a variety of objectives, and that these may at times conflict, is not in itself a criticism of that policy. But the reality behind the apparent multiplicity of objectives is not that the policy has a rather sophisticated rationale, but rather that it is lacking any clear analysis of purpose or effects; and hence any objective which seems achievable is seized as justification. The outcome is that no objectives are effectively attained, and in particular that economic efficiency - which is at once the most important of these and the most difficult to attain - has systematically been subordinated to other goals. (Kay and Thompson, 1986, p19).

Over recent years two distinct trends have emerged which create a dichotomy in policy making. In political terms there has been increasing pressure for deregulation and privatization. Meanwhile public concern with social and economic welfare, particularly in the context of the environment, has created a need for greater rather than lesser control. Both these trends have, within Europe, heightened the involvement of the state and supra-state in the transport industry. This collection of essays attempts to address these issues both generally and in respect of specific modes.

Note
1.   This discussion is based on Dempsey op.cit. pp36-8.

References

Bell, P. & Cloke, P. (1990), *Deregulation and Transport: Market Forces in the Modern World,* David Fulton Publications, London.
Dempsey, P. (1989), *The Social and Economic Consequences of Deregulation,* Quorum Books, New York.
Kay, J. & Thompson, D. (1986), "Privatization: A Policy in Search of a 'Rationale", Economic Journal, Vol. 96.
Marshall, A. (1892), *Economics of Industry,* Macmillan, London.
Ministry of Transport (1963), *Traffic in Towns,* HMSO London, (known as the Buchanan Report).
Savage, C. (1959), *An Economic History of Transport,* Hodgison Press, London.
Thomson,J. (1974), *Modern Transport Economics,* Penguin, Harmondsworth.

2 Collectivism and UK transport: The challenge of liberalization

John Sheldrake

Introduction

Since about 1800 the dialectic between the libertarian and collectivist tendencies has assumed the aspect of a diverse but growing dominance of the latter in all areas of political activity (Greenleaf, 1983, pp.28-9).

So claimed W. H. Greenleaf in the first volume of his monumental study of the British political tradition published in 1983. Self-evidently, it would be difficult (if not impossible) for anyone writing about British politics in 1994 to make a similar claim. The central element in the collectivist project (namely the state) has seemingly entered a period of retreat that shows no immediate sign of abating. This is not, of course, to imply that the state has become less dominant within the British polity. On the contrary, in many ways the reverse is true; the reduced strength of the trade unions and the declining status of local government being just two areas where the state (in the form of central government) has substantially limited the possibility of challenge in the years since 1979. Nevertheless, more than a decade of privatization, deregulation, contractualization - and, in a word, "liberalization" - have all served to constrain the boundaries of state activity and to redefine the parameters of the state's perceived responsibilities. Paradoxically (but not perhaps surprisingly) part of the Thatcher "revolution" was the use of governmental or state power to bring about a reduction of the state's role. Thus, bit by bit, legislation was passed with the intention of correcting (at least in the government's view) the collectivist tendency which had developed incrementally in British politics over the previous century. Central to this was the desire to refute the collectivist view which depicted the state as the key or (in some spheres) the only supplier of goods and services and the single employer of labour. The full extent and limits of the experiment are not yet known and the long term outcome of what has so far been achieved (however this is measured) remains to be seen. These are of course issues which will be considered, at least with regard to transport, in the chapters that follow. One thing that can be stated with considerable certainty, however, is that the changes of the Thatcher years have substantially eroded the notion that undiluted collectivism offers an ideology relevant to the present situation in Britain or indeed Europe. Of course, collapse of Europe's single major experiment in collectivism (viz. the Soviet Union) severely damaged the notion that collectivism had history on its side. Instead, a reassertion of liberal ideas including the benefit of market forces, the long term futility of protectionism and the utility of private enterprise over state ownership have been claimed as the ideology of the moment. None of this is to suggest that collectivism is dead or that libertarian values are wholly prevalent. What is certain, however, is that a decisive change of ideological mood has occurred, the climate of ideas shifted, and policy now being made using a different set of prescriptions than would have been deployed during the years of collectivist certainty. The remainder of this chapter will trace the long rise and rapid decline of collectivism in the British case and identify some of the outcomes of this process for transport policy.

The rise of collectivism

> Laissez faire was the ideal, state intervention the pragmatic reality (Brown, 1991, p.493).

This is Richard Brown's verdict on the state as it emerged in Britain during the nineteenth century up to 1850. Briefly, policy was driven by contradictory impulses. The desire on the part of radicals to strip away what they saw as the privileges of Old Corruption was constrained to run in tandem with the pressing need to respond to the problems of population growth, rapid urbanization, industrialization, destitution, immigration and the growing risks of epidemic disease. By the time the Corn Laws were finally repealed in 1846 a new "administrative" state was already emerging as an active force both as regulator and provider. In any case even Adam Smith himself, who in his purely economic analysis allocated a distinctly minimal role to the state, nevertheless considered that it should provide such public works as might be required to facilitate economic activity. Although believing that in providing public services the state should, as far as possible, attempt to stimulate market conditions, Smith conceded, in a much quoted passage from *The Wealth of Nations,* that such items as roads, bridges, canals and harbours were of such a nature, that the profit could never repay the expense to any individual or small number of individuals, and . . . it therefore cannot be expected that any individual or small number of individuals should erect or maintain (them) (quoted by Skinner, 1986, p.78). Of course, the eighteenth century response to this problem was divided between the joint stock company and the establishment of special statutory bodies such as turnpike trusts and improvement commissioners to supplement the activities of the historic parishes. After the passing of the Municipal Corporations Act 1835, however, responsibility began to be taken by the emerging local authorities, although ad hoc bodies continued to be established and operate throughout the nineteenth century and beyond (Byrne, 1990, pp.10-12).

In specific terms the urban local authorities, particularly the great cities of northern England began, from the 1840s onwards, to obtain private acts of parliament which gave them the necessary powers to purchase, construct and operate gas and water works. These powers were subsequently extended by central government and later complemented by legislation enabling the major authorities to construct (but not operate) tramways and also to provide the closely associated service of electricity supply (Sheldrake, 1989). Of course, the initial stimulus for the extension of local government's powers stemmed from concern about public health. It is estimated that infectious diseases accounted for over 30 per cent of deaths in the period 1835-75 and for a much higher percentage of infant, child and maternal mortality during the same years. Edwin Chadwick's *Sanitary Report* of 1842 condemned private enterprise water supply observing that out of the 50 largest towns scrutinized only six had supplies that could be deemed good, whereas over 30 were "so deficient as to be pronounced bad" (Waller, 1991, p.301). The numerous demands for improvements in urban sanitation coalesced into the public health movement of the 1840s and '50s. A pressure group for the improvement of public health arrangements, the Health of Towns Association, was established to campaign for legislation; cutting across political boundaries it has been described by McDonagh as "the first clear movement towards collectivist action on the part of the middle class" (McDonagh, 1977, p.143). However, having said all this, there was no official awareness that the modest expansion of central and local government activities was set on a collectivist, let alone socialist course. Perhaps informed opinion in the mid century was best summed up by John Stuart Mill when he stated in his *Principles of Political Economy* that "laissez faire. . . should be the general practice, every departure from it, unless required by some great good, is a certain evil" (Mill, 1985 edition, p.314). Mill's thinking subsequently developed (partly due to the promptings of his partner, Harriet Taylor) in a socialist direction which influenced the theorizing of the Fabians later in the century. Quite what Mill meant when he designated himself a socialist is a matter for debate and need not detain us here. More important for the present case, is the fact that he was from an early stage willing to compromise his laissez faire principles where issues relating to the public utilities and transport were concerned. As he put it, rather long-windedly perhaps, "There are many cases in which the agency by which a service is performed, is certain to be virtually single; in which a practical monopoly, with all the power it confers of taxing the community, cannot be prevented from existing. I have already more than once adverted to the case of gas and water companies, among which, though perfect freedom is allowed for competition, none really takes place, and practically they are found to be more irresponsible and unapproachable by individual complaints, than the government . . . In the case of these particular services, the reasons proponderate in favour of their being performed, like the paving and cleansing of the streets, not certainly by the general government of the state, but by the municipal authorities of the town, and the expense defrayed, as even now it in fact is, by a local rate. But in the many analagous cases which it is best to resign to voluntary agency, the community needs some other security for the fit performance of the service than the interest of the managers; and it is the part of the government, either to subject the business to reasonable conditions for the general advantage, or to retain such power over it, that the profits of the monopoly may at least be obtained for the public. This applies in the case of a road, a canal, or a railway. These are always, in a great degree, practical monopolies; and a government which concedes such monopoly unreservedly to a private company, does much the same thing as if it allowed an individual or an association to levy any tax they chose for their own benefit . . . The state should either reserve to itself a reversionary property in such public works, or should retain, and freely exercise, the right of fixing a maximum of fares and charges, and, from time to time, varying that maximum. It is perhaps necessary to remark, that the state may be the proprietor of canals or railways without itself working them; and that they will almost always be better worked by means of a company, renting the railway or canal for a limited period from the state" (Mill, 1985 edition, pp.327-8).

The rhetoric of "Radical Joe" Chamberlain is in stark contrast to Mill's characteristic circumspection. Self-made millionaire, mayor of Birmingham, president of the Board of Trade in Gladstone's second cabinet, president of the Local Government Board in Gladstone's third cabinet and, after splitting the Liberal Party over Irish home rule, Colonial Secretary in the governments of Salisbury and Balfour, Chamberlain was a political heavyweight. While mayor of Birmingham during the 1870s he presided over a municipal programme which enabled the council to take control of the local gas companies in 1875 and the water company in 1876. Chamberlain saw municipalization as both the means to generate the necessary funds for Birmingham's long overdue improvement and also a way of extending the prestige and influence of the council. During his period as President of the Board of Trade he was able to set the tenor of the Electric Lighting Act 1888, which gave local authorities the right to purchase private supply undertakings at cost after 21 years. In Chamberlain's view municipalization of the utilities, including road passenger transport, offered the best protection for the public against the dangers of private monopoly. Writing in 1894 he also claimed, in the passage which follows, that municipalization made sound commercial sense

> the supply of gas and of water, electric lighting and the establishment of tramways must be confined to very few contractors. They involve interference with the streets, and the rights and privileges of individuals. They cannot, therefore, be thrown open to free competition, but must be committed, under stringent conditions and regulation, to the fewest hands. As it is difficult, and, indeed, almost impossible satisfactorily to reconcile the rights and interests of the public with the claims of an individual, or of a company seeking, as its natural and legitimate object, the largest attainable private gain, it is most desirable that, in all these cases, the municipality should control the supply, in order that the general interest of the whole population may be the only object pursued (quoted in Jay, 1981).

By the 1890s the rise of collectivism and the concomitant demands for greater state intervention were already well under way. Of course, as Ensor commented in relation to the phenomenon of municipalization, it "had not been identified in the minds of its promoters with any collectivist principle. They were simply . . . facing public needs and trying to meet each of them specifically in what appeared the most practical way" (Ensor, 1936, p.128). In the case of the London based Fabian Society, however, the pragmatic decisions of what Ensor described as "empirical Englishmen" were interpreted as contributions to a gradual process leading to the establishment of socialism. Sidney Webb, for example, in *Fabian Essays* (1889) reviewed the historical basis of socialism and emphasized its unconscious development under the impact of continuous municipalization. Webb became a London County Council (LCC) councillor in 1892, representing Deptford in the Progressive cause. Not surprisingly he advocated greater public control as the means of modernizing the capital even though the newly created LCC's powers were somewhat limited. Nevertheless under the control of the Progressives the LCC did what it could, gaining among other things ownership of London's street tramways and converting them to electric traction. As Hibbs has observed

> The LCC, from its foundation in 1889 . . . turned its back upon the laissez faire policies of its predecessor, the Metropolitan Board of Works (and) the Progressives made tramway ownership a main plank in their platform. In this they reflected advanced political opinion throughout the country, which saw in the tramway a means of social reform. (Hibbs, 1968, p.86).

Having said all of this, however, the expansion of municipalization, eventually precipitated a campaign of opposition. A protest movement, the Liberty and Property League, presented during 1899 alone over 400 petitions to parliament demanding an inquiry into the development and appropriate limits of municipal trading. Further, an Industrial Freedom League was established with the purpose of combatting what it saw as the growing powers of local government. In 1900 a Joint Select Committee on Municipal Trading was appointed which took extensive evidence on the subject of municipal enterprise. Although the Committee made no final pronouncement, it nevertheless became clear that parliament had grown antagonistic to the further extension of municipal trading. In London the Progressives lost control of the LCC in 1907 to the moderates (i.e. Conservatives) who held control until 1934 when the Labour Party took over. Resistance to the further extension of municipalization did not, however, halt the rise of collectivism. By the end of the First World War attention was increasingly turning to central government initiatives rather than the localities. Even the Webbs, the sometime apostles of municipal socialism, were constrained to acknowledge the significance of the centralizing tendencies which had occurred as a result of the hostilities. In their *Constitution for the Socialist Commonwealth of Great Britain* (1920) the Webbs advocated a much enhanced role for the central state albeit reserving "as much as one half" of the country's industries and services for local government! However, the bulk of local authorities, certainly as they were constituted in 1920, were too small to operate the public utilities efficiently. By the 1930s Herbert Morrison (with the examples of the Port of London Authority and the Central Electricity Board in mind) was moved to observe in his influential *Socialisation and Transport* (1933) that

> for other than exceptional cases . . . we shall be driven to making a clean cut between the concerns of the municipality and the concerns of the State. After all, Great Britain is a small country, and it is hardly necessary to provide for intermediate joint municipal bodies . . . We have to find an organ of economic management and administration, not for all services but those of the more commercial . . . less routine character . . . We are seeking a combination of

> public ownership, public accountability and business management for public ends. (Morrison, 1933, pp.148-9).

The administrative structure which Morrison advocated was, of course, the public corporation. While freely admitting that it was a Conservative Party creation he claimed that it could readily be adapted to socialist purposes. Morrison, for all his local government credentials, became in the words of Addison

> a missionary for the gospel of the state controlled public corporation. Instead of a nationalised industry being run by a minister and a Whitehall department . . . it would be conducted by a largely independent public corporation, modelled on business enterprise and staffed by professional managers. Responsible to government for the outline of policy, the public corporation would take its place in the development of a planned economy. (Addison, 1977, p.50).

As well as providing a model for the Labour Party's post Second World War nationalization programme, Morrison's advocacy of planning was a contribution to the vast literature on the subject produced during the 1930s. As Booth and Pack have observed

> the concept of planning assumed the same status in economic prescription as the philosopher's stone had done in medieval alchemy. It was widely proclaimed as the panacea for all economic ills . . .(and) The Labour Party and the TUC advocated a statist model based upon the cumulative nationalization of key industries (Booth and Pack, 1985, p.148).

In practical terms Morrison's ideas came to fruition with the creation of the London Passenger Transport Board (LPTB) under the London Passenger Transport Act 1933. Morrison himself, as Minister of Transport in the Second Labour Government, initiated the legislation necessary to bring the capital's underground railway, tram and bus undertakings (both privately and municipally owned) into a single, public corporation. Although Morrison went out of office with the collapse of the Labour Government (becoming leader of the LCC, however, in 1934) his Bill was nevertheless enacted by Ramsay MacDonald's National Government. From 1 July 1933 the LPTB (or London Transport as it soon became known) took responsibility for operating all road and underground rail services within an area of almost 2,000 square miles with a population of 9.5 million. It brought together five railway companies, 14 municipal tramways and three private ones, and 61 bus companies. Continuity of management between private and public operation was ensured when Lord Ashfield (former chairman of the Underground Combine) was appointed inaugural chairman of the Board. Similarly, the first general manager was Frank Pick who had also held the same position with the Combine. John Cliff, assistant general secretary of the TGWU and former leader of the United Vehicle Workers' Union, joined the Board with responsibility for staffing matters. From its impressive corporate headquarters at 55 Broadway the LPTB was able to undertake the mammoth task of planning and co-ordinating transport across the entire metropolis. As Bagwell has observed

> the work of co-ordinating services, pooling receipts, standardizing equipment, services and charges went on apace. In the latter 1930s it proved possible to make substantial extensions to the tube railways - something that it had not been found possible to achieve in the 1920s. By the outbreak of war London's transport services . . . were the envy of many other countries. (Bagwell, 1974, p.270).

Certainly London Transport's scale of operation was vast and, by the 1940s, its labour force exceeded 100,000. It is perhaps worth noting that the model provided by the LPTB proved influential when, in 1939, the Conservative Government of Neville Chamberlain (viewing competition between Imperial Airways and British Airways on overseas routes as being against the national interest) merged the two organizations to form the British Overseas Airways Corporation.

With the onset of war, and the control of transport under the auspices of the Central Transport Committee of the Ministry of War Transport, "socialization"(or nationalisation as it was increasingly called) substantially gained in plausibility. Certainy nationalisation of transport had been a central part of the Labour Party's programme since the beginning of the 1930s, figuring in *The National Planning of Transport* (1932), Morrison's *Britain's Transport at Britain's Service* (1938) and, finally, in the 1945 election manifesto *Let Us Face the Future*. Further, at the 1945 Congress at Blackpool the TUC approved the report *The Public Operation of Transport* which argued that

> the transport services of the country must be operated as one system and must be so developed and so utilized that each separate service shall, as one complementary part of national transport, carry the traffic most appropriate for it, while transport as a whole must be capable of being used as an instrument in the carrying out of Government policies of national development and full employment

quoted in Bagwell, 1974, pp.304-5).

Here then was a statement for the times incorporating ideas not only of nationalisation, planning and central government control but also economic expansion and full employment. As far as Britain was concerned this was "socialism" and when Labour won the election of 1945 it set about implementing its plans for transport with the result that a comprehensive Transport Act was passed in 1947. The Act established the British Transport Commission which took control of all railways (together with the ships and hotels operated by the railway companies), canals, road passenger operations and some road haulage concerns on 1 January 1948. In the context of the immediate post-war years and the development of Labour's nationalisation programme, the Act brought the freight moving capacities of the railway system into public ownership alongside the coal mining industry, gas production and electricity supply. Although the British Transport Commission did not gain full control of road haulage, and was thus prevented from achieving the establishment of a fully integrated transport system, the 1947 Act probably marks the high (or low depending on your ideological view) point in the development of collectivized (i.e. publicly owned and operated) transport in the UK. Writing in the early 1970s Bagwell was moved to comment that "the Labour Party's victory in the general election of July 1945 was of decisive importance for the future of British transport". Although for those reviewing the situation some 20 years later, and in the light of what has taken place since 1980, the word "decisive" appears to have been something of an overstatement, things had nevertheless come a very long way from the era of qualified laissez faire and hesitant state intervention.

When the Conservatives returned to power in 1951 they sought to return a greater element of competition into the economy. In the sphere of transport, for example, they restored road haulage to the private sector and abandoned the attempt to plan transport across sectors. During the 1950s and '60s the increase in car ownership, the loss of freight to road haulage and the developmment of the motorway network all served to place great pressure on the commercial viability of the railways. Similarly, bus operators faced lean times as passengers were lost in the face of increased competition from the car. Of course developments in transport technology and the loss of markets that go with technical obsolescence were not new phenomena. The stagecoaches disappeared in the face of competition from railways; canals had suffered a similar decline as had the Thames passenger boats; horse buses had given way to the more efficient trams and the trams subsequently disappeared with the appearance of the more flexible motor bus and so on. Nevertheless a strong rear guard action was mounted in support of the railways and against road transport and the struggle continues. Although the pros and cons of the road versus rail argument are beyond the scope of this chapter, support for railways has often, tacitly or overtly, gone hand in hand with support for public transport per se. A single passage from Bagwell - a committed railway and public transport advocate - is enough to give the flavour. In the early 1970s he claimed that

> by the end of the 1960s it was becoming more apparent that the policies which had encouraged the largely unrestrained growth in numbers of privately owned motor vehicles threatened to wreck much that was of value in the life of the community, while not providing the British people with as efficient or as economic a system of transport as might have emerged if fragmentation of ownership had not been resorted to in the early 1950s. In 1970 Britain possesses a much under utilized railway system. British Rail has the capacity for carrying a much larger proportion of long distance passenger and freight traffic than that actually carried.... Great Britain has now reached a watershed in transport policy. The alternatives are either a blinkered policy of trying to make the railways pay . . . or a large expansion of investment in a thoroughly modern railway system based on the conviction that in the long run on both economic and social grounds this is an absolute necessity for civilized living. (Bagwell, 1974, p.379).

Laying aside the alarmist rhetoric, this passage demands rather more than a greater commitment to the railways. It also calls for greater state intervention, bigger subsidies, more regulation, direction, planning and, in a word, a return to the *collectivist* spirit of the immediate post-war era. As we now know developments since the 1970s have not restored the fortunes of the railways or public transport. Instead there has been an attempt by government to retreat from the whole notion of publicly owned transport and to stimulate competition and market forces. Consideration of these developments will form the subject of the section which follows.

The decay of collectivism

The Arab-Israeli war of October 1973 quadrupled the cost of Britain's oil imports stimulating, if not actually precipitating, a period of rapid inflation. Inflation rose from around 6 per cent in 1970 to peak at 25 per cent during 1975 before declining to single figures in 1978 and climbing once again to 18 per cent in 1980. One result of this was that the Keynesian consensus, which had dominated British economic policy since 1945, came under serious practical challenge as the phenomenon of "stagflation" (i.e. low growth going hand in hand with escalating inflation) raised the spectre of hyper-inflation and the dire social consequences associated with monetary collapse. As the governments of Heath, Wilson and Callaghan struggled to get the economic situation under control, Marxists and free market liberals from the left and right of the political spectrum proferred solutions that would hardly have gained a hearing in the days of "Butskellism" and consensus politics. Stuart Holland, for example, in *The Challenge of socialism* (1975) argued that the economic situation

> made imperative a programme of fundamental and effectively revolutionary reforms, transforming the injustice, inequality and inefficiency of modern capitalism. This includes not only a major extension of new public enterprise through the mesoeconomic sector, but also socialist planning in which new patterns of ownership and control are made possible (Holland, 1975, p.9).

Self-evidently a substantial intensification of collectivism and a much enhanced role for the "socialist" state was envisaged. By way of contrast, however, Hayek in the 1976 re-print of *The Road to Serfdom* (1944), claimed that

> the liberal argument is in favour of making the best possible use of the forces of competition as a means of co-ordinating human efforts . . . It is based on the conviction that where effective competition can be created, it is a better way of guiding individual efforts than any other .... Economic liberalism is opposed . . . to competition being supplanted by inferior methods of co-ordinating individual efforts. And it regards competition as superior not only because it is in most circumstances the most efficient method known, but even more because it is the only method by which our activities can be adjusted to each other without coercive or arbitary intervention of authority. (Hayek, 1976 edition, p.27).

As we now know it was the market liberal, rather than the socialist/marxist, view which prevailed as the Conservatives came to power in 1979 and subsequently won the general elections of 1983, 1987 and 1992. Meanwhile a badly divided Labour Party struggled to regain electoral credibility. The circumstances under which the Conservatives achieved electoral success in 1979 (following the debacle of the so-called Winter of Discontent) were not propitious for public transport or the public sector generally. In 1979 the Conservative Party's Economic Reconstruction Group had produced *The Right Approach to the Economy* which embodied much of what was later to be termed Thatcherism, including monetarism, public expenditure control, trade union reform and reduced taxation. As Martin Holmes has commented it

> was based on the critique of post-war Conservatism advanced by Sir Keith Joseph in the 1974-75 period when the Heath leadership was under challenge from the right. Joseph, Thatcher, John Biffen, John Nott and others on the economic right of the party had argued that the Conservative Party had not reversed the advance of socialism but had merely halted it temporarily whilst in office. The "socialist ratchet" critique saw middle way Butskellite Conservatism as participating in a process in which Britain at successive stages descended into an East-European-style economy and society, where political freedom along with economic free enterprise would ultimately fall into dissolution (Holmes, 1985, p.8).

The central thrust of the Conservatives' policy since 1979 has been largely based on the determination to reduce the activities of the state and constrain public expenditure. Operating alongside of this, there has been an attempt to increase labour market flexibility which has included, among other things, a legislative programme aimed at reducing the power of organized labour. Public transport with its dependency on central and local government and its historically high levels of trade union membership was pretty well bound to suffer under such policies and indeed this has proved to be the case. Although recession and an acknowledged mishandling of the economy during the late 1980s have stimulated government's need to spend, there has certainly been a marked reduction in the scope of state activity. The government's preferred method for reducing the size of the public sector was privatization, ideally disposing of assets through share flotations or direct sales. However, where such privatizations proved impracticable, a programme of contractualization, deregulation, reduced subsidies and, with the latest arrangements for Britlsh Rail, franchising has been pursued. In terms of transport alone all of this has impacted radically on road passenger transport; aircraft manufacture and civil aviation; shipbuilding, shipping, ferries and ports; automobile manufacture; railways and railway engineering. Interestingly there has been little opposition to all of this beyond the immediate complaints of the interested parties. In any case there now seems small prospect of the old collectivist certainties ever returning and there is little evidence of them even in current Labour Party thinking. The rapid decline of collectivism in the British case is yet to be thoroughly analysed but perhaps it is sufficient to say that, although collectivism certainly influenced people, it ultimately failed to win friends - or at least the friends who mattered.

References

Addison, P. (1977), *The Road to 1945*, Quartet, London.
Bagwell, P. (1974), *The Transport Revolution from 1770*, Batsford, London.
Booth, A. & Pack, M. (1985), *Employment, Capital and Economic Planning: Great Britain 1918-1939*, Blackwell, Oxford.
Brown, R. (1991), *Church and State in Modern Britain 1700-1850*, Routledge, London.
Byrne, T. (1990), *Local Government in Britain*, Penguin, Harmondsworth.
Ensor, R. (1936), *England 1870-1914*, Clarendon, Oxford.
Greenleaf, W. H. (1983), *The British Political Tradition: Volume 1, The Rise of Collectivism*, Methuen, London.
Hayek, F. (1976 edition), *The Road to Serfdom*, Routledge, London.
Hibbs, J. (1968), *The History of British Bus Services*, David & Charles, Newton Abbot.
Holland, S. (1975), *The Socialist Challenge*, Quartet, London.
Holmes, M. (1985), *The First Thatcher Government 1979-83*, Wheatsheaf, Brighton.
Jay, R. (1981), *Joseph Chamberlain*, Clarendon, Oxford.
McDonagh, O. (1977), *Early Victorian Government 1830-70*, Weidenfeld and Nicolson.
Mill, J. S. (1985 edition), *Principles of Political Economy*, Penguin, Harmondsworth.
Morrison, H. (1933), *Socialisation and Transport*, Constable, London.
Sheldrake, J. (1989), *Municipal Socialism*, Avebury, Aldershot.
Skinner, A. (1986 edition), *Introduction to Adam Smith's The Wealth of Nations*, Penguin, Harmondsworth.
Waller, P. (1991), *Town, City and Nation: England 1850 to 1914*, Clarendon, Oxford.

3 The context of choice and competition in transport: An overview of privatization in Western Europe

Paul Webb

Introduction

Contemporary interest in questions of choice and competition in the industrial, retailing and service sectors clearly reflects the changing economic, political and ideological context of the past twenty years. One enthusiast for privatization and deregulation situated ideologically on the neo-liberal right has suggested that

> The impetus has been the same throughout; to shake off the public sector and the confining grip which it places on development and growth, and to reduce the costs of state sector operations. (Pirie 1988: 295).

While it is hard to deny the truth of this view, regardless of one's own ideological orientation, there remains much to be added by way of elaboration. Such elaboration is essentially the task of this chapter. In particular, it will concentrate on an account of the economic, political and ideological contexts from which the privatization phenomenon has emerged in discussing the motives for, and patterns of, privatization found on the continent of Europe.

Observers of affairs in the UK will be only too aware of the political influence in these matters of the neo-liberal "New Right" for whom commitment to market values is virtually an article of faith. Such values have clearly provided impetus for the sale of state assets, tendering of public services to private sector contractors and de-regulation in a wide range of policy areas since the Conservative government of Margaret Thatcher was first returned to national office in 1979. Surveying the wider European scene since that time, however, inclines one to the view that these ideological instincts provide only part of the explanation for the attempts to inject greater reliance on market processes into the provision of public services such as transport. Nevertheless, one thing that strikes the comparative observer of such developments in Western Europe is that both neo-liberal zealots and pragmatists alike seemed to take their cue from the economic and industrial problems which have plagued the advanced industrial democracies since the middle of the 1970s. In particular, four developments stand out as being important background factors when seeking to understand the nature of the privatization phenomenon.

The economic, industrial and political context

The internationalization of capital and markets

The trend towards mergers and the rationalization of large firms, first evident in the 1960s, has served to enhance the multinational nature of industry and the international mobility of capital and investment. This has presented the national governments of Western Europe (and indeed, elsewhere) with at least two related problems. First, capital has often tended to flow away from Europe to developing economies (especially those of the Pacific Rim) where wage costs are significantly lower. Second, national governments are less able to exert autonomous control over their domestic economies than was hitherto the case. Nothing better illustrates this than the experience of the French socialist government which came to power in 1981. The expansionist policy that the socialists pursued initially was so badly out of step with government approaches adopted elsewhere in the industrialised world, that it swiftly generated over-priced French commodities in international markets, a balance of trade crisis and a run on the franc. Even more seriously, perhaps, it provoked a sharp reduction in private investment in the country. This demonstrated how crucial exports are to all modern industrialised economies and the extent to which capital is increasingly mobile across national borders.

The development of the Single European Market and the removal of nearly 300 physical, technical and fiscal barriers to trade which it entails only serves to underline the point. Moreover, the European Union is increasingly likely to impose further constraints on government intervention - for example, through limiting subsidies to industry (now regarded as "unfair" competitive practice) and general increases in public expenditure. In short, the European Union recognises that the future lies in encouraging European competitive success in the international market place.

The end of the "long boom" believers

The oil price shocks of the 1970s did much to spark the deep recessions that marked the end of Europe's long postwar boom in economic and industrial performance. During the economic troughs that ensued it became clear to policy makers across the continent that Keynesian demand management techniques had lost the efficacy for which they had been revered during the long boom. Instead, it has become increasingly orthodox for governments to resort to strategies designed to make their export industries "leaner" and more competitive in the international market place. This essentially supply-side approach has been operated by European governments in the hope that the region as a whole can better meet the economic challenges posed by America and south east Asia. Thus, a common effect of both the internationalization of capitalist markets and the end of the long boom has been the substitution of supply-side strategies for demand management by national governments. Privatization and deregulation form a central part of this supply-side responses.

Technological change

Observers such as Freeman and Perez have been influential in suggesting that modern economies have suffered from frictional dislocation as they shift on a Kondratieff style long wave pattern from one dominant technological and socio-institutional paradigm to another. These new paradigms are ushered in by clusters of innovations producing new forms of work, models of management and sectors of high growth. These innovations

> have such widespread consequences for all sectors of the economy that their infusion is accompanied by major structural crises of adjustment, in which social and institutional changes are necessary to bring about a batter "match"' between the new technology and the system of social management of the economy. (Freeman and Perez, 1988, p.38).

The development of micro-electronics and information technology represents such a paradigmatic innovation in the contemporary era because its range of application is so potentially and actually wide. Thus it implies the need to alter the dominant model of production from the Fordist mass-production one to a post-Fordist pattern of smaller units of production based on a skilled, "flexible" workforce and management, and geared to the output of rapidly changing and diversified portfolios of goods and services. Systemic change such as this clearly involves a significant degree of transitional economic, social and political difficulty, with particular implications for unemployment levels, patterns of labour organization and trade union power, and the training and skilling of employees. It has been argued, for instance, that this type of post-industrial transition implies the need to break the power of unions and corporatist models of industrial relations, and the reduction of unit labour costs

> The flexibilization of work organization, dismantling of collective bargaining and the welfare state, unemployment and growing income differentials are reinforcing a shift towards individualization. (Hirsch, 1991, p.72).

Such a context is clearly relevant to the renaissance of the neo-liberal agenda and to the emphasis on privatization and deregulation. In the UK, in particular, the large nationalized corporations were long regarded as bastions of union power and over-staffing; thus, in this country at least, the "flexibilization" of the workforce is directly relevant to the privatization phenomenon.

Governmental overload and fiscal crisis

In the 1970s political science became replete with interpretations suggesting that governments had "overloaded" themselves with the burden of too many responsibilities and financial commitments. Concerns about the political and economic effects of high levels of public expenditure, governmental overload, ungovernability, and fiscal crisis of the state were interrelated and considerable (see, for example, O'Connor 1973; Bacon and Eltis 1976; King, 1976; Rose, 1980; Birch, 1984). In the 1980s a further connected theme emerged with the development of the *public choice* school of public policy analysis, which appeared to offer an explanation of the relentless growth of public sector bureaucracy and spending. Based on rational choice assumptions borrowed from economic theory, writers like Niskanen argued that it was in the interest of both office-seeking politicians and budget-maximising bureaucrats to keep increasing public sector budgets; in doing so, voter demands could be met and bureaucrats' desires for more job and promotion opportunities, employment perks and pensions assuaged (Niskanen, 1971). Almost certainly, the various and related concerns apparent in academic works such as these have dovetailed with an ideological predisposition in favour of market values in the minds of British policy makers since 1979. To a lesser extent, this is also true of other European countries. Again, the result is a growing interest in the hiving-off of state responsibilities to the private sector.

This, then, is the background of economic dislocation and governmental overload against which advanced industrial democracies have been obliged to reappraise the political and economic orthodoxies which dominated what one noted French observer refers to as the "thirty glorious years" following World War Two (Fourastié 1979). This process of reappraisal has sometimes resulted in a diagnosis known as "Eurosclerosis" - that is, a perception that Western Europe as a regional block is suffering by comparison with the developing economies (especially those of the Pacific Rim) in terms of international competitiveness. To reiterate, attempts to account for and remedy Eurosclerosis do not necessarily have to produce the ideological reflexes of the neo-liberal right. Nevertheless, it is clear that such has been the most significant ideological response to the economic, industrial and political developments outlined above, and it is interesting to consider this important aspect of the ideological context of privatization and deregulation.

The ideological context of privatization

Ironically, the intellectual turning point in the political theory of the state's proper role in economic and industrial affairs probably came with the work of someone not necessarily associated with the New Right as such - the American academic Robert Nozick. Nozick's classic work *Anarchy, State and Utopia* was an ambitious and fundamental piece of work which, among other things, seriously reconsidered basic justifications for the very existence of the state and private property. His most startling conclusion was that only a minimal "nightwatchman" state which served to protect people's natural rights and to ensure that they are not coerced in any way could be justified on theoretical grounds. Nozick himself admitted to recoiling from these conclusions when he first arrived at them (Nozick 1974).

Although it would not be appropriate to regard Nozick's work as having directly influenced policy making in Western governments, it might be seen as something of an intellectual trigger for writers who did. Fortuitously, perhaps, *Anarchy, State and Utopia* was published at almost precisely the moment when the Keynesian-welfarist consensus was plunging into an authentic crisis, and it provoked a dramatic reaction in intellectual circles. Consequently, *Anarchy, State and Utopia* might be regarded as the catalyst for a serious reconsideration by intellectuals of whether the state was prone to too much intervention, and whether it represented any kind of a threat to individual rights and liberties.

This intellectual development coincided with economic and political developments to shift the terms of debate on to territory familiar to those who have subsequently become known as the neo-liberal or New Right. In the case of the best known guru of the neo-liberal intelligentsia in the United Kingdom, Friedrich von Hayek, it was to facilitate his rediscovery by influential politicians in the country. Hayek had published his widely known polemic against the interventionist state, *The Road to Serfdom*, as early as 1944 and his libertarian bible, *The Constitution of Liberty*, in 1960, but from the time of his early disputes over economic policy with John Maynard Keynes, he had distinguished himself by a consistent talent for running against the grain of prevailing political orthodoxy. The crisis of the postwar consensus earned him a new appeal in influential circles, however. Von Hayek's themes were essentially a twentieth century restatement of conservative individualism. Like the eighteenth century writers David Hume and Edmund Burke before him, his approach was characterized by the belief that humans were incurably ignorant and destined never to understand fully the mystery of society. This meant that aspirations to control and engineer social developments were essentially misplaced, and he therefore maintained that it was desirable to allow a spontaneous social and economic order to evolve through the market mechanism. Hayek argued that liberty was the supreme human value and that the dependency of individuals upon state provision and direction threatened their independence and freedom. Thereby lay "the road to serfdom". In particular, the pursuit of "social justice" through redistribution of income and wealth was a "mirage" which entailed the coercion of some individuals in order to benefit others (Von Hayek, 1976).

Writers like Von Hayek and the Chicago School of economists set the ideological tone for the neo-liberal agenda which was taken up so enthusiastically by the governments of Margaret Thatcher in the UK and Ronald Reagan in the USA. For ideological purists, privatization forms a crucial part of the Hayekian prescription for rolling back the state and enhancing liberty. However, ideological conviction has clearly not provided the sole motivation for privatization initiatives in Western democracies. What have been the others?

Firstly, there are a number of more narrowly defined *economic and financial* motivations. This category is probably the most significant from an international perspective and entails a number of themes. In particular, it centres around the desire to transform debt laden public sector companies into profitable competitors in the international market place. For many observers, privatization is the most dramatic and effective way of achieving this. As John Vickers and Vincent Wright have pointed out

> Uninhibited market oriented profit-seeking entrepreneurs are preferred to budget-maximizing bureaucrats and vote-seeking politicians (Vickers and Wright, 1988, p.6)

This could be expected to be especially important when it comes, for instance, to willingness to tackle trade unions on over-staffing. A closely related theme which falls under the heading of economic and financial motivations for privatization is the desire to tackle the problem of swollen public sector borrowing requirements and to enhance short run state revenues. This factor has been especially important in the UK, Austria, Italy and Belgium. Some governments have even been prepared to divest themselves entirely of publicly owned firms by sales to foreign corporations. For instance, the Spanish government sold its car production company SEAT to Volkswagen and the truck and bus company ENASA to General Motors in the 1980s (Pirie, 1988, p.300). It is interesting to note, however, that on the continent of Europe sales have not always necessarily been designed simply to increase the flow of revenue into government coffers. Instead, a model of partial privatization which enables state corporations and holding companies to raise extra capital has been preferred. For example, the Austrian national airline sold 25% of its stock in the late 1980s in order to raise new capital (Muller, 1988), and the Italian state holding companies' reduced their stake in firms like Alitalia and Aeritalia in the same period (Pirie, 1988, p.302). Revenue from these privatization initiatives was fed back directly into the companies concerned.

Privatization is sometimes motivated by *the desire to modify managerial relationships and autonomy*. Italy provides a perfect example of the way in which public sector industrial mangers can simplify their jobs by removing politicians and/or bureaucrats from the equation. It is clear that part of the impetus for privatization in Italy came from public sector managers eager to rid themselves of political intervention. This point can only be fully appreciated when one understands the wider context of postwar Italian political life, which has been characterized by the development of an extensive clientelistic spoils system. The widely used Italian word *partitocrazia* refers to the way in which the main political parties, led by the long-dominant Christian Democrats, have suffused the entire public sector with their presence to a degree unparalleled in Western Europe. Through a process of *lotizazzione* (inter-party bargaining over shares of the spoils) thousands of public sector jobs have been carved up and handed over to individuals carrying the appropriate party membership cards. This, in conjunction with a growing dependence on the national treasury for subvention as some companies sustained financial losses after the 1960s (Bianchi, Cassese and della Sala, 1988, p.98), generated conditions conducive to growing political interference in the running of public sector firms. As one noted Italian political scientist once observed the system with which the political class can expand its control over citizens, constraining them to become obedient subjects. (quoted in Vickers and Wright, 1988, p.13)

Escaping this pervasive - and many would argue, malignant - presence of the party politicians has long been a goal of some parts of the vast Italian state sector. Indeed, as Bianchi and his colleagues have pointed out, the early initiatives for privatization often came from the industrial managers rather than from the politicians. What is clear is that the profound crisis that the Italian political class has been submerged by thanks to the *tangentopoli* ("bribesville") scandals that have been revealed since 1992 present the public sector with a dramatic opportunity for reform. The public opprobrium and legal humiliation heaped upon politicians of nearly all parties and ranks has combined with the fiscal implications of the Treaty of Maastricht to catalyse a new drive for privatization. The first steps were taken by the government of Carlo Azeglio Ciampi (a non-partisan former Governor of the Bank of Italy) with the successful flotation of a number of public sector financial institutions on the Milan *Borsa* in 1993; further privatization was almost certain to follow.

The final type of motivation for privatizing publicly owned companies or services is *electoral-populist* in nature. In a number of countries, survey evidence suggested that nationalized industries were becoming increasingly unpopular during the 1970s and 1980s. There was a doubling of the proportion of British electors desiring further privatization between 1964 and 1983, for instance, although by 1987 there were signs that the majority felt privatization programmes had gone far enough (Webb, 1993, p. 115). Wolfgang Muller noted an even more dramatic rise (from 17% to 63%) in the percentage of Austrians wanting some privatization between 1979 and 1986. Equally, the proportion of Austrians turning against state financial aid to public sector firms increased from 17% to 56% (Muller, 1988, p.106). Such trends in public opinion are bound to be noticed by politicians, and quite possibly encouraged by them. Indeed, trends of this nature do not simply occur spontaneously, but reflect the themes pursued by political elites. Whatever, it seems clear enough that many citizens in Western democracies have been receptive to privatization arguments. In this respect, politicians seeking to exploit these popular attitudes have often only had to push against an open door. Clearly, there has been a potential electoral payoff for parties and politicians able to exploit this disaffection with the public sector. Such a perspective surely helps to explain the French Gaullist party's conversion to the cause of privatization and economic liberalism since the middle of the 1980s, for instance.

Patterns of privatization in Western Europe

Broadly speaking, it is possible to distinguish between two basic privatization scenarios in contemporary Western Europe. Firstly, there are countries which have indulged in relatively extensive experiments in privatization to the accompaniment of a significant amount of neo-liberal rhetoric. Secondly, there are countries whose experiences of privatization have generally been far more limited and pragmatic. Into the first category we can only place the UK and France with any degree of certainty, although a more equivocal case might also be made for the former German Democratic Republic.

In France, a limited experiment in partial privatization and the eradication of debt in public corporations was started in 1983 by the socialist Finance minister of the day, Jacques Delors (Boucek, 1993, p.79). However, it was the conservative coalition government of 1986-88 headed by prime minister Jacques Chirac that was responsible for launching a privatization drive that was dramatic by the standards of France's postwar traditions of *dirigisme* (state direction of the economy). The campaign embraced firms nationalized by the socialists between 1981 and 1986 and industries nationalized by de Gaulle's liberation government in the 1940s. Initially, some 66 firms were intended for privatization, with an estimated stock value of £30 billion (or some 25% of the entire value of the Paris *bourse*). In the event, approximately one third of the planned sales were achieved before the stock market crash of October 1987 halted progress. Since the return of the right wing to power in March 1993, the government of Edouard Balladur has launched a further privatization drive covering banking, insurance and industry; again, it is estimated that this should be worth a total of nearly £30 billion to the French state. Among the more notable enterprises set to leave the public sector are Air France and Renault (Webster and Christie, 1993, p.1).

The case of the ex-GDR after national reunification is somewhat different to either that of France or the UK. It is certainly not the case that the Christian Democratic led government of federal Chancellor Helmut Kohl generally demonstrated any obvious neo-liberal fervour during the 1980s. However, after 1990, Kohl did opt for a radical and speedy conversion of the east German economy to the market system of allocation. Amongst other things, this entailed a privatization programme that completely eclipses anything seen in France and the UK. The privatization agency (the *treuhandanstalt*) sold an average fifteen to twenty firms each *day* during 1991, especially in the retailing, construction, food processing and mechanical engineering sectors. By the year's end more than five thousand firms had been privatized. However, the impression of a neo-liberal economic crusade in the country has to be tempered by the high costs of the programme that the German state has had to bear

> The Bonn government has therefore found itself mired in subsidies and transfer payments of various kinds to keep eastern workers on short time, training and job creation schemes. This has affected taxes and interest rates...By the autumn of 1991 about 1,500 firms had gone out of business, but subsidies and other transfer payments to the east were estimated to have been DM153 billion in 1991. It is generally recognised that this level of payment cannot be maintained in the longer term. (Carter, 1993, p.27).

What of the European countries where the experience of privatization been more limited and pragmatic? What constraints have imposed themselves on the privatization urge in these countries? A number of factors stand out. In the first place, *there has been no underlying ideological impulse driving the privatization project forward* in many cases. In such countries the whole issue of the ownership of industry has lacked strong ideological connotations. This is especially true of places where nationalization was not carried out for ideological reasons in the first place. In countries such as Italy and Austria private capital was not developed enough to fund industrial development or postwar reconstruction to the extent that the government desired, so the state intervened to provide the resources and direction. This is quite unlike the British context, where the 1945-51 Labour governments saw nationalization as an essential component of the task that the party had set itself in 1918 - to secure social control of the means of production. Thus, where nationalization was not ideologically motivated, then neither is privatization in the contemporary era. And where the issue of public ownership is not widely regarded in ideological terms, then the impulse for privatization may well remain muted.

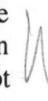

Second, *public control of industry is sometimes an important element of the national socio-political bargain.* In such cases, radical privatization programmes cannot be considered without risking the basic political stability of the country. We have already alluded to the Italian case, where public sector industry has long formed an essential part of the political spoils system which the main parties negotiated and operated between themselves. Similarly, some of the so-called "consociational" polities where society is divided along religious or linguistic lines (for example, Belgium, Switzerland or the Netherlands) also operate systems of patronage and the proportional sharing of public sector posts and offices. In a sense, the spoils system operates as part of the wider bargain that cements political coalitions together in such countries (Lijphart, 1977). Far reaching privatization schemes would be unthinkable viewed in this light, since they would threaten the national political balance. A somewhat different version of essentially the same point is provided by the institutional obstacle of federalism. Part of the reason for the relatively "timid" approach to privatization taken by the Federal Republic of Germany prior to 1990 lies in the fact that many of the regional states (*laender*) would probably have resisted even if the federal government had pushed for a more ambitious programme. Publicly owned and controlled industries in the regions represent part of the power base of the laender and even the Christian Democratic governed states are party to the "state capitalist" consensus. Thus, again we find that a certain degree of public ownership of industry is part of a national political bargain.

In a number of countries outside the United Kingdom, *privatization through a public flotation of shares on the Anglo-French model is simply unfeasible given the small size of the domestic stock exchange.* This is especially true of countries such as Spain, Portugal, Greece, the Netherlands, the Scandinavian states and even Italy. This helps to explain why privatization in such countries has either been very restricted or has taken the form of direct sales to large private sector multinational companies. Only in France could a right wing government seriously contemplate a major public flotation of public sector equity in the form pioneered by the Thatcher governments.

A fourth constraint on privatization is the fact that *it is simply irrelevant in countries where the industrial public sector has never been that big.* A rather surprising example of this is provided by Sweden, widely recognised as the most developed socialist state among Western democracies in the twentieth century. As Jon Pierre says

> To many outside observers, Sweden has become the epitome of the advanced welfare state based on extensive redistributive politics and a huge public sector, but *with the means of production essentially remaining in private hands.* (emphasis mine: Pierre, 1993, p.35).

This bargain between capital and labour held for nearly half a century, before the Social Democratic government's wage earner funds initiative threatened the consensus during the 1980s. These funds were to be drawn from a tax on company profits, controlled by trade unions and used to buy up equity in private industry. The goal was to socialize the means of production gradually over the course of several decades (Stephens, 1979). In fact, they were not a conspicuous success. The point is, however, that their very existence testified to the restricted nature of the Swedish public sector. Given this, radical schemes of privatization could never form a significant element of the political agenda in the country.

Fifthly, *nationalist concern has sometimes constrained privatization initiatives by blocking the sale of public assets to foreign investors.* British readers will recall that such a scenario formed the backdrop to the dramatic cabinet battle over the sale of the Westland Helicopter Corporation in 1985- Sixthly. Similarly, the nationalist right of the Bavarian Christian Social Union (a member of the government of the German Federal Republic) voiced concern over the planned partial sale of the Lufthansa airline in 1985. This said, it is interesting to note that transport is one of the areas that has experienced some privatization in western Germany, albeit modest. For instance, apart from Lufthansa, motorway facilities and trucking concerns have both been sold into the private sector (Pirie, 1988, p.301). In general, the consensus on public sector assets in the former Federal Republic has long been that they would remain public and were considered "indispensable for regional and industrial policy".

> Nevertheless, it is expected that all of these publicly owned businesses will be managed according to private business criteria and that they will work effectively and survive in the free market (Esser, 1988, p.71).

Conclusion: a retreat of the state in Western Europe?

So what has a decade and a half of experimentation with privatization achieved in Western Europe? Has it been a core element of a successful neo-liberal drive to withdraw the state from the private domain? There is little doubt that privatization has had a significant impact in some countries. This impact is most dramatic, as has been seen, in the former GDR. In the United Kingdom too it is hard to envisage any future left wing government returning public sector industry to its pre-1979 size in peace time circumstances. Between 1979 and 1990 the number of employees working for public corporations in the UK fell from 2,065,000 to just 778,000 (HM Treasury, 1990). This had a profound impact on transport, of course, with privatization in this period affecting Hoverspeed, the National Freight Corporation, Associated British Ports, Sealink ferries, British Airways and a number of regional bus operators. Central government also sought to reduce subsidies to operators and to local government (through the Transport Supplementary Grant), and to encourage private investment in public transport projects such as the Channel Tunnel (Shaw, 1993, pp.153-5). Indeed, the Labour Party has as good as acknowledged the impossibility and undesirability of turning the clock back in policy developments over the past few years (Webb, 1993). And yet it is as well to retain some sense of perspective about just how far the state has been rolled back across the continent during this period. For instance, research suggests that between

1979 and 1989 government consumption across 16 European democracies fell by an average of just 0.2%, while government sector employment actually increased on average by 1.3% (Oxley et al, 1990).

Moreover, even if Western political economy has moved broadly away from states and towards markets since the 1970s, a number of observers have noticed that the very process of privatization paradoxically tends to generate new forms of state intervention, through the growth of regulation. For example

> One of the most remarkable features of the "conservative turn" experienced in the UK since 1980 is the paradoxical emergence of extensive *re*regulation of economic activity in a period supposedly typified by dramatic *de*regulation...the Conservative governments since 1979 have presided over what can only be characterized as a renaissance of intervention. (Thompson, 1990, p.135).

Thus, we have witnessed the birth of new public utility regulators such as OFTEL, OFWAT and OFGAS. Maloney and Richardson have claimed that the regulatory pattern emerging in the UK is far from that envisaged by the Conservative government when the privatization crusade began. Not only is there no evidence to date suggesting that regulators have been "captured" by the industries they are supposed to constrain - a common development in the USA - but the newly privatized industries are often left perplexed by a sense that regulatory goalposts are shifting: "That the grip of the regulators *is* being tightened is beyond doubt" (Maloney and Richardson, 1992, pp. 18-19).

This phenomenon clearly applies to the domain of passenger transport. For example, the tendering out of many London bus routes to private operators is to be accompanied by the establishment of a passengers' charter, the introduction of traffic signal pre-emption schemes and a special "smartcard" ticket system to counteract the problems of services which have been slowed down by the removal of conductors from the buses. These initiatives represent a cost to the public purse, as do the increases in public subsidies paid to private bus operators (Aitchison, 1994, p.30). Plans to privatize British Rail entail the creation of a new Rail regulator, and passenger transport services still run by the public sector are now obliged to abide by the standards laid out in passenger charters.

Furthermore, the same regulatory pattern is currently emerging at the European level, with the European Commission assuming significant international powers of control in a number of areas of economic activity. One obvious such area concerns the content and conduct of mergers and take-overs involving major multi-national corporations; another relates to banking and financial services (Vipond, 1993). As Loukas Tsoukalis has pointed out, the creation of the Single European Market has often been portrayed as an essentially deregulatory exercise, but this is a little too simplistic

> At least in some cases the creation of the internal market will, inevitably, involve the adoption of a new regulatory framework at the EC level and, therefore, the transfer of powers to Community institutions. There will be more market in the new economic order, but also more European state; and the trade-off between the two will be determined in the future by a combination of economic and political factors, both internal and external to the EC. This is what we may call the political economy of liberalization and regulation. (Tsoukalis, 1991, pp.88-9).

The advent of the Single European Market has often been portrayed as a crucial feature of a liberalized and integrated European transport policy for the future. Until its introduction freight and passenger transport operators could rely on the protection of a variety of restrictive practices maintained by national governments, notwithstanding the rhetoric of the Treaty of Rome. For example, state owned Airlines could benefit from generous government subsidies, while road haulage was bound by a complex system of permits which, among other things, prevented hauliers from conducting local business in other countries. Many of these constraints on the market will be removed over the next few years in the name of an internal free market for the countries of the European Union. However, the prospect of regulation will not necessarily diminish. Rules governing transport may often be as strict as hitherto, if not more so, but they will have to be harmonized across national borders. Thus, fiscal rules covering, for example, vehicle excise duty, fuel tax and motorway tolls, will have to be common throughout the EU. Similarly, standards and regulations covering road haulage vehicle weights and sizes and also drivers' hours will be harmonized (Shaw, 1993, ch.14). In short, it may be broadly appropriate to foresee enhanced prospects of both choice and competition in European transport, but it is important to bear in mind the growing sigificance of the role played by the European state.

References

Aitchison, C. (1994) "No privatization without regulation: The Independent, 6 January.

Bacon & Eltis (1976) *Britain's Economic Problem: Too Few Producers* (Macmillan: London).

Bianchi, P. Cassese, S & della Sala, V. (1988) "Privatization in Italy: Aims and constraints': West European Politics, 11/4 (October).

Birch, A. (1984) 'Overload, ungovernability and deligitimation', British Journal of Political Science, 14/2 (April).

Boucek, F. (1993) 'Developments in postwar French political economy: the continuing decline of dirigisme?' in Sheldrake, J & Webb, P *State and Market: Aspects of Modern European Development,* (Dartmouth Publishing, Aldershot.

Carter, S. (1993) "The privatization of the former East German economy" in Sheldrake & Webb, op.cit.

Esser, J. (1988) Symbolic privatization: the politics of privatization in West Germany; West European Politics, 11/4 (October).

Freeman, C. & Perez, C. (1988) "Structural crises of adjustment, business cycles and investment behaviour" in Dosi, G., Freeman, C., Nelson, R.

Silverberg, G. & Soete, L. *Technology and Economic Theory,* Pinter, London.

Fourastié, J. (1979) *Les Trente Glorieuses, ou la Revolution Invisible de 1945 à 1975,* Fayard, Paris.

HM Treasury (1990) *Economic Trends* December, HMSO, London.

Hayek, F (1976) *Law, Legislation and Liberty, Vol.2* Routledge and Kegan Paul, London.

Hirsch, J. (1991) From Fordist to post-Fordist state in Jessop, B, Nielsen, K, Kastendiek, H & Pedersen, O. *The Politics of Flexibility,* Edward Elgar, Aldershot.

King, A. (1976) *Why is Britain becoming harder to govern?* BBC Books, London.

Lijphart, A. (1977) *Democracy in Plural Societies* Yale University Press, New Haven.

Maloney, W. & Richardson, J. (1992) "Post-privatisation regulation in Britain", Politics 12/2 (October).

Muller, W. (1988) "Privatizing in a corporatist economy: the politics of privatization in Austria", West European Politics, 11/4 (October).

Niskanen, W. (1971) *Bureaucracy and Representative Government,* Aldine-Atherton, New York.

Nozick, R. (1974) *Anarchy, State and Utopia,* (Basil Blackwell, Oxford.

O'Connor, J. (1973) *The Fiscal Crisis of the State* St. Martin's Press, New York.

Oxley, H. Maher, M, Martin, J, & Nicoletti, G. (1990) *The Public Sector: Issues for the 1990s* Working Paper number 90, OECD, Paris.

Pierre, J. (1993): Social Democracy, state and market in Sweden in

Sheldrake & Webb op.cit.

Pirie, M. (1988) *Privatization*, Wildwood House, London.

Rose, R. (1980) *Challenge to Governance: Studies in Overloaded Politics.* Sage, London.

Shaw, S. (1993) *Transport: Strategy and Policy,* Basil Blackwell, Oxford.

Stephens, J. (1979) *The Transition from Capitalism to Socialism*, Macmillan, London.

Thompson, G. (1990) *The Political Economy of the New Right*, Pinter, London.

Tsoukalis, L. (1991) *The New European Economy*, Oxford University Press, Oxford.

Vickers, J & Wright, V. (1988) "The politics of industrial privatization in Western Europe", West European Politics, 11/4 (October).

Vipond, P. (1993) "The state, the EC and banking regulation in Europe" in Sheldrake & Webb op.cit.

Webb, P. (1993) "The Labour Party, the market and the electorate" in Sheldrake & Webb op.cit.

Webster, P & Christie, A. (1993) "Sweeping £35 billion French sell-off to include banks and blue-chip firms The Guardian 27 May.

4 Travel and the assertive consumer

Stephen Shaw

Introduction

In transport, as in other sectors, the customers have grown more assertive. They have become more skillful, more sophisticated in uniting to challenge suppliers of goods and services. This chapter:

* explains the origins and development of consumerism
* discusses a successful user campaign
* assesses the future of consumer representation where transport services are being liberalized/deregulated.

It argues that independent user bodies are necessary to safeguard and promote the interests of passengers of all modes. Furthermore, they become more, not less important in a free market environment for transport.

The consumer movement

The word "consumerism" has acquired two quite different meanings. On the one hand, it can describe a culture based on unquestioning materialism and self-interest. In contrast, it can mean collective action to defend those who are ignored, disadvantaged or exploited by suppliers; i.e. "the protection and promotion of consumers' interests" (Oxford Reference Dictionary). Thus, groups and coalitions form to lobby for new or tougher safeguards. They may also demand a voice for the consumer; continuing dialogue with the suppliers and more radically active participation in decision making.

They may become the third corner of a triangle involving:

```
        suppliers              employees
        and trade              and trade
        associations           unions
              \                  /
              consumers and user organisations
```

Consumerism, in the altruistic sense of the word, became a "movement" which was well established in the United States by the early 1960s. At micro-level it questioned the imbalance of power between Big Business, and the individual as a buyer of goods and services. The latter might be in a weak bargaining position, unable to voice dissatisfaction with the high price of poor quality of everyday purchases. At the macro-level, consumerism raised doubts concerning the social and environmental worthiness of products offered by suppliers. Surprising perhaps, that such criticism should be levelled against an economic system apparently based on choice and competition, with the highest standards of living in the world.

By origin, consumerism was anti-establishment. The movement's activists were young, articulate and politically aware. The popular appeal and wide media coverage given to its chief protagonists such as Ralph Nader shocked and offended reactionary business executives. Many companies firmly believed that they were customer-orientated. Moreover, their products conferred wider benefits to society, i.e. "What's good for Ford is good for America". Widespread ownership of manufactured goods such as automobiles, and greater consumption of services such as air travel and tourism, would enhance the quality of life. These would be the very symbols of economic progress. Following the austerity of the Great Depression, the War and its aftermath, such adverse criticism of growth and abundance looked like downright ingratitude, if not subversion. However, some observers, nevertheless, interpreted these dissenting voices as warning signals. Suppliers who ignored the consumer movement would do so at their peril. Kotler advised the reactionaries to re-examine their philosophy of business. Consumerism was not a conspiracy by a small circle of agitators. It highlighted the increasingly strained relationship between standard business practices and long term consumer interests. It could not be ignored as a short lived "flare" of discontent. It would become a permanent feature of society. He understood it to be "an inevitable phase in the development of our economic system ... just as the labour movement started as a protest uprising and became institutionalised in the form of unions, government boards and labour legislation, the consumer movement, too, will become an increasingly institutionalised force in US society" (Kotler, 1972, p. 49).

Political legitimacy from the highest level was conferred on the movement by J.F. Kennedy in 1962. The President's Consumer Bill of Rights, outlined in his message to Congress, contained four main elements. All had particular significance for transport users:

* the right to safety
* the right to be informed
* the right to choose
* the right to be heard

These principles were more or less endorsed by Presidents Johnson and Nixon, and President Ford added a fifth: the right to consumer education (Preston and Bloom, 1980, p. 38). President Carter proclaimed himself to be "the Number One consumerist in the nation". During the 1976 presidential election campaign he actually played a game of baseball with Ralph Nader. In office, however, his administration's attempts to create an effective federal consumer agency resulted in a disappointingly "watered down, understaffed and toothless" bureaucracy (Richardson, 1980, p. 17).

There was, indeed, a good deal of disillusion with the use of rules, agencies and complaint-driven procedures to solve consumer problems. In the mid 1970s, public opinion in the United States swung against Federal intervention. In particular, it was considered that the deregulation of key industries, including banking, communications, and transport, would offer greater choice and lower prices for the customer. Value for money was an understandable concern at a time when inflation was running high and household budgets tight. Gialloreto (1988, pp. 19-20) describes the presentation of the case for airline deregulation as something of a crusade: pro-consumer and against the cartels of established commercial airlines, as well as against the bureaucracy of government agencies, in this case the Civil Aeronautics Board (CAB). Some 40 years of strict quantity licensing was ended at one stroke. Domestic airlines which satisfied the "fit, willing and able" requirements would be free to enter the market place. They could fly new routes, and withdraw them gain if they wished. They could charge whatever fare they considered commercially appropriate. President Carter was reaching the mid-point in the term of his administration. Inflation was running high and the cost of air travel increasing faster than the normal pace. The creation of an "Open Skies" regime, through the Deregulation Act of 1978, was the promised saviour for consumers of air travel. Indeed, in the early years of deregulation, a new entrant such as People Express could position itself as the consumer champion: the low price/no frills carrier during a period of recession. On the North Atlantic services, Laker Airways offered similar promise. The innovative Skytrain concept targeted price-sensitive leisure traffic. It was rightly anticipated by Laker that, if the fares were low enough, a substantial latent demand for trans-Atlantic travel would materialise. Yet both People Express and Laker faced merciless retaliation by established air carriers, and both were doomed to failure.

Liberalization itself led to public disillusion in air transport as in other sectors. Deregulation led to greater consolidation within the airline industry. Although some carriers such as American Airlines developed a corporate strategy based on internally generated growth, others did so by mergers and acquisitions. An initial increase in the number of competing carriers was a short lived phase. By 1988 only ten "mega carriers" survived (Pickrell, 1991, p. 23). By the early 1990s it was observed that "the results of US airline deregulation have been the opposite of what was expected: a few big sharks have gobbled up all the small fish... it is feared that the price advantage will disappear as a few dominant airlines push through fare increases and cut back services to smaller cities" (Morris, 1992). The issue of which consumers would be getting the lower fares was never quite fully explained to the travelling public. In a free market system, the only services where an airline has to compete on price are those where there are other carriers who are doing the same thing. In many smaller markets in the United States, competition did not increase. Deregulation was a signal to some carriers that they could now abandon the less profitable markets (Gialloreto, 1988, pp 20-1). Thus, the question of where and how much to deregulate has become an issue of considerable debate. Deregulation remains a possibility: "dissatisfaction with the results of deregulation (from communities that have lost all airline service, for example) will inevitably emerge, just as complaints about deregulation itself did in the past. Calls for continued or renewed regulatory activity will become more frequent" (Preston and Bloom, 1980, pp 48-9).

In the UK, consumerism found expression in the Consumers' Association. From humble beginnings, it has become highly institutionalised. Its *Which?* magazine provides information and advice on the price and quality ratings of a wide range of consumer products and services. Surveys relating to transport and travel in recent issues (1991-1993) have included: cars and other vehicles; carhire; express coaches; ferries; domestic airlines; and railways. It should be noted that these include some markets where choice is considerable, and others where choice within the mode is non-existent. Public monopolies have, however, become a major focus of concern, particularly in the transport sector. The price, quality and safety for Britain's rail services, for example, have been discussed with regularity in the pages of *Which?* magazine since 1977 (Consumer Policy Review, 1991, pp 176-82). The arguments have been supported by the Association's own research. Thus, a telephone survey of 500 Network South East commuters, published in 1990, yielded a somewhat negative response. Nearly two out of five passengers thought that the service represented "poor value for money". During the previous twelve months as one in four had complained verbally to British Rail, and one in 14 had sent a written complaint. When the commuters were asked if they considered complaining, without actually doing so, six out of ten said "yes". The majority of these had failed to take their complaint to the rail operator because they "did not think it would do any good". When asked whether they thought commuter services on their regular route had improved or deteriorated in the last three years, two-thirds felt they had deteriorated.

In the early 1990s both the Conservatives and Labour Party acknowledged consumer anxieties over the quality of services offered by British Rail and other public utilities such as the Post Office and National Health Service. Consumerism was raised several notches on the political agenda. As Cartledge has commented (1992, pp 35-6), the sudden eruption of consumerist themes onto the centre of the political stage caught many consumer activists unawares: "To be courted by politicians and civil servants for ideas that might form the centrepieces of future manifestos was an unprecedented and possibly unnerving experience. To find their traditional preoccupations - choice, access, information, safety, representation, and redress - entering the currency of parliamentary debate was an exhilarating departure. To find Government and Opposition jockeying for position to determine whose consumerist credentials were the stronger was a fascinating spectacle".

On this occasion, the proposed solutions to consumers' problems were to lie with "Charters" for the users. The Conservative version known as the Citizen's Charter initiative, was launched by Prime Minister Major in 1991. According to the Conservative Manifesto of the following year this "…. addresses the needs of those who use public services, extends people's rights, requires services to set clear standards, and to tell the public how these standards are met". Thus the British Rail Passengers' Charter pledges with regard to Network South East services that: "… if we fail by more than a small margin to meet our punctuality and reliability standards, you will be entitled to a discount when you renew your monthly or longer period season ticket" (British Rail, 1992). Different targets were set for different routes within the network, reflecting the age and condition of the infrastructure and rolling stock. Although the principle of target-setting and redress for service failure was generally acclaimed, the narrowness of the criteria used to measure quality, and the restrictive "smallprint", received a sceptical reception from consumer groups and from the media. The case study discussed in the next section of this paper provides an example of active participation by user groups in the policies and practices of a metropolitan public transport operator. In this case the initiative for action came from the passengers' group.

User campaign: transport and personal safety for women

In North America, public services such as municipal transport have received attention from agonised consumers who demand the basic taxonomy of rights: to safety; to be informed; to choose; and to be heard (Enis and Yarwood, 1980, pp 153-64). Compared to the UK, however, there has been a much greater emphasis on the connection between consumer rights and human rights in the provision of services. A notable example was the campaign led by disabled Vietnam war veterans for accessible public transport: action which led to far-reaching legislation in the mid 1970s. The following case study was researched in Canada by the author and his colleagues Fiona Colgan and Sue Johnstone. For the broader context of equity in transport and other sectors, the reader is referred to the forthcoming book *Women in Organisations* edited by Colgan and Ledwith (1994). Safe, convenient and affordable public transport has particular significance for women since many are wholly dependent on it for access to paid employment, childcare, education, health services, leisure provision and so on. And yet "...the transport world has been slow to see the relevance of women, women's needs or women's issues to the plans and decisions which they make" (Hamilton and Jenkins, 1992, p. 57). These points have also been emphasised by women in Canada. "Women have a major stake in the design and operation of the public transportation system, because women are more than twice as likely as men to use public transit. The provision of transportation alternatives and options is the result of both policy decisions and non-decisions. These decisions should receive continued public scrutiny to determine how they may favour or ignore the needs of one gender over another" (Rutherford and Wekerle, 1987, pp 3-4).

The Toronto Transit Commission (TTC), the second largest public municipal operator in North America, received particular criticism: "... the TTC uses models and criteria which are "objective", gender-blind, and largely indifferent to the larger (defined as non-transportation) needs of its clientele. This not only ignores the gender of the rider, but removes from the concern of the public transit agency the constraints, needs and costs borne by one gender over another." (Rutherford and Wekerle, 1987, p. 4). Many women have justifiable fears of being assaulted or harassed while using public transport. Such anxieties, experienced by other groups including ethno-racial minorities and the elderly, may deter them from travelling at all, especially at night. Over a period of ten years from 1983 to 1993 public transport users in the city of Toronto have voiced these concerns to the senior management of the TTC. They are now achieving some measure of success. Our study examined the process of change and focused on the following questions:

* how were personal safety concerns made known to the public transport operator?
* what programme of action resulted?

Public concern for the personal safety of women and children was highlighted during the early 1980s. An horrific series of rapes and murders in the metropolitan area and surrounding suburbs led to widespread expression of outrage. The women's movement in Canada was already very well organized and a number of local groups came together demanding action. The TTC have a longstanding commitment to high safety standards and had carried out a safety review with the Toronto Police Force in 1976. This had resulted in a number of changes including the installation of passenger assistance alarms on subway trains and public telephones on station platforms. Nevertheless, as women's groups emphasised, the safety audits hitherto had not addressed the issue of sexual assault and harassment. As a first step, the Metropolitan Council set up a taskforce chaired by legal expert Jane Pepino. This conducted a comprehensive investigation of the underlying problems, and the TTC participated in the work of its subcommittees. In 1984 the taskforce published its recommendations which included the creation of a permanent specialist body funded by Metro but independent from it. Thus, the Metro Action Committee on Public Violence Against Women and Children (METRAC) was established. The vulnerability of women and children to sexual assaults on public transit has been an important concern of the organization since its inception. METRAC has worked closely with Prof. Gerda Wekerle and her colleagues at York University who developed a methodology for assessing the personal safety hazards of sites such as subway stations and transit stops, and for identifying possible improvements.

METRAC used this research as the focus for discussion at a public meeting on women and transportation in 1987. The meeting was held at a time of great anxiety over a series of rapes in the Scarborough area of the city, where the assailant had followed women from bus stops. Jane Pepino, now President of METRAC and a Police Commissioner, then approached Al Leach, the TTC's newly appointed Chief General Manager, in order to discuss the way forward. This led to a unique collaborative project between the TTC, METRAC and the Police Force to promote safer public transit. Despite the shared goal, it was recognised that the three organisations had no shared philosophical perspective to provide a natural starting point: "Traditional police crime prevention programmes had not included sexual assault prevention; transit authorities' safety initiatives had not specifically focused on sexual assault, and women's rape prevention initiatives had rarely embraced traditional institutions dealing with crime prevention and general safety issues or transit safety". Working together would not be easy. Nevertheless, as the project developed "... all involved found that our effort to make transit safer for women was better because it was a shared venture" (Toronto Transit Commission, 1989a, p. 6). As draft recommendations were being prepared in summer 1988, the TTC hosted a meeting with the local women's organizations. The discussion enabled those attending to express their concerns and to review progress. As a result, a number of priorities for action were highlighted, especially:

* physical safety measures, including alarm systems, CCTV and voice intercoms on all station platforms, and the installation of better lighting and mirrors for all "blind" corners;
* staffing measures, including sensitivity training for all staff and more TTC security or police officers to patrol the system;
* public education to inform women about the safety features, where to seek help, and about their rights to safety.

An important feature of the collaborative project was that the audit process should be informed by surveys, meetings and focus group discussions. Feedback was sought on a step-by-step basis. Thus, publication of the draft recommendations at the end of 1988 was followed by extensive consultation, and a well-attended public meeting attended by senior managers of the TTC. As a result, a number of modifications were made before the final recommendations and programme of action was drawn up in 1989.

The centrepiece of the physical improvements has been the installation of Designated Waiting Areas (DWAs) in all subway stations, which were completed in autumn 1992. The aim has been to offer women a safe location, allowing two-way communication with transit staff who can provide assistance. Members of METRAC were fully involved in the piloting of the scheme, and other women were invited to comment on the experimental DWAs in selected stations. Three different prototypes were tried and tested. The one option favoured by METRAC was subsequently adopted despite its relatively high cost. Its essential features are: increased lighting; seat alarm button; inter-com to collector's booth; CCTV monitored by collector; public telephone; and an information panel.

Plans for all new stations, and refurbishment of existing ones, are submitted to an architect whose responsibility is to examine the proposals from a personal safety perspective. The current postholder is a woman whose work has received praise from METRAC. The process enables modifications to be made at an early stage of design. Other physical improvements throughout the system have included extra mirrors, signage, and features such as extra benches, and public art to "humanize" the subway. It is recognised that care must be taken to avoid obscuring sightlines or creating any new hiding places for potential assailants. Another feature which is being added on METRAC's recommendation concerns the yellow alarm strip. System-wide, the word harassment is being added to the list of emergency situations where the alarm should be pressed. The current expression 'passenger safety and security' is now considered too vague.

Surface transport has also received attention. In 1989 the TTC was approached by two organizations from an area of the city where a serial rapist had followed his victims after they had alighted from TTC buses. The Scarborough Women's Centre and Scarborough Women's Action Network initiated a safety review of surface transport, supported by METRAC in co-operation with the TTC. (Toronto Transit Commission, 1991a, p. 5).

The recommendations included a Request Stop Programme, to enable women and others to get off TTC vehicles at locations other than bus stops, when travelling after dark and early in the morning. The proposal was tried out, but the initial use of this facility was lower than anticipated. Following discussions with METRAC it was given greater publicity and demand increased. As a result of the pilot scheme in Scarborough, the Request Stop Programme was extended system-wide for all surface transit operated by the TTC.

The auditing process and dialogue with women's organizations highlighted the need for the TTC's front line staff to respond effectively and sensitively to the victims of sexual assault. They must also be alert to the dangers faced by women using public transit and thus help reduce such risks. It was recognised that many TTC staff might be uncertain of their role, and how best to deal with issues of personal safety for women, as well as fearful of their own safety in some circumstances. A programme of action to provide more precise guidelines for TTC staff has been developed by the Safety and Security Department with advice from Equal Opportunities staff. Throughout the system the staff have received instructions on how to respond to an incident of sexual assault with sensitivity to the emotional and physical reactions of the victim. It has been made clear that this does not just mean actual or attempted rape but also harassment such as a woman being followed, stared at with menace, or touched.

Safety improvements must be given appropriate publicity using media and messages which the various audiences can understand. Women passengers should be informed how to move about the system in greater safety, and how to use the new features such as DWAs. Toronto is a cosmopolitan city and many of its residents and visitors do not speak English as their first language, if at all. Women who are members of ethno-racial minorities are vulnerable to racial as well as sexual assault and harassment. A general user guide *Your TTC* includes some basic safety information and is now produced in 15 languages. It has been promoted in the multi-cultural media. Nevertheless, distribution has not been fully effective in reaching the target audiences. In 1993 the TTC Equal Opportunity and Marketing Departments were developing a manual and video, again to include safety messages. This will be used by community organisations as a resource facilitated by TTC outreach staff.

The campaign for safer public transport in Toronto eventually led to positive responses from municipal government, and from the public transport undertaking. The climate of city politics was favourable, but this is not always the case. As Richardson has argued (1980, p. 20) consumer organizations cannot set the agenda of public policy. Rather, they must adapt to their environment. Their influence depends a great deal upon: media access; saleable ideas in the public policy arena; and a believable claim to consumer authenticity. Some user groups have become highly skilled at gaining attention. Nevertheless, in the UK context Cartledge (1992, p. 35) draws the gloomy conclusion that consumer concerns have tended to be a minority issue, and that consumer representatives generally languish in obscurity, especially when compared with their business and trade union counterparts: Lacking recognition, funding, organization and political clout, the consumer movement has remained fragmented and ineffectual. Profree market governments have put far more faith in the power of market forces to satisfy consumer demands than in the type of consumer representation demonstrated in Toronto. How valid are their arguments?

Liberalization and user bodies

The final section of this chapter examines the role of user bodies in the context of the regulation/deregulation debate. Freedom of choice has become enshrined as a fundamental consumer right. Nevertheless, in many countries, transport services are provided by monopolies. In the case study discussed above, the majority of women passengers were wholly dependent on public transport: obliged to use the TTC's services, or else not travel at all. Where markets are captive or semi-captive, consumers may encounter indifference and resistance to change. There is therefore a need for user bodies to protect passengers' interests, to voice their opinions on operators' policies and practices, and to lobby for improvements.

To the political right, such problems are inherent where markets are distorted by State intervention. To free marketeers, consumer voice is a poor substitute for consumer choice. Thus, user bodies are considered necessary, only where economic regulation has restricted market entry, artificially fixed the prices charged to the customers, and imposed a route network, timetable and service level through centralized planning by the "nanny" State. According to this doctrine, competition or the threat of it, provides a more powerful and immediate incentive to respond to the needs and wants of customers than advice from user representatives. In the UK, special-purpose user bodies have been set up by central government or its agencies to represent:

* airline users
* rail users
* public transport users in the London region.

Today, all modes are affected by actual or proposed liberalization. Will the free market environment render such consumer organizations redundant?

Airline users are represented by the Air Transport Users' Council (AUC). Originally set up in 1973, it assumed its current terms of reference in 1978. The AUC is sponsored by but independent from the Civil Aviation Authority (CAA), the UK's regulatory agency for air transport. Members of the AUC are appointed by the CAA, and full time staff at the time of writing consisted of the Director General, his personal secretary and three other executives. The AUC's function is to make reports and recommendations to the CAA "... furthering the interests of air transport users including the investigation of complaints against the suppliers of air transport services ..."

Nevertheless, the AUC also makes representations to the government, European Commission and other agencies. The AUC reviews the policies and practices of airlines, airport authorities, regulatory agencies and other bodies whose decisions affect air transport users. Issues closely monitored by the AUC include: air safety; passenger security; airport slot allocation; runway capacity; surface access to airports; and facilities for disabled passengers. As has been noted the user body's terms of reference include the investigation of complaints. In principle, this embraces all scheduled and charter services into UK airports, regardless of the nationality of the airline: a throughput which has peaked at over 100 million passengers a year in recent times. Given the AUC's limited establishment it "does not set out to be a complaints bureau" (Air Transport Users' Council, 1991, p. 25). It has therefore adopted a rather low profile in this respect. Nevertheless, it does investigate over 1,200 cases each year. The most common complaints relate to: flight cancellations and delays; tickets; baggage; reservations; and in-flight services (Shaw, 1993, pp 204-06).

One of the most important issues for the AUC is the liberalization of air services within the European Union. The new "freer skies" regime, which came into effect in January 1993, was warmly welcomed. In essence it means that airlines will have the freedom to set their own fares, and be able to fly between any airports in the European Union (EU). The AUC supports the principle that "competition provides the best available mechanism to ensure that the users always have a choice and that the services provided by the industry are of high quality and reasonable price" (Air Transport Users' Council, 1992, p.9). To some free marketeers it might appear, at first sight, that the user body are arguing themselves out of a job. Learning from experience of total deregulation in the United States, the AUC emphasise that fair competition is essential to consumers' interests. The AUC will therefore monitor very closely the effectiveness of the EU competition rules. They are mindful of the view of some critics that after some initial instability the European airline industry ... will consolidate into no more than four of five mega-carriers who by tacit collusion on fares and by their grip on slots at the main Community airports, will ensure the consumers do not reap any real benefits from liberalisation (ibid, p.14). There are important safeguards to prevent either collusion over fares or predatory pricing, but their effectiveness must be demonstrated. The European Commission is empowered to take prompt action in the form of a "cease and desist" order to prevent one carrier from jeopardising the services of another". The AUC therefore regards... "the existence of comprehensive competition rules, fearlessly and effectively applied by the Commission, to be a vital corollary of the liberalization process. However, the real test will lie in the Commission's willingness to exercise these powers when the need arises" (Air Transport Users' Council, 1991, p.8).

Consumer education is an expanding aspect of the AUC's work. In contrast to rail commuters, most airline travellers make very few flights per year. Some find the process bewildering, if not daunting. Mindful of the practical limits to its complaints investigation role, the AUC is aware that much dissatisfaction stems from ignorance of what the consumer can reasonably expect for his/her money. In 1993 the AUC published a *Passengers' Guide to Planning and Using Air Travel*. This provides valuable information on how consumers can avoid expensive mistakes, their basic rights and responsibilities, and how to resolve any problems that arise. The AUC is also active in supporting any actions which can help disabled passengers to travel with the least discomfort and inconvenience. It has produced its own advice booklet for disabled air travellers *Care in the Air*.

Rail users are represented by eight, regionally-based Transport Users' Consultative Committees (TUCCs). Such bodies were originally set up in 1947 when large sections of the transport industry were nationalized, though their remit has been modified by subsequent legislation. Implementation of the 1993 Railways Bill will change their role and function once again, to take account of the government's proposals to privatize/commercialize British Rail. Their name will change to Rail Users' Consultative Committees (RUCCs). Formerly multi-modal in their remit, their current title has been a misnomer for many years, since they deal almost exclusively with passenger railways viz British Rail services and land networks such as the Tyne and Wear Metro and Manchester Metrolink. The broader picture for the national network is reviewed by the Central Transport Consultative Committee (CTCC) whose membership includes the Chairperson of the TUCCs. All report to the President of the Board of Trade as the Minister with responsibility for consumer affairs. For nearly 20 years this arrangement has given them some independence from the Secretary of State for Transport who has direct responsibility for British Rail.

The TUCCs and CTCC monitor and review the decisions of the rail operators, as well as those of the government and other agencies. Matters of direct concern to the user bodies include: passenger safety and personal security; quality of train services and the passenger environment on stations; staff conduct; provision for passengers with special needs and so on. They also monitor various aspects of performance including: punctuality; level of cancellations; overcrowding; response to enquiries and so on, although with limited resources, they have to rely a great deal on data supplied by the rail operator which may not be satisfactory for the user bodies' purposes. They may also initiate and commission their own surveys and studies as their budgets permit. They are debarred, by statute from considering fares. Nevertheless, the CTCC has recently commented in its Annual Report that they ".... deplored the Inter City and Network South East fare rises introduced in January 1993. Average increases ... three times the prevailing rate of inflation amounted to an exploitation of a monopoly position". (Central Transport Consultative Committee, 1993, p.21). The TUCCs' functions include a quasi-judicial role. If the rail operator wishes to close a passenger station or line, the TUCC for that region is required by law to consider any objections and report to the government on the hardship that would result. The proposed closure cannot be implemented unless the government has given consent, having considered the TUCC's report and recommendations.

TUCC also handle a considerable caseload of complaints, comments and suggestions from the travelling public. These individual cases are referred to them where a passenger is not happy with the response of the rail operator. If the TUCC considers the passenger's case to be justified, it can make representations to the operator, who may be persuaded to offer an apology, explanation and/or compensation. The TUCC's review of policy matters as well as the overall pattern of complaints will suggest a number of problems and issues which the user body may pursue with the rail operator/government/other agencies. On some matters TUCCs take a critical stance. For example, the CTCC Annual Report (1993) highlighted the withdrawal of certain through Inter City services; punctuality of trains on Sundays; ticket office queues; inadequate waiting rooms, lack of/dirty toilets and so on. On the other the CTCC was supportive on a number of points. The Chairperson's statement commented "... I am often surprised that British Rail has done as well as it has, bearing in mind the age of some rolling stock and the restraints on improvements to the rail infrastructure .... BR staff deserve credit therefore for keeping the overall national standards at an acceptable level ..."

The government's proposals for privatizing British Rail dominated the work of the CTCC in 1992/3. The White Paper *New Opportunities for the Railways* was published summer 1992, confirming the basic framework set out in the Conservative Election Manifesto. In the first phase, train operation will be separated from the infrastructure which is to be run by Railtrack: a state-owned agency which will charge the rail operators, and be expected to earn a profitable return on its assets. The three main elements of the regulatory framework will be the Rail Regulator to ensure "fair play"; a Franchising Director to oversee the disposal of the service elements of the passenger businesses into franchises, and an enhanced role for the Health and Safety Executive. Later, some routes will become open access services, meaning that different rail operators would compete for passenger markets on the same track. The subsequent consultation document *A Voice for the Passenger* allayed fears that consumer committees would simply be wound up. Nevertheless the CTCC expressed concern that they would, seemingly, be excluded from representing passengers on open access services. Sponsored by the Rail Regulator, they might find it hard to exert their independence. They would have to "take account of value for money from the point of view of the public purse". Furthermore, they would be prevented from considering fares and charges, and from commenting on franchise specifications (CTCC, 1993, p.10). Continuing provision for disabled passengers was a further concern. The CTCC resolved "... that all rail operators should be required by legislation to accommodate the needs of disabled passengers, and in particular safety, access and comfort". The CTCC did not oppose the principle of privatization. Nevertheless it has remained anxious concerning the scale of such changes which have not been tried and tested in any other country. Following the White Paper, it became increasingly anxious about the lack of firm guarantees on the retention of network benefits such as through long distance train services; scheduled connections at interchanges; interavailability of tickets and the national information and reservation system. (CTCC, 1993, p.8).

Public transport users in the capital are represented by the London Regional Passengers' Committee (LRPC). Set up in 1984, it has a parallel reporting structure and functions as the TUCC for other regions, with regard to British Rail services, but additionally covers all services run by or for London Transport: London Underground; bus services (including tendered routes); Victoria Coach Station; with special arrangements for Docklands Light Railway. It enjoys a high profile in the media as consumer watchdog for passengers, and holds its meetings in public. It has campaigned long and hard to improve the level of funding for investment in London's public transport network, and strongly criticised the government's reduction of project expenditure for 1993/4. With regard to Network South East's forced economies in operating budgets, a particular concern has been the destaffing of London stations which has escalated in recent years. With regard to rail privatisation, LRPC has spoken in concert with its fellow TUCCs through the CTCC whose delegation gave evidence to the House of Commons Transport Committee's hearing on the subject. LRPC are especially concerned to resist any reversal of the progress towards greater integration of London's public transport, for example in joint information systems and the all-operator multi-modal Travelcard. The latter has long been regarded by the LRPC "as its most important campaigning success. By common consent, Travelcard has played a crucial part in retaining and winning passengers for London's public transport system" (LRPC, 1993, p.8). Neither British Rail nor London Transport has been willing to give a guarantee about its survival. Stored value ticketing (modelled on phonecards) offers a technical solution, as the system is progressively privatized and fragmented. The operators do not, however, appear to be in a position to meet the cost of installing it system-wide.

The LRPC holds no collective view on the privatization of the London Buses subsidiaries. It is, however, vehemently opposed to deregulation in the capital. The LRPC believes that the existing tenders regime has delivered benefits in terms of improved quality of service; reductions in unit costs and subsidy; retention of ridership; and stability of service "... which far outweigh the somewhat nebulous claims made for the positive impact of deregulation in comparable conurbations elsewhere". (LRPC, 1993, p.11). The user body had even more cause for dismay, since according to the Department of Transport document *A Bus Strategy for London* (1991, para. 27) the LRPC would lose its watchdog role for buses, except for the residual "socially necessary" services. In its evidence to the subsequent House of

Commons Transport Committee's inquiry into the government's intentions for buses in London, the LRPC reported that this proposal attracted almost universal opposition, mainly on the grounds that the difference between commercial and tendered services would not be apparent or relevant to bus passengers. As many as 53 out of 57 respondents to the consultation paper, including London Transport, wanted LRPC to have a locus standi in respect of commercial services too. (House of Commons Transport Committee 1993, para 108).

Passengers in the UK are also represented by a number of campaigning voluntary organisations specific to the transport sector or to particular modes. At national level, these include Transport 2000, the Railway Development Society and the National Federation of Bus Users. Such organizations have very limited resources, especially when compared to other interest groups whose policies and arguments they may oppose, notably the British Roads Federation. Consumer pressure in public transport is often expressed at local level. There are, for example, over 100 such groups in the London area, (London Regional Passengers Committee, 1990 p.3). Some voice to concerns of passengers using particular stations or lines, for example, the Southend Rail Travellers' Association and the Bishop's Stortford Ticketholders' Association. Some local groups have been formed to campaign against service closure, and in particular to defend those who have no other means of transport for essential journeys. For example, a user group successfully argued against closure of the North London Line in the 1960s, and carried out surveys demonstrating the large numbers of children who travelled to school on it. Supporters of the Settle and Carlisle Line have defended their railway for 30 years. Such local groups sometimes affiliate to the national organizations already mentioned and may thus receive wider support and publicity for their action. Some user groups are concerned with transport for people with special needs such as those whose mobility is impaired by a disadvantage such as blindness, deafness or arthritis. For example, the London Dial-a-Ride Users' Association publicise the problems experienced by people dependent on a specialized form of transport for which demand greatly exceeds supply. Their surveys have shown that even an initial telephone call to book a journey can require persistence and patience (Shaw, 1993, p.207).

Consumerism is an established and developing feature of the political and economic life in North America, the UK and other OECD countries. The institutions which provide a voice for consumer interests are, nevertheless, weak relative to their counterparts which represent capital and labour. In passenger transport, many user bodies were set up by the State or by voluntary effort as a countervailing force against benign but monopolistic public undertakings. It is quite wrong to assume, however, that the process of liberalization and the unleashing of market forces will render such bodies superfluous. Passengers will continue to need well-organized, adequately-resourced bodies to speak for them. These must genuinely represent a broad cross-section of passengers, especially those who are disadvantaged socially and economically.

Some consumer concerns are common to regulated and deregulated markets for passenger transport:

* it is desirable for an independent body to monitor the policies and performance of operators, and to provide a forum for constructive criticism;
* the individual may be in a weak bargaining position, and require a channel for complaints, comments and suggestions, independent of the operator;
* inexperienced travellers may lack adequate information to make a rational decision;
* user bodies may highlight issues which should be included on the operator's agenda, eg the particular needs of blind/partially sighted people, the elderly, parents with small children, ethnic-racial minorities.

In liberalized markets, commercial carriers may compete for customers; introduce or withdraw services; raise or lower fares; and determine the frequency/capacity of service, all according to the operator's commercial judgement. In theory, this should result in customer choice and motivate the innovative, market-oriented entrepreneur. Yet in practice, the markets for some transport services may be very different from the economist's ideal of perfect competition - a fair contest between a multitude of suppliers for the custom of well-informed buyers. Competition may be neither free nor fair and, in the longer term, customers may find themselves in a weaker bargaining position.

In some modes, big operators may use anti-competitive predatory tactics against smaller fry. Furthermore, the customers often require through transits, and expect good co-ordination between different routes within a network. They also expect the advertised services and prices charged to have reasonable stability. (Shaw, 1993, p.2). The free play of market forces may not be able to satisfy important user requirements. There are therefore some additional reasons for consumer representation:

* without ownership or regulatory control by the State, the public can no longer influence service provision through central/local government or its agencies;

* market instability may create a great deal of uncertainty over the continuity, level and quality of some services;
* the benefits of integrated services such as through-ticketing and service co-ordination may be lost;
* the rules and procedures to prevent unfair competition in the various modes have yet to prove themselves as effective guardians of consumer interests;
* the market may respond positively to effective demand, but there is a need to protect disadvantaged consumers whose transport needs may not be catered for.

It can also be argued that from a transport operator's point of view, user groups may provide a source of fresh ideas and valuable information. Other sectors such as retailing, hotels and catering recognise that their customers have become more discerning and more articulate in voicing opinions. Choice and voice are not mutually exclusive. Such suppliers often pay panels of consumers to discuss and criticise their products! Combined with other forms of market intelligence, they help build up a picture of how their offerings are perceived and received. Constructive dialogue between transport operator and user body requires time and skill to develop. Both parties need patience and open-mindedness to work together and achieve results in the medium to long term.

Conclusion

Consumerism has been expressed in different ways in different countries and different cultures. It has, perhaps, moved at a different pace in different industries, even within the transport sector. It has become, or is becoming, a significant force in air, rail and road passenger transport, regardless of the actual competition or degree of choice available. Operators may find it hard to understand and interpret, but they cannot ignore it. Some may harness it to their advantage. To return to Kotler's analysis "My assessment is that consumerism will be enduring, beneficial, pro-marketing, and ultimately profitable. Consumerism mobilises the energies of consumers, businessmen (sic), and government leaders to seek solutions to several complex problems in a technologically advanced society. One of these is the difference between serving consumer desires efficiently, and serving their long-run interests" (Kotler, 1972, p. 57).

References

Air Transport Users' Council (1991), *Annual Report 1990/1*.
Air Transport Users' Council (1992), *Annual Report 1991/2*.
British Rail (1992), *Passengers' Charter*.
Cartledge, J. (1992), "Consumerism and public transport" in *Travel Sickness: The Need for a Sustainable Transport Policy for Britain*. ed. Roberts J. etal, Lawrence and Wishart, London.
Central Transport Consultative Committee (1993), *Annual Report 1992/93*.
Colgan, F. & Ledwith, S. (1994), *Women in Organizations*, Macmillan, Oxford.
Consumers' Association (1991), 'Action Stations Campaign' in *Which?*, August.
Consumer Policy Review (1991), *Data from the CA. The Quality of Service in Utility Industries, Part 2: British Rail*, vol. 1, no. 3, July.
Department of Transport (1991), *A Bus Strategy for London: Consultation Paper*, HMSO, London.
Enis, B. and Yarwood, D. (1980), 'Consumer Protection in Public Sector Marketing: A Neglected Area in Consumerism' in Bloom, P. & Smith, R. (eds) *The Future of Consumerism*, Lexington, Massachusetts/Toronto.
Gialloreto, L. (1988), *Strategic Airline Management: the Global War Begins*, Pitman, London.
Government of Ontario (1989), *Human Rights Code, 1981*, as amended, Ministry of the Attorney General.
Hamilton, K. & Jenkins, L. (1992), 'Women and Transport', in Roberts, J. et al, op.cit.
House of Commons Transport Committee (1993), Fourth Report, *The Government's Proposals for the Deregulation of Buses in London*, Volume 1, HMSO, London.
Kotler, P. (1972), 'What Consumerism Means for Marketers', in Harvard Business Review, 50, May/June.
Lancaster, G. & Massingham, L. (1988), *Essentials of Marketing*, McGraw Hill.
London Regional Passengers Committee (1990), *About Turn*, LRPC, London.
London Regional Passengers Committee (1993), *Annual Report April 1992 - March 1993*.
Morris, B. (1992), 'Competition Leaves US Airlines on the Critical List' The Independent on Sunday, 13 January.
Preston, L. & Bloom, P. (1980), 'Concerns of the Rich/Poor Consumer' in Bloom, & Smith, op cit.

Richardson, S. (1980), 'Evolving Consumer Movement: Predictions for the 1990s' in Bloom, & Smith, op cit.

Rutherford, B. and Wekerle, G. (1987), *Equity Issues in Women's Accessibility to Employment: Transportation, Location and Policy,* City of Toronto Equal Opportunity Division, Management Services Department.

Shaw, S. (1993), *Transport: Strategy and Policy,* Blackwell, Oxford.

Toronto Transit Commission (1989a), *Making Transit Safer for Women.*

Toronto Transit Commission (1989b), *Summary of Departmental Responsibilities*

Toronto Transit Commission (1991a), *Making Transit Stops Safer for Women: Scarborough Moves Forward.*

Toronto Transit Commission (1991b), *Annual Report 1990.*

Toronto Transit Commission (1993), *Equal Opportunity Report.*

5 Local government and road passenger transport

Kevin Hey

Introduction

Local government has been involved with the public road passenger transport industry for well over a century. The period of this involvement covers great technological developments, major alterations to local government structures, and a reorientation of local government from direct service provider to service purchaser. These changes have caused significant alterations to the functions and role of local government in respect of public road passenger transport and this chapter considers some of the key aspects of these changes. The chapter outlines the constitutional position of local government and explains the various forms of authority granted to the locality. The key roles of local government in respect of public road passenger transport are then considered in turn. By examining the origin, history and development of each role, together with present arrangements it is possible to view the involvement of local government in public transport from different, yet often related, dimensions. The paper concludes with some comment on the reduced role which local government now performs in respect of public transport. Some of the similarities between the present and past nature of the various roles are observed to the extent that the return of local government to a more distant stance is less radical than sometimes assumed.

Local government

Modern local government is a creation of parliament which delegates certain functions to the responsibility of local government on the specific competency principle. Indeed local government can only undertake those functions for which specific parliamentary authority exists. Actions by local government not covered by such authority are subject to the doctrine of ultra vires and are therefore illegal. Parliament grants authority of action to local government through statute in the form of general public or local Acts of Parliament, or through some other delegated parliamentary authority procedure. Thus parliament places duties upon, and grants powers to local authorities in respect of a wide range of functions. Duties impose an obligation whilst powers provide an element of discretion, although the distinction is not absolute since duties can also permit local discretion (Foulkes, 1986, p.163). The greater discretion associated with local government powers rests on the form which such powers take, viz, obligatory, permissive or adoptive. Obligatory powers compel local authorities to exercise the powers contained within the statute. Permissive powers give local authorities discretion to exercise the powers contained within the statute. Finally adoptive powers allow local authorities to specifically acquire the powers contained within the statute only after undertaking prescribed steps.

Although the duties and powers determine the functions which local authorities perform, the discretionary nature of parliamentary authority allows variations of service delivery at local level which are then magnified through the local political process. This in part explains the complex development of local government involvement in public road passenger transport and the differences which exist between localities in the degree or manner in which certain elements are performed.

From an analysis of the public transport functions undertaken by local government a number of key roles can be identified - regulator, constructor and owner, operator, financial supporter, policy coordinator, and representor. These roles are not constant or uniform, or indeed discrete, since they are each performed under specific parliamentary authority with a different allocation between tiers of local government on the basis of locality typology.

However, there are some discernable features:

* the removal of local government from direct to indirect role executions through the creation of separate executive bodies to perform certain public transport functions previously undertaken by local government;
* the imposition of duties as well as powers which serve to focus the attention of local government upon key issues;
* the erosion of local discretion over public transport issues through increasing central control to ensure the supremacy of the latter over the former (Hepworth, 1984, pp.67-8, Loughlin, 1986, p.77).

Regulator

The role of public road passenger transport regulator was initially undertaken by local government - except in the metropolis where the function was vested in the Metropolitan Police. A number of provincial local authorities had powers covering the regulation of hackney carriages which were subsequently consolidated in the Town Police Clauses Act 1847, Public Health Act 1875 and finally extended to omnibuses through the Town Police. Clauses Act 1889. Glaister and Mulley (1983, p.3) summarize the position that powers were granted to town and district councils. However, there were wide variations in the application of these powers between localities and this made coordination difficult (Hibbs, 1989, pp.108-11). It should be noted that the granting of omnibus regulatory powers to local government was at a time when ownership and operation of omnibuses was by the private sector. At this stage there was clear role separation within and indeed between modes as initial tramway schemes were promoted by private enterprize. When local government tramway construction became accepted practice and direct municipal operation of public passenger transport was conceded, the regulator role was to come into conflict with the additional roles since local authorities were able to use powers of regulation to protect the direct operations of the authority from competition (Hibbs, 1989, pp.108-111).

Although a review of public road passenger transport regulation after World War One was prompted by concern for public safety rather than any desire for uniformity or coordination (Glaister and Mulley, 1983, p.22), the result was to remove the regulator role from provincial local government under the Road Traffic Act 1930. A system of largely autonomous Traffic Commissioners was established on a regional basis throughout the country with responsibility to regulate route, service and fares of omnibuses. Local authorities retained a very minor involvement with the Traffic Commissioners covering the locality by providing nominees to a panel of additional commissioners for the region.

Constructor and owner

As previously observed, public road passenger transport facilities were originally owned and developed by the private sector. Early tramway schemes promoted by private enterprize through local Acts of Parliament often provided for the local authority to acquire ownership of the tramway after a specified period (Robson, 1935, p.320). Local government was able to take a greater role as a result of the Tramways Act 1870 which allowed municipal construction and ownership of tramways through Provisional Order of the Board of Trade subject to parliamentary confirmation. Furthermore, a local authority could secure ownership of privately owned tramways within the locality, at structural value, through adoptive powers of compulsory purchase (s.43). These powers acted as a disincentive for private capital (Hibbs, 1989, p.45) particularly with the development of tramway electrification since private enterprize was reluctant to embark on such schemes without extended security of tenure. Accordingly an increasing number of local authorities exercised the powers of compulsory purchase and the concept of municipal tramway construction and ownership provided a foundation for the general development of municipal public passenger transport.

Notwithstanding the ideological differences surrounding the issue of municipal public road passenger transport ownership, local government was able to extend such powers to include the construction and ownership of trolleybus networks and omnibuses in due course. However, subsequent changes introduced by parliament or entered into on a voluntary basis by localities were to considerably reduce the number of local authorities involved with public transport. The structural changes implemented by parliament initially related to the metropolis and then later during the postwar period to more general local government reorganization. In the metropolis, the creation of a public authority under the London Passenger Transport Act 1933 in the form of the London Passenger Transport Board (LPTB) acquired ownership of no fewer than 11 local authority public transport undertakings within the area. Elsewhere, postwar local government reorganization proved to have a major effect upon the public transport roles of local government. In the conurbations it was recognized that reorganization of public transport could not await local government reform (Cmnd. 3481, 1967, p.3). The ensuing Transport Act 1968 allowed for the creation in each conurbation of a Passenger Transport Executive (PTE) to which ownership of municipal undertakings in the area were transferred. This removed a further 19 local government transport undertakings and one municipal joint board in England, plus 1 local authority undertaking in Scotland. More fundamental changes to the structure of local government in England and Wales outside the metropolis occurred as a result of the Local Government Act 1972. This established a two tier local government structure and the change further eroded the number of local authority undertakings. The initial PTEs were extended, two new PTEs were created, and whilst ownership of the remaining municipal public transport undertakings was vested in the lower tier authorities, many were amalgamated into larger units. The net result was to reduce the number of local authority owners of public road passenger transport undertakings to a rump of 49.

In addition to these general changes were those arrangements entered into voluntarily by local authorities. These were of three types:

1. Joint ownership with railway group;

2. Joint ownership with other local authorities or territorial bus company;
3. Transfer of ownership to territorial bus company.

It must be remembered that changes in ownership also meant similar changes in respect of the operator role although in all but the latter typology, a local authority retained ownership albeit on a shared basis and through a separate body. Examples of these arrangements were the Joint Omnibus Committee (JOC) in the case of railway involvement, Joint Transport Committee (JTC) when local authorities acted jointly, or a jointly owned company or committee arrangement between a municipality and the private sector. The nationalization of the railways and some of the territorial bus companies under the Transport Act 1947, with the remaining major company operators coming under state ownership after the Transport Act 1968, brought the centre and locality into joint ownership in these areas. These latter changes allowed local authorities to promote further adjustments in the form of either extended or complete ownership of the erstwhile joint arrangements, or divesting ownership of some or all of the joint arrangements to the state sector.

Although the number of municipalities involved in ownership of public road passenger transport had declined dramatically during the century, the Transport Act 1985 in effect removed the role by requiring each local authority transport undertaking to be established as a Passenger Transport Company (PTC) under the appropriate company legislation (s.67). In these circumstances, the local authority role is that of shareholder and hence owner of the PTC which as a body corporate has ownership of the former municipal undertaking. Measures were put in place for disposal of these units into the private sector (s.75), subject to the approval of central government, and many local authorities have exercised these powers. Authorities have varied in the manner in which disposal has taken place, some opting for a management and/or employee purchase, or selling the PTC direct to an existing private sector group or operator. Central government has indicated that it requires the remaining local authority PTCs to be disposed from municipal ownership in the near future and it is likely that local authorities will have to comply with this desire.

Local government is currently involved in promoting guided transport systems, notably light rail. In the metropolis and conurbations the separate executive bodies have promoted schemes but elsewhere it is local authorities which have obtained parliamentary sanction. Such authority was usually secured through a private Act of Parliament or the provisions of the Tramways Act 1870. However, this latter statute was inadequate and inappropriate for the purpose. Central government responded by simplifying the procedure for acquiring powers through the Transport and Works Act 1992. This legislative change mirrors the situation of over a century ago when the promotion of tramways was similarly made less onerous. The Act covers guided transport systems and local authorities can seek an Order in respect of the construction of such systems (s.20). There are currently a number of schemes under consideration covering some of the main urban centres of Great Britain, for example in Leeds (in conjunction with West Yorkshire PTE), Lothian and Nottingham.

Operator

The local government role as local public road passenger transport operator is closely connected with the constructor and owner role since the former was an extension of the latter. However, the development of the operator role was initially more complex and not immediately conferred upon local government. When it was finally conceded by parliament it contained inherent tensions.

The Tramways Act 1870 which granted construction and ownership powers to local government in respect of tramways specifically stated that "nothing within this Act shall authorize any local authority to place or run carriages upon such tramway" (s.19). Robson, (1935, p.321) explains that although this was construed as prohibiting municipal tramway operation, the statement merely defined the limits of local government power. The statutory framework clearly separated construction and ownership from operation since the former was a permitted role for local government whilst the latter was undertaken through lease by private enterprize. Reference has already been made to the powers of compulsory purchase available to local government, which coupled with technological innovation in the form of electric fraction discouraged private enterprize. The matter became an issue when in 1882 the Huddersfield Corporation were unable to obtain a lessee for the town tramway. The municipality challenged the interpretation of the legislation and applied to the Board of Trade for power to directly operate the system. This was granted on the proviso that no acceptable lessee was available and until such time as a suitable lessee came forward. Thus direct municipal public road passenger transport operation was conceded only after private enterprize failed - a point which supports the contention that public sector provision was a "last rather than first resort" (Butcher, Law, Leach and Mullard, 1990, p.9). Nevertheless, the change of central attitude was crucial and although the power was extended to other local authorities it was not without refusal in some localities (Robson, 1935, p.321). The principle was finally accepted by virtue of the Light Railways Act 1896 which gave local authorities adoptive powers to construct and operate a light railway. These powers were used by a number of tramway promoters, including local authorities, although it is clear that this was not the specific intent of parliament (Klapper, 1974, p.34). It perhaps serves best to illustrate the difficult task of framing legislation in terms of distinguishing between a tramway and light railway, and the ingenuity of local government in utilizing a range of statutory provisions to maximum advantage.

The acceptance of municipal public road passenger transport operation marked a period of role combination in that regulation, construction and ownership, and operation were all authorized roles for local government. However, local authorities had to secure separate powers to operate each mode of public road passenger transport, namely - tramways, trolleybuses and omnibuses. Not all applications for powers were successful and one of the most notable was the inability of the London County Council to secure approval to operate trolleybuses and omnibuses. Those municipalities which did secure powers to operate omnibuses were often restricted to operating such vehicles within the administrative boundary of the authority and confined to regular local stage carriage services as opposed to the private hire of vehicles and excursions, although there were some prominent exceptions. However, the position of local government operators was substantially altered under Part V of the Road Traffic Act 1930 which granted permissive powers to operate omnibuses on any road within the district. Operation outside the district was framed as an adoptive power since it required the consent of the Traffic Commissioners. In comparison to company operators the restrictions upon local government systems were a major constraint upon development and the problems became increasingly acute as spatial expansion of urban areas gathered pace.

The tensions surrounding the operation of direct municipal public passenger transport services centred in part upon the primary motive of such trading activity. The provision of municipal water and gas services were justified on the grounds of public health and safety respectively (Keith-Lucas and Richards, 1978, p.38), but the rationale for municipal public transport was less clear. The key element was the extent to which such trading was a commercial or social activity requiring local government financial support. At this stage there were no statutory duties placed upon municipalities in regard to operational policy other than local provisions included within private Acts of Parliament. In general, operational policy was a matter purely for local authority discretion. As we shall discover, tensions between the commercial and social approaches were to become so acute that it eventually brought central and local government into direct conflict.

Once the local government operator role was established subsequent development of the role followed that of constructor and owner with, as already explained, the number of municipal operators reduced considerably by postwar local government reorganization. It is however worth noting that prior to such reorganization, municipal operators had considerable discretion over operational issues. Under the reorganized system outside the metropolis and conurbations of England and Wales, public transport responsibilities were divided between both tiers of local government with the operator role conferred upon the lower tier. However, municipalities were required to operate the undertakings in accordance with the policies of the respective higher tier authority. This created potential for further tensions in that it removed the control over operations which municipal operators previously enjoyed and divided the roles between authorities which were distinct political entities. The reorganized system in Scotland, outside the Clydeside conurbation, avoided such division since all the public transport roles were vested in the higher tier authorities.

The Transport Act 1985, which as previously observed removed the local government ownership role, also specifically extinguished the operator role by stating that local authorities "shall not have power to provide a service for the carriage of passengers by road which requires a PSV operators' licence" (s.66). The current arrangement does at least clarify the position since a PTC is required to operate within a competitive environment on a commercial basis. This fundamental cultural shift was to prove easier to accomplish by some municipalities than others and not all local authority operators completed the transition successfully.

Financial supporter

The local government financial supporter role of public road passenger transport originated through the construction and ownership of tramways. This developed further when local authorities exercised an operator role. The tensions in the operator role between commercial and social approaches have already been mentioned. Local authorities had discretion over the operational approach to be followed, however, the distinction between commercial and social philosophies was not absolute. A local authority would not normally pursue maximum surplus or undertake operations on the basis of unlimited subsidy. Nevertheless, commercial operation implied the generation of a surplus of income over expenditure, or as an alternative a situation in which income was balanced with expenditure, whilst social operation required varying degrees of revenue support. The decision on such matters was determined by each municipality according to the political complexion of the local authority and the operating circumstance of the locality. This is not to suggest that particular political parties always adopted a certain policy approach but the differences were split broadly along party lines. Nevertheless, political parties did have a disposition in favour of a certain approach which reflected the core value systems of the respective party and with increasing political polarization these differences became acute.

The financial supporter role became of major significance in the decades following World War Two as passenger numbers declined and operating costs increased. Local authorities were forced into a combination of responses which included reduced service levels, increased fares and/or higher levels of revenue support. The Transport Act 1968 which created Passenger Transport Authorities (PTAs) in the conurbations composed of nominated members of the constituent authorities, formalized the position. The PTA was allowed to precept the local authorities in the area to meet any operational deficit of the PTE (s.13), although the Minister of Transport had reserve power to restrict the total amount raised by this method.

Meanwhile, the structural changes in the metropolis strengthened the position of local government in respect of public transport. The LPTB had been brought under state ownership after World War Two and subsequently reconstituted as the London Transport Board (LTB) following the Transport Act 1962. The LTB was altered to the London Transport Executive (LTE) and operations in the metropolis were transferred from state to local government control under the recently created Greater London Council (GLC) as a result of the Transport (London) Act 1969. The GLC had a duty of promoting "integrated, efficient and economic transport facilities and services" (s.1) within the area and was given power under section 3 to make grants to the LTE and British Rail. Similar duties and powers were assumed by the Metropolitan County Council (MCC) authorities formed in the conurbations when they were granted PTA status under section 202 of the Local Government Act 1972. Elsewhere in England and Wales, powers to subsidize public transport were bestowed jointly upon both tiers of local government (s.203). Provisions were made for the higher tier authorities to financially recompense municipal operators within the area which suffered disadvantage as a result of adhering to the policies of the former authority.

The financial supporter role was adjusted under the Local Government Act 1974 which amended the arrangements for central government grants to local authorities for financial assistance to public transport. Hepworth (1984, pp.67-8) points out that these grants came to be determined more in relation to national constraints than the merits of local requirements. In addition there were doubts about the equitable nature of the distribution, particularly between the metropolis and conurbations, and the rest of the country. Moreover, central government increasingly used the system to influence local policies and the degree of local discretion was thus moderated by the additional power which the centre was able to exercise over the locality in respect of funding issues.

A number of MCCs under Labour majority embraced public transport policies which had a greater degree of social orientation. The most radical was South Yorkshire MCC which had been under Labour control since inception and from 1975 had maintained a heavily subsidized fares policy. The GLC and some of the other MCCs had experienced periods with different political parties in control but by 1981 were all controlled by Labour administrations. The GLC was committed to reduce LTE fares by twentyfive per cent under the "Fares Fair" policy which was subsequently introduced in October 1981 financed by a supplementary precept. Merseyside and West Midlands MCCs were notable for embarking upon similar schemes. These were all legally challenged by lower tier local authorities in the respective areas and a detailed account is given by Loughlin (1986, pp.68-78) of the various judgements and ramifications. In short the GLC policy was declared unlawful whilst in the case of West Midlands MCC the social fares policy was altered prior to judgement. However, the legal challenge to Merseyside MCC failed. Part of the reason for the different judgements between the GLC and Merseyside MCC resulted from a variation of wording in the separate statutes applicable to the metropolis and conurbations, nevertheless the position of local authority financial support for public transport clearly required clarification. Central government responded in the form of the Transport Act 1983 under which a limit to the amount of financial support which could be given to public transport in the metropolis and conurbations was determined by the centre. The limit known as the Protected Expenditure Level (PEL) provided a figure which was the maximum sum which could be allocated in financial support by the locality with immunity from legal challenge. Loughlin, (1986, p.80) argues that the objective of central government "was not to resolve legal uncertainties, but rather to exploit them in order to coerce Authorities into compliance with the Government's guidelines on acceptable levels of revenue support".

Meanwhile there was increasing pressure to not only remove LTE from GLC control but also for the abolition of the entire higher tier of metropolitan local government (Byrne, 1992, p.90). In the event the LTE was removed from GLC control and reconstituted as London Regional

Transport (LRT) by virtue of the London Regional Transport Act 1984 and placed under state control. Local government in the metropolis reverted to a more distant position and the financial supporter role was removed since LRT is funded from central government with a levy from the centre upon local authorities in the area. This change was followed by structural reorganization of local government in the metropolis and conurbations as a result of the Local Government Act 1985 which abolished the GLC and MCCs in 1986. The public transport functions of the MCCs were transferred to joint boards known as Metropolitan County Passenger Transport Authorities (MCPTA) composed of nominated members from the constituent local authorities. In the English conurbations, therefore, the financial supporter role was removed from elected local authorities to a nominated local government approach. Central government exercised powers to limit the expenditure of each MCPTA which ensured a greater degree of central direction over local desire. By comparison, continuation of the two tier local government structure in the conurbation of Scotland ensured that the financial supporter role remained under the direct local authority model.

In addition to the reorganization of local government in the metropolis and conurbations, the financial supporter role of local government was fundamentally changed as a result of the Transport Act 1985. Firstly, restrictions were placed upon the extent to which a local authority could grant financial assistance to the PTC which it owned. Secondly, changes were made to the process by which local government provided financial support for public transport. It must be remembered that the Act abolished quantity controls on local bus services except in the metropolis. Bus operators are now required to register details of the routes and services which they will provide without direct local government financial support. Local authorities are under a duty to secure "the provision of such public transport services as the council considers it appropriate" (s.63). The local government role is therefore of a residuary nature through ensuring the provision of those routes and services deemed necessary but which are not provided by operators on a commercial basis. The role is framed in such a manner which still allows considerable local discretion between the extremes of a minimalist and maximalist approach. However, local authorities have a duty to secure "the best value for money from their expenditure on public transport taken as a whole." (s.88). The procedure for providing local government financial support is now through the process of competitive tendering (s.89). The tenders are for the operation of specific routes and services to be provided on a contract basis for a given period of time.

The concept of competitive tendering although not new either to local government or indeed transport, is a radical alternative to the characteristic method of financial support of direct service provision by local authorities. This activity is more than the mere application of the procedural construct since the arguments surrounding the technique centre as much upon ideology as other considerations (Hampton, 1991, p.73). As far as public passenger transport is concerned we have observed that initial operations of tramways owned by municipalities was by lease to private enterprize which then provided services on the entire network as a commercial activity. This contrasts with the current practice of competitive tendering on three counts. Firstly, only individual or groups of routes are placed out to competitive tender as discrete entities rather than a complete network. Secondly, the route and details of service provision are stipulated by the local authority. Thirdly, unlike the tramway lease arrangements where a company agreed terms for acquiring the lease, an operator receives payment from the local authority for the service provided. By comparison, the tendering process has some similarities with the leasing arrangements of the last century in as much as a fixed term contract provides for periods of instability on account of the future determination of the contract at the point of expiry. Whether or not this acts as an incentive upon operators is open to debate but the potential instability inherent in the procedure represents a weakness of the system. An observation which should be made, however, is the point by Mather (1989, p.225) that the competitive tendering process provides a regulatory role for local government. From a terminology perspective this would seem to be a return for local government to the role previously performed in the latter part of the last and earlier part of this century. However, the new regulatory role is very different from the historical version since it relates to only the residual function of retrieving deficiencies in the commercial network through the process of specifying, purchasing and facilitating such provision. Nevertheless, it still provides for local government to take a positive rather than a passive role in local public road passenger transport and to some extent it involves a planning role which is complementary to that of policy coordinator.

Policy coordinator

Local authorities which provided municipal public road passenger transport services also performed a policy role through the determination of operational matters. However, local government received a wider role in the form of general policy coordinator. Initial references to the role are to be found for the conurbations and metropolis authority in the Transport Act 1968 and Transport (London) Act 1969 respectively. In the conurbations the role was exercised by a PTA which as we have observed were initially composed of nominated members from the constituent authorities. By contrast, in the metropolis the role was performed by local government since the duties were conferred upon the GLC during the period of responsibility for the LTE. As previously explained, the Local Government Act 1972 brought the conurbations closer to the metropolis model by placing each PTA under a solitary authority in the form of an MCC. Outside the conurbations, the Act was also notable for giving the higher tier authorities a duty to 'develop policies which will promote the provision of a coordinated and efficient system of public transport' (s.203). A similar duty was placed upon the higher tier authorities in Scotland under section 151 of the Local Government (Scotland) Act 1973.

The policy coordinator role is interesting for as with the financial supporter role, it covers all modes of local public transport and not just those operated by local government - since some operations were provided by state or other local state bodies and executives. The various statutes also placed a duty on such organizations to cooperate with the policy coordinating authority. In the event, the coordinating authorities were able to exercise this role in conjunction with others, notably that of financial supporter. Where an authority pursued an active financial supporter role it was able to exercise considerable powers over those operators dependent upon such support, although this was not without tensions particularly in England and Wales where, as previously noted, municipal operations were the responsibility of separate political entities.

The policy coordination role was given further status through the Transport Act 1978 which placed a requirement upon the Traffic Commissioners to take account of the public transport policies of the appropriate local authority when considering road service licence applications.

This led Mackie (1987, p.112) to declare the Act as the "high-point of local authority influence over local bus transport". The zenith of such influence was to prove transitory when in less than a decade the Transport Act 1985 deregulated local bus services, removed municipal transport operations, redefined the financial supporter role, and diluted the policy coordinator role to that of developing policies for securing socially necessary services. Local authorities must frame such policies and conduct themselves "as not to inhibit competition" (s.63). Although local authorities have no direct legal powers to interfere with the commercial activities of operators they are able to advocate suggestions and amendments to routes or services where these are seen as desirable. However, the most public manifestation of the role is through the provision by local government of local public transport information in the form of route maps and timetables where these are not provided by the operator.

Representor

Local government has a distinguished history of representing the views of the locality on various issues either to central government or other bodies. Local authorities received such a role in respect of public road passenger transport during the period of tramway development when the Tramways Act 1870 required private tramway promoters to obtain the consent of the appropriate local authority before submitting proposals to parliament (s.4). It is interesting to note that a similar requirement was not included in the Light Railways Act 1896 although a local authority could always raise specific objections using other procedural methods.

Local government in the metropolis has long performed a representor role in respect of local public road passenger transport. When the London and Home Counties Advisory Committee (LHCAC) was established to advise central government on transport matters in the area, local government received statutory membership under the London Traffic Act 1924. The larger local authorities each had membership along with representatives of each category of smaller authority. In addition, local authorities were able to appeal against ministerial regulations on public transport matters (s.6). These arrangements were altered when the LPTB was created and the Railway Rates Tribunal was given some responsibilities over the services and charges of the new body. Local authorities in the area were granted statutory power of access to the Railway Rates Tribunal on matters such as fares and service facilities under section 30 of the London Passenger Transport Act 1933. This arrangement was modified when the LPTB was nationalized as the LTE under the Transport Act 1947 and the Railway Rates Tribunal was reconstituted as the Transport Tribunal. Changes were again made under the Transport Act 1962 to reflect the separate status of the LTB and the provisions were finally repealed when the LTE was transferred to GLC control. With the return of public transport in the capital to central government control in the form of LRT in 1984, the new body was given a duty under the London Regional Transport Act 1984 to inform local authorities of fares and service arrangements (s.30). Although a statutory representor body in the form of the London Regional Passengers' Committee was established, members are appointed by central government and there are no specific provisions for local authority membership.

Elsewhere, local authorities received a representor role through the road service licensing system. The Road Traffic Act 1930 required the Traffic Commissioners to take into consideration any representations made by any local authority affected by any licence application or modification (s.72). In effect, local authorities were able to make representations on route, service and fares levels. Sometimes, a local authority would pursue an objection to the point of a public hearing by the Traffic Commissioners, on other occasions the operator would consult with the local authority and modify proposals in order to accommodate the points raised by the locality. The deregulation of public road passenger transport removed much of the statutory representative provisions. Firstly, the control of fares by the Traffic Commissioners was removed under the Transport Act 1980 except in certain circumstances to protect the public or regulate competition (s.7). Local authorities were thus restricted to representations on route and service issues until these were finally removed with the abolition of road service licensing under the Transport Act 1985.

Thus as far as commercial operations are concerned the representor role of local government which previously had statutory support is now considerably diminished. The role has been eroded by both privatization and deregulation. Firstly, the removal of the operator role also reduced the representor role since local authorities are no longer able to explicitly direct operational issues. Secondly, the abolition of road service licensing removed the regulatory framework within which the representor role of local government had statutory support. More recently, however, local government has received a new representor role in respect of guided transport systems. The Transport and Works Act 1992 grants powers of objection to local authorities to any proposals submitted for the locality (s.11). It should be noted that the determination of any such proposals rests solely with the Secretary of State but nevertheless a local authority is one of the few representors that can force a public inquiry. Whilst the Act does not require promoters to obtain the consent of a local authority as was the case with tramways, it does provide local government with the power to ensure that the representor role is one that can have a meaningful impact upon events in the locality.

Conclusion

The various roles of local government associated with public road passenger transport stemmed from an initial involvement with regulation. As each role developed they often brought others with them - such as operator and financial supporter. Subsequently, these roles have suffered variable fortunes. Some of them, such as regulator, were withdrawn entirely, whilst the operator role was gradually eroded and then finally removed. On the other hand the financial supporter and policy coordinator roles were enhanced. When the various structural changes to local government are taken into consideration the overall effect has been to weaken the locality as an entity, and also in relation to the centre. The changes to these roles reflect the deficiencies of local government. Nearly every role is reliant on parliamentary legislation which whilst providing role authority is also a fundamental defect since the centre is able to remove these powers. The events of the last decade have vividly exposed the weakness of the local government position when confronted with a determined central administration. Of course this is partly a function of the diffuse nature of local government with structural differences between and within each part of the UK - in short, local government is not a single entity. Finally, the revenue base of local government was inadequate for the service functions granted to local authorities. As public road passenger transport became generally unprofitable this required increased financial support from the locality, which in conjunction with reliance of local government upon central government grants focused attention on the conflicts between central objectives and local desires. This finally resulted in increased restrictions upon local discretion which served as confirmation of the supremacy of the centre over the locality.

Nevertheless, some of the similarities between current roles and those of a century ago are notable so that the return of local government to a more distant stance can be viewed as less radical than recent changes would suggest. The current period is one therefore of local government adjusting fully to the new and revised roles. Local government history demonstrates that authorities if so disposed are quite able to adopt a maximalist rather than minimalist approach. However, current duties and powers are such that the centre has undoubtably circumscribed the degree of discretion exercisable by the locality, to an extent not hitherto seen, yet there is still scope for positive development. The financial supporter role necessitates a new regulator element, whilst the policy coordinator role is already coming to the fore as the limitations of a deregulated environment become more obvious. The genesis of an environment more conducive to public transport, particularly in the metropolis and conurbations, should provide further stimulus to the development of these roles. Meanwhile, the representor role although largely devoid of statutory status, is still a valuable activity for local government to perform. Whilst a return to direct local authority service delivery seems rather remote and the locality continues to be restricted by control from the centre, there is sufficient evidence to support the contention that local government can still perform a positive role across a broad range of public transport issues.

References

Butcher, H. Law, I. G. Leach, R. & Mullard, M. (1990), *Local Government and Thatcherism*, Routledge, London.

Byrne, T. (1992), *Local Government in Britain*, Penguin, Harmondsworth.

Cmnd. 3481. (1967), *Public Transport and Traffic*, HMSO, London.

Foulkes, D. (1986), *Foulkes' Administrative Law*, Butterworths, London.

Glaister, S. & Mulley, C. (1983), *Public Control of the British Bus Industry*, Gower, Aldershot.

Hampton, W. (1991), *Local Government and Urban Politics*, Longman, Harlow.

Hepworth, N. (1984), *The Finance of Local Government*, Allen and Unwin, London.

Hibbs, J. (1989), *The History of British Bus Services*, David and Charles, Newton Abbot.

Keith-Lucas, B. & Richards, P. (1978), *A History of Local Government in the Twentieth Century*, Allen and Unwin, London.

Klapper, C. (1974), *The Golden Age of Tramways*, David and Charles, Newton Abbot.

Loughlin, M. (1986), *Local Government In The Modern State*, Sweet & Maxwell, London.

Mackie, P. (1987), "Policy Paper 7: Transport" in Parkinson, M. (ed.) *Reshaping Local Government*, Transaction Books, Hermitage.

Mather, G. (1989), "Thatcherism and Local Government: An Evaluation" in Stewart, J. & Stoker, G. (eds.), *The Future of Local Government*, MacMillan, Basingstoke.

Robson, W. (1935), "The Public Utility Service" in Laski, H. Jennings, I. & Robson, W. (eds.), *A Century of Municipal Progress 1835-1935*, Allen and Unwin, London.

6 Planning in an unplanned environment: The Transport Act 1985 and municipal bus operators

Alan Whitehead

Introduction

This chapter examines the intellectual origins of the Transport Act 1985, and compares the vision with what has so far happened. It draws some conclusions about the validity of the underlying intentions of deregulation and provides an analysis that has been either neglected or obscured in the welter of statistics that have arisen from evidence of bus activity throughout the country following deregulation. What, then was the Act trying to do? There has been no shortage of opinion about its essential intentions from friend and foe alike, many of which it has to be said, have been delivered with the benefit of hindsight. Evans considers it was about competition, or at least the threat of it. He states

> The main provision of the British Transport Act 1985 was to allow operators to compete freely in providing commercial bus services, except in London. It was believed that, whether there was active competition or not, incumbent operators would be so disciplined by the threat from potential entrants that they would always provide the best pattern of services and fares (Evans, 1990, p.255).

Other commentators detected a financial basis to the legislation. Stanley, for example, detects a hidden agenda behind the legislation, over and above that of general competition. He suggests that these "other ends" concern the level of public finance received by the industry, an aim to increase the flow of funds into the Treasury, and to reduce wage levels in the bus industry. Overall, he considers that "such savings would constitute a substantial part of the government forecasts that cost reductions of the order of 30% are feasible in a deregulated industry" (Stanley, 1989, pp.16-17). In this he has the support of Farrington who lists competition and cost savings as the two motivational factors

The proposals are consistent with the Government's ideological aim of introducing competition and private capital into economic and service activity. They are also put forward by the Government in the belief that they will result in savings in public expenditure because of increased operating efficiency due to competition (Farrington, 1986, p.259).

But do these somewhat differing accounts, even taken together, constitute a full background to the intention of the legislation? Closer examination of the legislation, and some archaeology of its intellectual antecedents suggest not. In order to understand what these antecedents were, it is necessary to consider the legislative atmosphere within which the Transport Act was conceived. The Thatcher government was still in the first flush of ideological fervour, still in the early stages of what Mrs. Thatcher saw as her mission to roll back the state.

Rolling back the state: the influence of the 'think tanks'?

Remarkably for a UK government, Mrs. Thatcher had little truck with the permanent government of the civil service "mandarinate". She was determined to stamp the ideological authority of the government upon legislation, and not succumb to the option papers traditionally placed in front of ministers when they announced their intention to legislate to their permanent secretaries. Mrs. Thatcher had, in 1983, dispensed with the Central Policy Review Staff and was embarking upon a relationship with the civil service that was to culminate in the Hibbs Report and the *Next Steps* initiatives. The key items of legislation - privatization of the massive state industries, laws to curb the activities of trade unions, assaults upon the alternative poles of power represented by local government - were left to trusted lieutenants and, as Transport Minister, Nicholas Ridley was regarded as at the centre of the trusted group ideologically committed to the Thatcherite project.

The natural allies to turn to for specific details of outline legislative programmes under these circumstances were not, therefore, the Civil Service, but the "think tanks" which had played a central role in the creation of Mrs. Thatcher's "New Right" brand of conservatism. These organisations viz the Institute for Economic Affairs, the Centre for Policy Studies and the "outside right" Adam Smith Institute had produced, in the 1970s and the early 1980s a stream of publications outlining a radical programme for a Conservative government. One document by the Adam Smith Institute, for example, *Reservicing Britain* by Michael Forsyth (now a Minister) contained in outline most of the Government's subsequent legislative programme on local government service provision, "contracting out" tendering and other activities that occupied much of the 1980s.

In the period immediately prior to the production of the *Buses* White Paper in June 1984, the "think tanks" had been very active in producing pamphlets and monographs about transport - a subject that had attracted little attention in right wing circles previously. As Hibbs suggested in the 1982 IEA pamphlet *Transport without Politics?* "'British Transport policy, such as it is, may be characterised as protectionist at the national level and interventionist at the local, irrespective of which political party is in power." (Hibbs, 1984, p.15). Hibbs pamphlet was a development of a previous work for the IEA *Transport for Passengers* published in revised form in 1971, and credited in the introduction to his later work as having "played a part in making the deregulation of the bus and coach industry practical politics". (Hibbs, 1984, p.10). Hibbs acknowledged the assistance of Gilbert Ponsonby with the 1982 pamphlet. Ponsonby had published *Transport Policy* for the IEA in 1969.

Transport Without Politics presents a detailed critique of the history and practice of regulation in the transport industry, and argues that

> There is no justification for the convention that assumes transport to be in some way unsuited to the disciplines of the market......the time has now come to put an end to over-government and to harness the neglected advantages of the market economy (Hibbs, 1984, p.10).

Although the author provided some pointers to legislation, such as an urgent call to end "cross subsidisation" in transport, the pamphlet did not really present an itemised programme of legislation in itself. This was left to a remarkable 1984 Adam Smith Institute pamphlet by Gabriel Roth and Anthony Shepherd, entitled *Wheels Within Cities*. This was largely a re-publication, with specific recommendations for the U.K. of a 1982 pamphlet *Free Enterprise Urban Transportation* published by the US Institute for Environmental Action. There is little doubt (both in terms of the content of the pamphlet itself and of the connections that exist between the work and all stages of legislation) that *Wheels Within Cities* represents the blueprint for the 1985 Transport Act.

The striking similarities between the work of the "think tanks" and the progress of this particular piece of legislation do not, though, end with the clearly close similarity between Roth and Shepherd's pamphlet and the *Buses* White Paper. The White Paper itself departed radically from more traditional presentations of government intentions in two ways. First, it announced legislative proposals in uncompromising tones which indicate a high degree of commitment to an ideologically based programme. This in itself jars with the measured, civil-service-ese of most similar publications. Second, it used a curious collection of right wing academics and "think tank" references to bolster the intellectual case presented in the first part of the White Paper. Furthermore, an annex was included entitled *Regulation, Subsidy and Cross Subsidy - a Critique* by Beesley, Glaister and Buchanan. Beesley and Glaister subsequently engaged in an extended polemic in *Transport Reviews* on the merits of complete deregulation as against route franchising with Gwilliam, Nash and Mackie of the Institute for Transport Studies at the University of Leeds. Reading the language employed in the polemic, one is hardly filled with conviction about Beesley and Glaister's impartiality on the matter of cross-subsidy. This impression is further confirmed by the sources Beesley Glaister and Buchanan used in their White Paper critique. Uniquely in White Papers (as far as I am aware) two IEA publications (the aforementioned Hibbs and Ponsonby Hobart Papers) were cited in support of the critique. Hibbs returned the compliment in his paper, citing Glaisters work in support of his own. A.A. Walters also made a contribution to the debate, through his paper *Costs and Scale of Bus Services* (written in 1979 as a World Bank Staff working paper), which is in turn cited by Roth in his pamphlet. A.A. Walters is, of course the same A.A. Walters who famously precipitated the departure of Nigel Lawson over his role as Mrs. Thatcher's economic adviser, and who produced an earlier Hobart Paper (no 44) for the IEA. Whilst one should be wary of "ad hominem" arguments, and should give the arguments of academics respect based on the soundness of argument rather than political allegiance, the strong impression remains of a hermetically sealed academic loop feeding into the thought-processes behind the White Paper.

Before turning to the surfacing of this debate in the columns of Hansard during the passage of the Transport Bill itself, it is worth considering whether this array of evidence linking the White Paper closely with the work of the right-wing "think tanks" should cause us to review our conclusions about the purpose of Nicholas Ridley in promoting the legislation. One might ask - was the vision for the future of transport held by Nicholas Ridley the same as the purposes attributed to the legislation by various commentators on the Act, and can we draw any conclusions about this question from the discussion of "think tank" involvement that has been set out above? In this context, it is important to establish the nature of the assumptions made about the likely behaviour of the travelling public and the future transport operators, both from the previously public sector and those entering the market for the first time following deregulation. These can be identified fairly robustly from the acknowledged ideological influences of both the IEA and the Adam Smith Institute.

Ideological influences

Two aspects of such ideological influences might be thought of as pertinent. First, there is the Hayekian notion of "spontaneous order", which is a central theme of his political and economic system. Hayek himself contributed a number of papers to the publication list of both the IEA and the ASI and it is surely no accident that Roth uses the specific phrase "spontaneous order" in the context of an integrated transport system arising without the attentions of transport planners. For this is what the concept means essentially: that the world as a whole, and therefore "the market" will impose a logical order upon itself by the unknowing inputs of thousands of individuals undertaking what they see is the most rational course of action for themselves. Hayek argues that, because of the impossibility of anyone having available to them complete knowledge about the circumstances under which these individual actions will be taken, interference in the market by means of attempted planning will only serve to distort and harm it, and will produce in all cases, a less optimal outcome than had "spontaneous order" been allowed to arise. Under these circumstances, the only duty of government, Hayek suggests, is to create the circumstances which will entail the least impediment to its development. In other words, government's only role is to dispose of road blocks and regulate the market to prevent distortions arising from "market-fixing" or crime. In this light, the uniquely anti-statist tenor of the 1985 legislation can be seen as an attempt to create conditions for "spontaneous order" in the transport industry. The logical actions of the thousands of small entrepreneurs likely to invade the market following deregulation would make it happen.

This line of reasoning can be seen in the White Paper, as well as the passages I have illustrated from the pamphlets that preceded it. One brief quote will illuminate the point well:

> If one operator fails to provide a service that is wanted, another will. They will be stimulated to provide a greater variety of services, using different types of vehicles running on different routes or frequencies, offering more choices to meet peoples needs. Competing minibuses may offer a fast and frequent service in city centres. shared taxis may provide transport for people in villages.

This passage also serves to highlight another key assumption of both the "think tank" academics and the White Paper. This is that in transport, there is little or no advantage to be gained from economies of scale.

Hibbs is concerned to establish this point theoretically in his contribution.

He states

> The issue of scale has received much attention from academic economists. Those who have examined the transport industry broadly agree that economies of scale cease to apply fairly early in the growth of the firm, and this contention appears to be borne out by the absence very large firms in the unregulated sector. (Hibbs, 1982, p.40).

Roth's exhaustive survey of unregulated competition and his conclusion that successful transport providers tend to be small firms, often owning one or two vehicles also nails his colours to the mast on the issue of size: both authors, and plainly, the White Paper, believe that, in conditions of free competition, the small operator or market entrant, with low overheads and a few small vehicles will inevitably be at a market advantage. The vision from the point of view of operators, therefore, is that deregulation will bring in its wake a revolution in transport in which the large over-extended traditional operators, running large buses on networked routes will rapidly be supplanted by large numbers of small, lean operators, in some instances operating minibuses and in other instances running shared taxis. Together, perhaps through the mechanism of route associations, a network would come into being, but on a very different basis from the assumptions or practice of network creation and management prior to deregulation.

The second key ideological consideration, however, sheds some further light on the presumed validity of this assumption. This is the identification of the Adam Smith Institute in particular with the Public Choice school of societal and political motivation. Public Choice is now a rambling and many faceted school of political theory, but at its heart can be reduced to some central propositions. As Dennis Mueller states in his key work *Public Choice 2*. "The basic behavioural postulate of Public Choice, as for economics, is that man is an egoistic, rational, utility maximizer" (Mueller, 1989, p.2). Clearly, Roth's ideas, and those of the White Paper assume a general public motivated according to this description in order to produce the customers for the momentous changes that were envisaged in the supply of service. Passengers would, for example, need to shop around for best bus prices, switch services in order to reward more efficient operators and punish less efficient players and trade the comfort of the larger buses for the more frequent headway and better penetration of the minibus and so on. Most importantly, for services on the margin to become profitable as a result of more effective competition, new customers would have to make the rational choice to switch to bus services and away from other forms of transport. In this respect Hibbs expressed some reservations, noting that deregulation would only work effectively if there was a level playing field of choices when rational calculators able to choose between modes of urban transport

> ...The system inhibits a rational choice of transport modes. The bus passenger perceives that his daily journey would be faster by car and makes his arrangements accordingly. He is then followed by others until the resulting congestion makes his journey more time consuming than it had been by bus. By now, however, the bus takes even longer. But in the meantime, the incremental change that has culminated in this absurd situation cannot be reversed unless a sufficient number of motorists return to the bus en bloc. It is a sort of prisoner's dilemma. (Hibbs, 1982, p.66).

He thus advocates, among other measures, the introduction of road pricing, a measure which is only now surfacing as an option at government level.
At the time, however, this concern was not shared by the White Paper or subsequently, Nicholas Ridley in advocating the legislation in Parliament.
One could raise the objection that although the anticipated behaviour of passengers might be underpinned by a faith in Public Choice theory, what was being attempted was the marketisation of a previously non-market based activity, and that the aim was therefore to anticipate that the public would behave as rational economic actors. To this it might be countered that Public Choice theory is relevant to the extent that the public, given a choice of supply which for the first time would allow them to make rational choice should behave as the theory suggests. However, there is another equally important aspect of Public Choice theory which I would suggest is a further key assumption in the system of legislation proposed. This is the assumption that bureaucrats always act to maximize the bureau which is under their control. This aspect of Public Choice theory is most readily associated with the work of William Niskanen, who, incidently published an summarised version of his book *Bureaucracy and Representative Government (1971)* as an IEA pamphlet in 1973 under the title *Bureaucracy: Servant or Master?*
Niskanen makes two key points in his analysis of bureaucracy. Using the familiar argument about the impossibility of an individual possessing full knowledge, he claims that: "It is impossible for a single bureaucrat to act in the public interest because of limits on his information and the conflicting interests of others, regardless of personal motivation" (Niskanen, 1972, p.23). Instead, Niskanen argues, the bureaucrat will be motivated by: "salary, perquisites of office, public reputation, power, patronage, output of the bureau, ease of making changes, and ease of managing the bureau." Furthermore, government (or local government) will exercise very little real

control of this process because it will be a "passive sponsor which knows the budget it is prepared to grant for a given quantity of services but does not have the incentive or the opportunity to obtain information of the minimum budget necessary to supply it" (Niskanen, 1972, p.17). If these premises are true, the final part of the process can be satisfactorily analyzed. Inevitably, being non-market led bureaus, bus service agencies, and particularly those under the control of local authorities will be "budget maximising" bureaucracies that will inevitably have grown too large for their function because of their relationship to their sponsor. A combination of a service that would be in no position to compete, potential small and lean entrants who can capture dense urban routes, and a pool of passengers willing to act as rational calculators would provide the motive force (both negatively and positively) which would make the legislative proposals work. Niskanen's views have been subject to attack, most notably by Patrick Dunleavy in the UK. However, it is not the purpose of this paper to argue theoretically for or against Niskanen; it is sufficient to establish that the framers of the 1985 legislation believed that mechanisms of the sort proposed by Public Choice theorists would work, within the framework of a market that would, in time, generate "spontaneous order" as it developed. It is plain that Nicholas Ridley was fully convinced of these premises when introducing the Transport Bill in February 1985. It is also clear that the Labour opposition had no real understanding of the premises to which Ridley was working, and therefore concentrated their attack on targets which did not exist as problems, at least from the point of view of the vision of the proposed legislation.

What is remarkable about both the *Buses* White Paper and the debates in Parliament on the legislation itself is the absence of doubt in the text or on the government Front Bench that the measures would work, a certainty rare in political activity more normally hedged with carefully crafted caveats, and which can be explained by Nicholas Ridley's grasp of the theoretical essentials of the systems I have described. Opening the Second Reading debate he was confident that the ills of the bus industry had been caused by regulation, and that deregulation, in itself, would liberate the logic of the market and rational choice to transform matters. In winding up the debate, his deputy, David Mitchell produced a peroration similar in its glowing certainty to that of the White Paper. The legislation, he suggested

> ...represents opportunity because it will provide for the removal of barriers to new bus operators and enable small businesses to be born and to grow, providing a service to the public (House of Commons, Hansard, 12 February 1985, col. 259).

To summarise, therefore, one can conclude that the intention for the working and result of the new legislation based on the analysis here was

* The creation of a deregulated market that would disadvantage bus companies, particularly municipal undertakings, that had previously been run as bureaucracies. These companies would either slim down substantially or physically break up in order to survive: many municipal companies would simply disappear.
* This would be because a new generation of small cost-effective operators would enter the market, competing successfully for routes, predominantly in the urban areas. These operators would, over a period of time, band together in their own interest to formulate an informal network to replace the previously planned arrangements.
* The combination of small operators and the need to serve the customer wherever appropriate by increased route penetration and improved headway would entail the substantial demise of big buses and their replacement by minibuses. The principle would be extended to shared taxi routes on lower volume routes and at marginal times of the day.
* The rational response of the travelling public in choosing both to patronise this combination of cheaper, more journey-effective modes than hitherto and to switch to buses from other forms of transport would secure the success of the revolution and reverse historic passenger decline.

Outcomes

It is something of a commonplace to state that the story of the deregulated system of public transport in the U.K. has not proceeded along these lines. On the other hand, neither have the blood curdling predictions of the opponents of the legislation come to pass either. Although one can perhaps recognise fragments of their predictions more readily than one can discern the success of the grand vision offered by Nicholas Ridley. Ibanez and Meyer summarize the predictions of the Act's opponents thus

> Those opposed to the reforms expected competition either not to develop or to be wasteful if it did. They contended that many communities would end up dominated by entrenched local bus monopolies, which, being unresponsive to users and no longer inhibited by Government oversight, would raise local fares and cut

services. If competition did develop, they said, it would be concentrated on a few profitable routes where competing firms would offer wasteful duplicative services, so that costs would escalate and productivity decline. Services would deteriorate on unprofitable routes, they predicted, particularly in low density areas and off-peak hours, generating and accentuating a general disintegration in the system of co-ordinated services operated under the previous regime. As a result, they argued, bus ridership would decline, and auto use and traffic congestion would increase (Ibanez and Meyer, 1990, p.11).

Some of the predictions of both sides can be conceded. Minibuses have, supplanted big buses to some extent but not under the conditions envisaged by the framers of the legislation. Ridership has declined, but not to the catastrophic extent envisaged by the Acts opponents. Peripheral services have survived to a larger extent than predicted, largely because of effective tendering processes instigated by County Councils. The companies operating transport throughout the UK bears a high degree of resemblance to those operating prior to deregulation, and especially so in non metropolitan urban areas. In effect, the resulting structure of public transport bears little resemblance to the scenarios painted by either side.

Why should this be so? The reasons for the non-appearance of the doomsday scenario of may of the Acts opponents can be accounted for fairly swiftly. One can conclude with some certainty that they did not appreciate the complexities and the holistic system of deregulation that was planned, or the extent to which the institutions of the previously functioning system might adapt to it. Instead they envisaged the "Titanic" of the previously fully regulated system meeting the iceberg of deregulation, and could envisage little else than a mighty collision followed by the loss of all hands. Whilst one can excuse much of the opposition pronouncements on the grounds that they were attempting to create conditions of maximum opposition to the legislation by attempting to make the flesh creep, the charge of failing to read the sub-text of the legislation properly an be laid at their door.

What requires more detailed examination, and which will be attempted in the rest of this chapter, is why the application of a range of rigorous theoretical positions, applied to an industry with great ruthlessness and care for detail, failed to produce the anticipated results. In making this appraisal, I shall refer both to existing research and, with specific reference to municipal transport, to primary research undertaken by myself and my collaborators at the Southampton Institute of Higher Education (SIHE).

The questions I will discuss can be summarised as follows:

* Why did the hoped for small operators not enter the market in large numbers?
* Why did the traditional bus companies, and especially the municipals, prove so comparatively resilient?
* Why did the public not behave in the way predicted by the legislation?

Perhaps the first place to look in such an examination is the Hereford and Worcester "experimental deregulation" which preceded the passage of the legislation itself. Whilst the experiment in three trial areas (viz. Hereford and Worcester, Norfolk and Devon) was hailed as a success by the *Buses* White Paper, such claims addressed themselves more to surface effects than to underlying developments which might have acted a more of a warning for the long-term development of deregulated services nationwide. Andrew Evans, in his study of the experiment published in 1988, looks closely at both the short and long term trends illuminated by the events of September 1981 - October 1986, when the special status of the area was superseded by the effect of the enactment of national legislation (Evans, 1990, pp.284-306). He considers that

> though the trials were influential and interesting, they were not conclusive, and the Governments later decision in the "Buses" White Paper to go for full deregulation was based mainly on more general arguments and presumptions.

Perhaps the most important factor in the trials, as will be underlined later, is that the local authorities involved were all volunteers, actively wishing to pursue aspects of deregulation for their own purposes. In fact they were the only volunteers; all other relevant local authorities, despite being canvassed, declined to take part. Hereford and Worcester, as Evans records, were keen to try out a scheme to tender competitively for subsidised services, and the county-wide scheme they devised was adopted for the legislation. But despite all these fair winds, long term operator reactions to the new liberalized regime did not fit with the theory: larger companies could fight and win wars, and it did not seem that the flexibility of small scale operation countered the advantage of initial size.

Evans concludes that rational behaviour by operators is in fact rather more pragmatic.

> Once a route is operated competitively, each operator has an interest in getting rid of the others. This may lead to mutual loss-inducing wars... A war makes sense only if the instigator hopes to knockout

the other(s) quickly: otherwise a competitive equilibrium-seeking strategy might be better... operators have a mutual interest in keeping off each others patches: it is better for two operators each to have one of two routes than to compete on both.

In other words, even in the Hereford experiment, operators decided that, unless the incumbent was enfeebled to the extent that a swift end to free competition could be achieved, the incursion was likely to be more damaging to the smaller interloper than to the incumbent: some form of covert "franchising" was therefore preferable to the stability of both sides than a debilitating route war. Evans attempted further analysis of this phenomenon in a study of deregulation in Preston, Lancaster and Stockton, published in 1990. Commenting on the general level of competition in the three years following deregulation, Evans concludes that

> Active competition has occurred on only a minority of routes. About 3 per cent of bus-kilometres were involved in direct on the road competition immediately after deregulation...this figure increased about threefold in the following year, but now appears to be declining. Active competition has therefore always been the exception rather than the norm, and now seems set to remain so (Evans, 1990, pp.255-281).

The problems of entry, Evans suggests, seem to have produced this result, particularly in urban areas with a strong municipal presence. In the three years of his study, Evans furthermore observed a surprising non-correlation with one key phenomenon of competition, namely the increased frequency of service that a period of intense competition on a route would bring. Surprisingly, Evans could find no evidence of increased patronage as a result; a finding that flies in the face of the Public Choice prediction that a rational calculator would respond to such an opportunity by switching to the plentiful service and away from other forms of transport. Instead, buses ran at double the frequency with half the previous passengers each: clearly a situation which would make it impossible for both operators to cushion the losses of the fight with an injection of new passenger patronage.

Evans applies games theory to assess what the reaction of entrants to the circumstances might be, and with the objective circumstances of the market turning out very differently from theoretical predictions, concludes that aggressive entry, except in the short term and with a strong probability of early success is not a rational strategy. He concludes

> Local bus markets have remained highly monopolized after deregulation. Active competition is relatively rare, and probably now well past its peak. ....in contrast to the governments expectation, the effect of potential entrants in controlling the monopoly operators is weak (Evans, 1990, p.277).

Balcombe, Astrop and Fairhead's 1992 report on competition underlines Evans conclusions with current and comprehensive statistics. Whilst they accept that the threat of competition has restrained operating costs and provided competition for subsidised services, they state definitively that

> So far, not more than a few per cent of bus services have been in direct competition with others, and so the proportion of passengers who have been able to choose between competing bus operators has been correspondingly small (Balcombe, Astrop and Fairhead, 1992).

The report catalogues the incidence of competition across the industry since deregulation, and examines the details of those cases where competition has ended. Overall, some 50% of incidents of competition had been resolved by the time the report was compiled, and of these, the vast majority had been won by larger incumbents. The report cites the startling statistic that, in 217 recorded cases of incumbents "winning", 177 cases were won by the larger operator. In most instances of completed competition, the incumbent beat off the competition, and in some instances settled. Only vary rarely did they "lose". In the case of former NBC companies, this figure amounted to a 78% "win" rate. Municipals were less successful, but still "won" in 55% of cases, and settled in a further 27%. These latter figures have to be regarded with some care however, since only 197 cases of competition altogether involving municipals as first or second operators have been recorded since 1986 - representing only four or so cases per company over a five year period. Balcombe, Astrop and Fairhead conclude that such low levels of competition have now,it seems, become the norm: "A dynamic state of equilibrium seems to have been established, with new cases of competition replacing those which come to an end." Contrary to predictions, therefore, larger companies are systematically succeeding against challenges by smaller entrants, and in any event, entrants in general are deciding not to enter the market, except perhaps in very peripheral "niches" of subsidised services, which do not challenge either the networks or the finances of the larger incumbent operators.

A further surprising observation (for supporters of the expected outcome of deregulation) concerns the position of municipal or former municipal bus companies in the years following deregulation. It is these companies which, according to Public Choice theory, would be over-large bureaus, and likely to fail spectacularly once external subsidy and internal cross-subsidy gave way to the discipline of the market. Whilst there have been one or two disasters, such as the liquidation of Maidstone Transport and Taff-Ely, by and large, the municipals have performed surprisingly well. Indeed, in 1990 -91, the sector as a whole is reported to improved their pre-tax profits over the previous year by 23.4% (Cheek, 1992, p.12). Not only have municipals not disappeared as might have been anticipated, but they have not "slimmed down" as might alternatively been posited, at least if the number of buses operated is regarded as an indicator. The number of municipals operating prior to deregulation is somewhat disputed: Hibbs records 51 in 1980, and the *Buses* White Paper lists 49 in 1983. Ibanez and Meyer state that "about 44 of the larger Cities in the Shire Counties had a Municipal Bus Company" prior to deregulation. I will take as definitive the Department of Transport *GB Transport Statistics 1985-6* which lists 47. The author and his collaborators tracked these companies to 1993: 35 remained in local authority ownership; 5 had been sold as ESOPs; one had been sold commercially, and six had been liquidated (in some cases after being sold). Incidently, the "attrition rate" of municipals is almost the same in the period running up to the legislation as in the period after it: between 1975 and 1985 five 'municipals' had ceased operating. These "survival" figures in a very difficult operating climate do not bear out the theoretical direction the municipal sector might have taken. Neither does a comparison of operating sizes between 1983 and the present. The *Buses* White Paper produced a table of operator size in 1983 (table 3 p.27). The SIHE team have compiled a comparable list up to 1993 based on a variety of sources, including the *Municipal Yearbook* and direct information from operators. Table 1 depicts the results.

Table 1
Fleet sizes of municipal or former municipal bus operators (1983 - 1993)

Fleet size	No. of Companies 1983	No. of Companies 1993
less than 41	9	2
41 - 70	15	8
71 - 100	8	8
101 - 150	7	11
150 - 200	3	5
201 - 250	5	0
over 250	2	4
Size not known	-	3

Whilst these figures should be treated with some caution, since they may conceal switches away from traditional fleets and towards mini and midi buses, they do not, nevertheless, demonstrate the degree of radical "slimming down" predicted by Roth, at least. The validity of these statistics is given some weight by the high degree to which networks previously operated by municipals prior to deregulation have been maintained by their successor companies.

Three other area of "prediction" might briefly be surveyed.

* Whilst it is true that bus service support has fallen between 1985 and the present, the crude figures disguise an initial steep fall, followed by a period of very shallow falls in support and then slight increases. Table 2 displays these figures.

Table 2
Trends in bus service support 1985 - 1991

1985-6	£262.8m
1986-7	£148.7m
1987-8	£142.1m
1988-9	£131.0m
1989-90	£131.2m
1991-2	£133.9m

Source: *Bus Industry Monitor 1992,* Transport Advisory Service.

It can be suggested that subsidies have been redistributed as they have fallen, but this is not borne out by records of county council tendering activity. Certainly, it does not appear that Nicholas Ridley's buoyant predictions of decreasing subsidies as competition improved the profitability of routes has happened.

* Passenger numbers continue to fall.
* Shared taxi schemes are virtually non-existent and never succeeded in entering the market. This is perhaps unsurprising in the light of the assumption among supporters of Transport Act that shared taxis would supplement the activities of the more intensely used sectors of an informal route network.

So why have all predictions been so wide of the mark? Opponents of the Act cannot claim that it is simply because deregulation broke a working system: it has not overall, and in any event as has been pointed out the predictions of the opponents of the Act were as wide of the mark as those of its proponents. What has happened it appears, is the arrival of a hybrid unanticipated by all parties to the dispute over the 1985 legislation. The whole scene has metamorphosed, but in unanticipated directions. I will attempt here a partial answer to this question, based largely upon the SIHE research programme into the activities of municipal or former municipal bus undertakings since 1985. This project aims to interview leading actors from County Councils, District Councils and in the Bus Companies themselves, in all of the districts supporting municipal bus companies upon deregulation, and thereby gain an impression of the interplay of bus companies and various authorities not perhaps fully emphasised by the more traditional method of statistical evaluation.

I would suggest that a number of actions, not all connected, cohered together to defeat the "logic" of a Public Choice driven "pure market" in road passenger Transport. Some of these activities were motivated, as I will identify by "mission" and some by self-interest, but as with most examples of the application of a simplistic theory to a complex reality, the cumulative effect of a variety of identifiable (and often, in truth, predictable) actions to accommodate the reality to the theory usually ensures that the outcome does not conform to stereotype. I would identify five significant reactions to the legislation which together created this outcome.

1. Municipal operators registered an unexpectedly high proportion of their existing networks upon deregulation. This is estimated by Peter Stanley to average 75% of previous bus mileage (Stanley, 1989,

p.28). They did so in covert defiance of "cross subsidisation" regulations, and initially, perhaps acted to defend what they saw as essential networks in a manner that would not be regarded as entirely rational on an economic basis. However, this strong assertion of the value of the maintenance of a network, and a rejection of the vision of a "spontaneous" recreation of a network at an unidentified futurepoint found an echo in the new county council regulators most of which began to design their tendered routes around the logic of the networks thus preserved. Of the fourteen county or regional authorities interviewed by SIHE researchers, all but one indicated their regard for the defence of networks, and by implication the relationship of tendered routes to them.

2. County authorities have not performed the disinterested "regulatory" role anticipated by the legislation. Instead, (and often regardless of political affiliation) they have seen themselves as very pro-active in the promotion of public transport within their areas. This has manifested itself in the widespread assumption of a promotional role through the issuing of timetables, travel "hot lines" and various other activities which built upon the idea of stable and predictable patterns of public transport. SIHE found that ten of the fourteen counties surveyed provide an active bus promotion service of this kind.

3. County authorities have also been active in effectively "fixing" the market marginally in favour of the larger and more historically recognised companies through a surprisingly active policy of County based travel concession schemes. Whilst these schemes are theoretically available to all operators, their application across Counties, and not on a "patchwork" basis in district authorities means that the providers of effective networks are more likely to benefit form passenger patronage. SIHE found that seven county authorities actively provide a financial input to county wide concession, and two more co-ordinate the financial input of districts to achieve a similar effect.

4. County tendering practices, whilst fair to all-comers according to the letter of the Act, largely assist the network operators not only by attaching tendered routes to networks, but by "bundling", tenders, or at least encouraging linked bids for tendered routes. In a number of instances this is done with acknowledgement that such practices deter the "cowboys" when it comes to placing acceptable bids. SIHE found that nine county councils appeared to support, or at least condone "bundling" practices.

5. District authorities which have historically maintained a municipal transport undertaking have largely maintained a very pro-public

transport stance subsequent to deregulation. In a number of instances the council has clearly taken great pains to restructure failing municipal successor companies, using resources of advice and planning to do so which are not sourced from within the company concerned. However, district councils have undertaken "bus-supportive" schemes on a much wider basis, which have clearly benefitted and sustained incumbent operators, whilst theoretically being available to all-comers. These include new bus priority schemes (in six district councils out of ten interviewed) new park and ride schemes (six authorities) and measures to curb the car in town centres (four authorities). The practice of providing financially important concessions, is, of course widespread (eight authorities, with the other two relying on their county scheme) and four authorities are recorded as providing their own tendered routes to supplement those of the county.

Taken together with evidence from Evans and from interviews with transport managers that the travelling public is far more resistant to changing their bus-riding patterns for the sake of a perceived fare of headway advantage than theoretical predictions would suggest, these factors have clearly created a protective "mesh" supportive of identifiable and familiar services which can, in the publics mind, be trusted to convey them to their destination. It is this recognition on the part of bus operators that has, in effect produced a de facto "franchise" pattern across most areas of the country as operators concentrate on developing long-term brand loyalty and reliability instead of attempting to drive their immediate competitors off the road. In most parts of the country, illuminated both by many of the research reports I have cited, and by our own interviews with transport managers, there is little stomach for further competition, and a recognition that there is more advantage to demarcated mutual survival than in "bus wars". This is not to say that companies are not "competitive" or now lack ambition, but this is channelled largely through the medium of acquisition (for example the exploits of Stagecoach and Badgerline) leading to even further consolidation of no-competition franchising, instead of the "Darwinist" competition that the Transport Act aimed to set up. In brief, the experience of the past seven years demonstrates that Public Choice simply does not work when it comes out of the hands of pamphleteers and into the realms of practical legislation.

References

Balcombe, R. Astrop, A. & Fairhead, R. (1992) *Bus Competition in Great Britain Since 1986 : a National Review,* TRL Research Report No. 353.

Cheek, C. (1992), "Virtuous Circle for Buses Still Faces Funding", Local Transport Today, June, London.

Evans, A. (1988), "Hereford: a Case Study of Bus Deregulation", Journal of Transport Economics, September, London.

Evans, A. (1990), "Competition and the Structure of Local Bus Services", Journal of Transport Economics and Policy, September, London.

Farrington, J. (1986), *"Deregulation of the British Bus Industry",* Geography Vol. 71, London.

Hibbs, J. (1984), *Transport Without Politics?,* Institute of Economic Affairs Hobart Paper, London.

Ibanez, J. & Meyer, J. (1990), "Privatising and Deregulating Local Public Services", APA Journal, Winter, London.

Mueller, D. (1989), *Public Choice 2,* Cambridge University Press, Cambridge.

Niskanen, W. (1972), *Bureaucracy: Servant or Master,* Institute on Economic Affairs, London.

Roth, G. & Shepherd, A. (1982), *Wheels Within Cities,* Adam Smith Institute, London.

Stanley, P. (1989), *All change: a Study of Bus Transport Planning Deregulation and Privatization in Seven Towns,* SEEDS, London.

7 Urban transport: Recent European experience

Martin Higginson

Introduction

This chapter analyses the evolving structure of transport in urban areas in the UK, which are compared with examples from mainland Europe. The period covered is that since the end of World War II, when public transport use was at its maximum. Developments between the late 1940s and the present are summarized, with particular reference to recent changes. The chapter concludes with an assessment of options for the future, and their likelihood of being selected for implementation.

Developments in policies are illustrated by reference to developments on the ground: changes in public and private transport use, in land use and demographic patterns, and in technical and operational capabilities and characteristics. The emphasis throughout is on public passenger transport.

Historical perspective

In the late 1940s and early 1950s, when life was getting back to normal after the six years of World War II, the principal mode of passenger transport in Britain was the bus. Buses and the rapidly dwindling numbers of trams accounted for 42% of all passenger kilometres by mechanised transport in 1952 (Department of Transport, 1993a). By 1959 the market share had dropped to 30%, although at 81 billion passenger kilometres, it was still close to double the present level of bus usage, 43 billion passenger kilometres in 1992. Perhaps of greater significance than the absolute decline, is that the reduction has taken place in an expanding travel market, of which buses now only account for 6%. In 1950, there were under two million cars on Britain's roads, compared to twenty million in 1992. Yet the portents of future traffic congestion were already to be seen; the total distance travelled by cars in 1949 (20 billion kilometres) was already five times that of buses and coaches. Bus and coach kilometres have remained broadly constant over the following forty years; but cars have seen a seventeen-fold increase to 335 billion kilometres.

The four main railway companies, after carrying increased loads under difficult operating conditions, and suffering from a lack of capital investment as well as a maintenance backlog, passed quickly from wartime government control to full public ownership in 1948 (Bonavia, 1987). In the few years between the end of the war and nationalization, the railways had already begun to pick up the trail of modernization, that had been abandoned in 1939. Work was completed to electrify the main suburban line from London's Liverpool Street as far as Shenfield in Essex; and orders for experimental diesel (London Midland and Scottish and Southern railways) and gas turbine (Great Western) (Robertson, 1989, p11) locomotives were a further indication of the beginnings of a move away from steam traction.

In Britain, many urban rail routes were converted to diesel traction, rather than being electrified, under British Railways' modernisation programme. Although further routes have subsequently been electrified, such as Birmingham's Cross City line in the West Midlands, re-equipment with new diesel rolling stock has even taken place in the 1990s on high frequency routes such as London's links to Salisbury, Aylesbury and Oxford. On the continent, steam was more commonly replaced directly with electric trains and intensive diesel operated suburban services are rare. High capacity can be provided within the more generous loading gauges in most other European countries by running double deck trains, for example in Paris (including through the cross city Reseau Express Regional tunnels) and in increasing numbers of German cities. Although subsequent operating costs may be lower, the high capital cost of electrification is a prime reason why Britain has lagged in this area. Whilst atmospheric pollution in urban areas is cut by electrification, whether or not emissions are reduced overall depends on the cleanliness of electricity generation.

Lifestyle changes have had a major impact on transport; and the converse is also true. As standards of living have improved, more people have been able to afford their own homes, more consumer durable goods, better food, longer and more exotic holidays. Residential densities have fallen, most noticeably as car ownership has facilitated a move to a suburban or rural location. Long distance commuting has become an accepted feature in the lives of thousands of Britons, able to exploit new motorway links and frequent, fast commuter railways. The M25 motorway now provides for orbital commuting around the outer fringes of London to an extent that causes embarrassment; the intention had been to provide a London bypass for long-distance traffic, not an incentive for firms to foresake central London offices reached by rail for green-field locations accessed by car.

Buses: technical evolution

The bus made enormous technical progress during the interwar period. The first covered topped double deckers (Sommerfield, 1933) and buses fitted with pneumatic tyres only appeared on London's streets in 1925, yet the smoothly contoured RT type emerged just fourteen years later, in 1939 (Barker and Robbins, 1974, p217). The spread of suburbs had taken city catchment areas well beyond the ends of many tram routes and into locations not served by rail (Jackson, 1973). In the days before mass private motoring, the bus was the natural means of meeting the travel needs of the new populations. Whilst some new buses had been constructed during the war, mostly to utility designs, major investment only restarted after the end of hostilities.

Technical developments have been a mixed blessing in the bus industry. Underfloor engines became universal for single deckers from the early 1950s. This is fine for coaches, where passengers appreciate the high vantage point and later designs have exploited the opportunity to accommodate luggage below the floor too. Boarding and alighting takes place infrequently, so the delay as passengers negotiate steep entrances is of little significance. For bus work, however, a high floor is a source of delay and inconvenience, which has still not entirely been obviated, despite the development since the early 1970s of rear engined vehicles such as the Leyland National.

On the continent, especially in Germany, ultra low floor single deckers are now commonplace, with step heights so low that pushchairs, prams, shopping trolleys and even wheelchairs can easily be admitted. Britain has been slower to adopt the low floor bus. Experimental services began in Liverpool, Tyneside and Dundee in 1993 and the first major conversion, with 68 purpose designed vehicles, in London in 1994 (London Transport, 1994). Bus operators in Britain, who have been concerned to keep costs down in the face of competition, have had difficulty since 1986 in keeping pace even with normal capital investment in vehicles and have been wary of purchasing untried, technically more complex and more expensive types. It is significant that the first substantial investment has been made for use in a regulated environment by London Transport's Unit for Disabled Passengers, with the aid of special government funding.

Whilst the investment has been undertaken under the auspices of the Unit for Disabled Passengers, the importance of the low floor bus is that it enables a larger proportion of the population to use buses. Easier entry and exit also reduces delays to passengers and other road users at stops; if the improvement in operational speed is sufficient to reduce the number of buses needed to provide a given level of service, this will go some way towards reducing the cost differential with conventional types of bus. Series production will in any case be cheaper than the cost of prototype vehicles. In a competitive environment, it is essential for new vehicles to be commercially attractive and technically reliable if operators are to be convinced of their worth. The price differential, currently around 20-25% for limited runs of prototype vehicles, could fall to as little as 2-5%.

The design of double deck buses was revolutionised by the introduction of rear engined types from the late 1950s and encouraged by the availability of New Bus Grant from the government from the late 1960s until 1983-84. A rear engine and front entrance allowed for the operation of double deck buses without a conductor, at a considerable saving in cost but, with the separate payment of graduated fares, at a cost in terms of delays at stops and thus of overall journey speeds. Although mitigated by the simplification of fare structures and by prepaid ticketing, one person operated buses are still slower in some urban situations than those with a conductor. London alone retains conductor operation on a large scale, for services to and from the busiest parts of the West End. A few other operators have effected their re-introduction as part of a competitive strategy, although in most cases this policy has been short-lived, as the revenue gain has unfortunately been outweighed by the additional staff costs.

Faced with still rising car competition, there is still a need for the dilemma of cost of operation versus service speed to be resolved by bus operators. Whilst modern buses are more comfortable and better appointed than older types, and in-vehicle time may represent a small proportion of total journey time (including access and waiting time), it is unsatisfactory to require the bus to remain stationary while fares are collected. Smart card technology, enabling pre-purchased tickets to be decremented automatically as passengers board or leave the bus, (another developmental area in which its regulated environment has enabled London Transport to lead the way), may bring about this long-awaited development.

Conventional tramways

Although trams had been given an extension of life by the war in a number of British cities, including London, Manchester and Newcastle, and continued to operate in declining numbers in most of the larger cities, investment in their modernisation was small in Britain. Extensions of tramways to serve new suburbs had been rare, even in the 1930s. London's last tramway extension was in Eltham in 1932 and Sunderland's shortlived reserved track Durham Road extension, opened 1949 and closed in 1954 (Irwin, 1990, p47), was one of the last in Britain. Only small numbers of new trams were constructed, for example for Sheffield, Leeds and Glasgow. Many tramcars dating from the Edwardian era were still in service, increasingly obsolescent in appearance and expensive to maintain. In most cities trams were viewed unfavourably; they were antiquated, their crown of the road tracks and stopping places inconvenient for their passengers and for other road users and increasingly, their routes did not link people's homes and workplaces.

Thus, as investment in new buses caught up after the wartime backlog, tramway closures recommenced. In London it was five years before sufficient buses were available for the programme of tramway abandonments to be recommenced in 1950 (Joyce, 1987). Final closure of the London tram system came in 1952, a decade later than would have been the case had the war not intervened (Higginson, 1993). The remaining systems gradually succumbed; Bradford and Manchester (Yearsley, 1988) in the late 1940s, Birmingham, Liverpool and Leeds by the end of the 1950s, for example, and finally Sheffield in 1960 and Glasgow in 1962, leaving only the untypical Blackpool coastal route to bridge the gap between the traditional British urban tramway and the new generation of light rail systems. Use of trams in Britain fell from two billion passenger journeys in 1948 to one billion in 1953 and only 16 million in 1963 (Munby, 1978, p300).

The pattern of tramway abandonment was matched in many other countries, such as France and the USA, where most of the conventional tramway systems were closed. In Germany, however, despite substantial war damage, most of the larger cities, and in the former German Democratic Republic, many smaller towns too, retained their trams. Tramways have also been retained and extended in the principal Dutch, Italian, Swiss and Austrian cities, in Eastern Europe, Scandinavia, Belgium and Portugal.

Light rail

Modernisation has included the construction of substantial underground sections in some city centres, including Hannover, Essen, Stuttgart and Cologne and upgrading to semi (Cologne) or full (Brussels) metro standards. Although the trams are freed from road congestion, sub surface stations are less accessible than above ground stops and sometimes unpleasant places in which to wait. The resultant mixed feelings about light rail and tram subways have led to policy reversals, for example in Cologne (Hall and Hass-Klau, 1985), where some surface level routes have been retained in the city centre. Apart from London's Kingsway subway (1906-1952), no British city ever acquired tramway tunnels, although they were planned for Leeds in the 1940s. On grounds both of expense of construction and of accessibility, it is therefore pleasing that the new generation light rail systems in Manchester, Sheffield and Grenoble are entirely above ground.

The closure of its tramways may be seen as an early example of Britain's folly in following American rather than European practice in transport policy. Had Britain's larger urban tramway systems survived another decade or so, this would have taken many of them into the age when urban road construction and the capacity of cities to accommodate all potential demand for car use and parking places, were beginning to be questioned, for example in (Sir) Colin Buchanan's prophetic *Traffic in Towns* report of 1963. In some cities, notably Liverpool, extensive sections of reserved track tramway were abandoned. Here and in other cities, it would have been possible gradually to extend the off road tramways into city centres, as older properties were demolished. Instead, inner city clearance has all to often given rise to space-consuming highways, cutting through, rather than meeting the needs of the remaining inner city communities in areas such as the southern approaches to Leeds and adjacent to London's elevated Westway motorway, along which no local bus services are operated.

Railways

The role of railways had already begun to decline before World War II, as buses (and, earlier, in some inner urban areas, electric trams) caused the withdrawal of uneconomic passenger services, mostly from branch lines in sparsely populated areas, or where the railway afforded an uncompetitively circuitous route compared to road, or where formerly competing routes offered duplicate services, such as in parts of South Wales and the East Midlands. Even where they offered competing services whose rationale dated from the pre-grouping era, before 1923, all main rail routes remained open in the early post war period. In 1947 rail travel accounted for 1.1 billion passenger journeys, 8% less than the typical annual figure for the 1930s. A further 8% fall in passengers took place over the 1950s, to one billion passenger trips in 1960. Subsequently, rail travel has stabilised at around 700-800 million trips annually. Unlike bus travel, which fell in absolute as well as proportional terms, rail passenger kilometres have remained relatively stable; 39 billion in the early 1950s and 38 billion in and 1992. The buoyancy of rail travel is largely attributable to increasing long distance commuting and to competitive inter city services; passenger travel lost as a result of line and station closures accounted for a relatively small share of rail's market.

Financial support for urban public transport

Urban public transport is generally more heavily subsidised in continental Europe than in Britain at present. External support meets between half and three quarters of costs in many cities, such as Paris (53%), Berlin (61%), Brussels (65%) and Stockholm (64%), compared to 29% for London's buses, 39% for London Underground and between two and twenty percent in deregulated British cities, where support is payable only for tendered services. Consequently, pressures on continental operators to cover their costs out of revenue are less. Simple, flat or zonal fare systems, often allowing transfer between vehicles and modes, blocks of tickets available for pre-purchase, and system-wide travelcards make the payment of cash fares (for which a surcharge is usually payable) a less common feature than in Britain. Outside Britain, passengers are often trusted to validate their own tickets in an on-vehicle machine.

Rather than considering subsidy as something to be avoided if at all possible, cheaply priced city public transport is seen in mainland Europe as conferring environmental advantages, for example in Switzerland and in Freiburg, Germany. In Britain, a distinction is drawn between capital and operating subsidies. Capital support is preferred, since it enables operators to be furnished with the necessary capital equipment to run good services, without removing the discipline for efficient operation. Over the past decade, the emphasis has moved further away from subsidising direct operations, to support for external facilities such as bus priority schemes and bus-activated traffic signals.

Government criteria for supporting investment stress the need to obtain non-user benefits and, increasingly since the late 1980s, look to the private sector to contribute at least part of the cost. Lack of familiarity with transport projects, which typically have a long payback period, has resulted in delay to several major projects. These include London Underground's Jubilee Line extension, finally authorised in late 1993, and several projects for which finance has still not been agreed at the time of writing (January 1994): the Channel Tunnel rail link and second London terminal (which have received a promise of partial government funding), new trains for urban rail services in Strathclyde and West Yorkshire, and the east west Crossrail in London.

Cycling

Cycling has experienced the most severe reduction of all the mechanised transport modes. In 1952, an estimated 23 billion passenger kilometres were travelled by bicycle; by 1992 this had fallen to 5 billion. Cycling accounted for more than one passenger kilometre in ten in the early 1950s, but has only accounted for 1% each year since 1968. Cycling has lost out, mainly to the car, for two reasons. Firstly, car ownership has risen as personal wealth has increased; but increases in car use and the implementation of policies designed to make motoring faster and easier have made the environment less attractive and less safe for the cyclist.

Cycle use remains high in some cities, notably Cambridge, Oxford and York, and this encourages the local authority to make provision for cyclists in their traffic and highway plans. In York, for example, the city council has constructed cycle routes linking the city centre with residential suburbs, using a combination of quiet streets, a road along the banks of the River Ouse which has been closed to motor traffic, and specially constructed and surfaced pathways. A comprehensive map of cycle routes in the city is produced. In most cities cycling facilities are wholly inadequate and where cycle lanes are provided, they commonly fail to provide for through journeys. The following example from London is all too typical. An isolated pair of bicycle lanes occupy the kerbside in each direction across Waterloo Bridge; but they end before the roundabout at the southern end of the bridge.

Ownership of cycles is increasing, but their use has fallen in recent years. This contradiction, which is clearly linked to perceived and actual worries over the safety of cycling, is shown in the returns of the 1989-91 National Travel Survey. The proportion of households with at least one cycle rose from 25% in 1972-73 to 36% in 1989-91, or from 14 to 27 cycles per hundred persons (Department of Transport, 1993c, Chapter 7). Annual mileage cycled fell from an average of 51 in the mid 1970s to 41 (for all households). Average annual distance travelled per bicycle fell by nearly half, from 295 to 153 miles between 1972-73 and 1989-91. 70% of households recorded no cycle journeys during the survey week and an average of only 21 cycle journeys per year was recorded. The use of cycles is changing. Perhaps surprisingly, commuting still accounted for 37% of cycling in 1989-91, but it had been overtaken by leisure, 40%, since 1985-6.

Use of the bicycle for educational trips has fallen by a third, to 7% of all cycle trips, over the past fifteen years. Parents taking children to school by car, to avoid the need for a "dangerous" bicycle trip, present a dilemma which goes to the heart of the problem of present day car use. The individual safety of the children taken to school by car increases the danger to those continuing to walk, cycle, or go by bus, causes obstruction and congestion at schools and on the roads at peak times, and reduces children's independence and freedom. The Safe Routes for Schools campaign is intended to encourage local authorities to implement improvements to walking and cycle routes and pedestrian crossings used by children on their home to school journeys; projects are currently in hand in Hertfordshire and Avon, with a further scheme centred on road safety training in progress in Gateshead.

Cycling is also now receiving greater attention from government policy makers. The government's *Planning Policy Guidance for Transport* requires local plans to "include policies that encourage the implementation of specific measures to assist people to use bicycles, particularly in urban areas" (Department of Environment, 1993, Appendix A, paragraph 11). Although expenditure is small compared to road schemes, councils are beginning to devote more resources to cycle facilities; Berkshire and Suffolk County Councils each plan to spend to spend around £600,000 on cycle routes by 1999 (Berkshire County Council, 1993; Suffolk County Council, 1993). Perhaps of greater importance, though, will be the extent to which cyclists benefit from the much greater amounts to be spent on general road and traffic schemes, such as new road construction, junction improvements and local safety schemes. The example of Ipswich emphasises the still relatively very low expenditure specifically devoted to cycling. Out of a package totalling £13 million, improvements at 32 key road junctions account for £4.8 million and cycle facilities a mere £361,000 (Suffolk County Council, op. cit. p.123).

The statistics for cycle ownership indicate a potential increase in cycling in Britain, but it is difficult for local authorities or the government to justify substantial expenditure in the absence of effective demand. This is a classic chicken and egg situation; although there is evidence of government awareness of the desirability of helping cycling, and of some dedication of finance, this is still minimal compared to expenditure on highways for motor traffic. In Holland the continued popularity of cycling, has made it easier to devote resources to it and The Netherlands has a comprehensive national network of cycle routes (Sustrans, 1992).

Walking

Walking accounted for 30% of all journeys and 81% of those under a mile in 1989-91 (Department of Transport, 1993b, Chapter 6); yet it receives disproportionately small attention from policy makers and transport engineers. On average, each person makes almost one walking trip per day (6.3 per week), of which half are less than half a mile and four fifths are under a mile in length. Average annual mileage walked has fallen by 4% since 1975-76, but that by children by between 20% (5-10 year olds) and 13% (11-15s). The main driver of a household car walks less than half the distance covered by a person from a non car owning household, 160 compared to 327 miles per year. Taking again the examples cited with regard to cycling, Berkshire's medium term plan envisages expenditure on footway schemes of £530,000 up to 1999 and in Suffolk, £200,000 is earmarked for improved pedestrian facilities in Ipswich. Despite claims such as that the 39% reduction in local delays brought about by junction improvements in Berkshire "are of benefit to all road users" (Berkshire County Council, op. cit. p.106), the principal objective of such developments is clearly to enhance motorised traffic speeds.

The more comprehensive pedestrianisation of many city and town centres in other European countries than Britain is noticeable in France, Germany, Austria and the Netherlands, for example. The shopping streets in the centres of cities such as Stuttgart, Munich, Utrecht, Salzburg and Cologne, are substantially free of traffic. Some British cities have followed this model, notably Birmingham, where pedestrians may traverse the city centre without crossing a major road, yet penetration by buses has been substantially retained. Central London has seen minimal progress, with heavy, through traffic continuing to use many main shopping streets, such as Regent Street. London is at last beginning to catch up with progress elsewhere; success has been achieved in reducing traffic in the City of London, albeit at the initial instigation of the City Police as a means of reducing the likelihood of terrorism. In the rest of central London, the government-appointed Traffic Director for London's proposals for implementation by the late 1990s, including extensive bus priorities and improved pedestrian conditions may succeed where the democratically elected boroughs (especially Westminster City Council) have failed.

The destruction of many continental European cities in World War II facilitated the construction of inner ring roads on a scale not possible without extensive and controversial property demolition in most British cities. Plymouth, the centre of which was largely destroyed in the war, is an exception; another is Coventry, and both have untypically modern centres, which have more easily been pedestrianised. In general, the removal of traffic from town centres has been more gradual in Britain, but most provincial cities now have substantial pedestrian core areas. Developments such as plans for the completion of an outer-central ring for general traffic and an inner public transport circuit (perhaps eventually to be used by trams) around Leeds city centre, indicate that progress is still being made. The planned introduction of more bus priority streets in central London, and proposals to reduce traffic and assist pedestrians in central Edinburgh, are signs of impending and overdue change in two British capital cities which have so far lagged behind.

Cars

Undoubtedly the greatest change in personal travel in the past fifty years has been the rise of mass motoring. In 1951, 14% of British households had a car; by 1991 this had risen to 68%. In southern England, excluding London, over 75% of households have cars, compared to just under 60% in Scotland and the north of England. In the early 1950s, travel by car, van and motorcycle accounted for around 30% of all mechanised travel. The watershed year for motoring was 1959, the year in which the number of passenger kilometres by car, van and motorcycle first equalled the combined total for buses, railways and cycling. By 1992, motoring's share had risen to 87% (Department of Transport, 1993a).

Access to a car does much more than allow a change of travel mode; it opens up a previously unthought of range of journey opportunities. The roots of today's traffic congestion are clearly seen in the statistics for car availability and use. Since the early 1950s, passenger kilometres by car have risen ten fold and are currently almost three time the total amount of travel by all modes in 1950. The number of cars licensed is also some ten times higher than in 1950. Road network capacity, which has increased by 25% since the end of World War II, has nowhere near kept pace with the expanded demands placed on it, notwithstanding the construction of some 3,000 kilometres of motorways since the late 1950s (Starkie, 1982), the dualling or widening of many other roads, and developments in traffic management.

The growth of motoring has proceeded in parallel with demographic changes. Post-war new towns such as Harlow, Stevenage and Crawley facilitated greater car use than traditional urban and suburban residential areas (Ratcliffe, 1981, pp.53-65). Although bus services were moderately good, dispersed residential and employment locations and lower population densities than in older centres emphasised the speed differential in favour of the car. Later developments, epitomised by Milton Keynes, saw maximum provision for the car (White, 1986, p86), with road structures geared to almost universal car use and buses consigned to a residual role (although to some extent smaller buses have retrieved the situation, by facilitating higher frequencies and better penetration of communities). The dispersal of population into erstwhile rural areas is a further consequence of motorised society. Most towns have their greenfield housing satellites, often remote from shops, health facilities, employment and education which, being beyond convenient walking distance and without good bus services, are predominantly accessed by car. Out of town shopping centres, once considered to be a characteristically French feature, are now common in Britain; but the traffic and transport problems they have generated are now recognised to detract from their beneficial attributes, and both in the UK and in France they are now viewed less favourably by planning authorities.

Statistics published by the European Conference of Ministers of Transport (ECMT, 1993) show growth in car use to be highly correlated with the state of economic advancement. Between 1965 and 1989, passenger kilometres travelled by car increased by around six times in Spain and Italy, 2.9 times in France, 2.5 times in the United Kingdom, 2.3 times in Belgium, 2.1 times in Germany and 1.9 times in Denmark. By 1991, many of the wealthier European countries, including Belgium, France, Italy and West Germany had more motor vehicles per head of population than Britain, which, along with The Netherlands, had 0.405 vehicles per person (British Road Federation, 1993, Table 51).

With road construction unable to keep pace with the rise in vehicle numbers, the number of vehicles per kilometre of road has increased throughout Europe since the mid 1970s. Britain's 2.9% per year average increase was exceeded by Germany (3.6%), France (3.7%) and Italy (4.7%), but was greater than the rises in Belgium, Denmark and The Netherlands. In 1991, Britain had 67 vehicles per kilometre of road the second highest after Italy (98) of the above countries (BRF, op cit, Figure 10).

Freight

Freight transport has undergone a similar revolution. Rail's share of goods moved fell from 42% in 1952 to 7% forty years later, whilst that of road rose from 35% to 61% (Department of Transport, 1993a, Table 9.3). The decline in domestic and industrial coal use and in heavy industrial output such as iron and steel; and rise in lightweight, high value goods such as electrical and electronic equipment and consumer goods, with increasing requirements for packaging and precisely determined delivery times, are key elements in this process of change. Road transport's ability to provide door to door service, with the product under personal control throughout, and without the expense and susceptibility to damage and loss brought about by transhipment, is an advantage which rail has striven without success to achieve for most commodities. Rail freight has lost much of the advantage it once had of depots close to town centres, with the result that most railborne freight that is not passing to or from a private siding at a port or works now requires a lengthy road haul, often through urban areas unsuited to modern lorries. Freight depots such as those at Kings Cross and Paddington in London (both still vacant or semi-derelict sites, and thus, given the necessary finance and political will, capable of being reactivated), together with numerous smaller terminals, brought goods close to where they were needed, and road distribution therefore typically took place only over short distances. The closure of dedicated freight centres such a these, accessed directly by rail from outside the cities, without the need for goods to travel on congested and environmentally sensitive urban and suburban roads, is a serious loss to Britain's transport network, which it would be difficult, but not impossible, to bring back into operation.

The collapse of the Speedlink network of fast, mixed freight trains in 1991 (Modern Railways, February 1991, p98) was one of the final indications of the railways' inability to compete with road except over long distances and for heavy, bulk flows in the present political and business environment. In recognition of road freight's ascendancy, the railways were relieved of the common carrier obligation by the Transport Act 1962 (James, 1980, p.287).

As with passenger travel, so the quantity of freight moved has increased over the past 40 years. Despite a reduction during the recessionary years since 1989, freight tonne kilometres in 1992 were almost two and a half times their 1952 level. Tonnage lifted, without taking distance into account, had only risen by 60%, which shows the effect of our more dispersed lifestyles in the motor age. Goods are both manufactured and consumed in more widely separated locations. In truth, these figures underestimate the dispersion effect, as they relate only to domestic transport. The effects of the largely new trade in manufactured goods from the Far East and of increased intra European trade outweigh reductions in trade with the Empire and Commonwealth.

Goods vehicle kilometres have increased more slowly (2.5 times more vehicle kilometres since 1952) than the quantity of goods moved (4.1 times more tonne kilometres), as heavier lorries have been permitted. Mileage per vehicle has also risen. The number of goods vehicles licensed is actually slightly less than it was 40 years ago (1952: 450,000, 1992: 437,000).

Although some European countries continued with the economic regulation of freight transport long after it was abandoned in Britain, road transport's market share is rising rapidly, with rail and inland waterways struggling to maintain absolute levels of traffic (Department of Transport, 1993a, Table 8.5).

Organisation and ownership

In 1948, a new nationalized conglomerate, the British Transport Commission (BTC) was set up, as the largest transport organization Britain had ever seen. BTC was charged under the Transport Act 1947 with the duty of providing and integrating transport and port facilities for passengers and freight; and was organized into five Executives: Railways, Road Transport, London

Transport, Hotels and Docks and Inland Waterways. Much of BTC's portfolio, including bus, waterway, road freight and hotel interests, as well as the railways themselves, derived from ownership by the former "Big Four" railway companies. BTC's existence was dogged by a remit that, whilst in some respects too wide, in others gave it insufficient power. Its empire was unmanageably large the hoped for co-ordination and integration proved unachievable, in particular as individual Executives tended to act independently. Gourvish (1986, p39) describes the relationship between the Commission and the Railway Executive as "uncertain" and portrays an uneasy balance of power between the two bodies. Aldcroft (1968, p.113) considered the BTC's functions to be too centralised, "since final power lay with the Minister of Transport". On the other hand, to succeed, BTC would have needed complete control over road transport, which almost certainly could never have been achieved. Nor would the size of the inevitable bureaucracy have been conducive to operating an efficient transport system, capable of quick response to customers' needs. The BTC inherited only the former railway portion of the bus industry and London Transport's bus interests, leaving the remaining services in the hands of local authorities and privately owned operators, including the major British Electric Traction group of companies (Hibbs, 1968, p.208).

The ownership and use of private cars, which was set to resume rapid growth in the 1950s, was untouched by BTC, and controls on cars at this time were minimal; few parking restrictions, no parking meters, no "MoT" test, little traffic management, and certainly no thoughts of road pricing. On the freight side, "own account" operations, vehicles carrying firms' own goods, remained outside BTC control and it is perhaps not surprising that much of road haulage was denationalized under the Conservatives' Transport Act 1953. The rump of the former BTC road haulage sector became British Road Services, which subsequently became part of the National Freight Corporation and was eventually sold to its employees in 1982 (McLachlan, 1983). The 1953 Act confirmed that aspirations for a fully co-ordinated system of transport were to be abandoned and, except with regard to passenger transport in the London area, BTC's requirement to co-ordinate and integrate transport was removed. The Railway Executive was abolished, leaving BTC in direct control of British Railways.

In 1955, British Railways made a loss for the first time, and the annual deficit exceeded £100 million in 1962, the final year before the BTC's replacement by separate organizations for each of its former constituents. The 1947 Transport Act and the BTC have been criticised for failing to produce a blueprint for the long term future of transport in Britain (Aldcroft, 1968, p115). Its investment expenditure was insufficiently directed or prioritised. On the railways, it amounted to an attempt to maintain the status quo and the 1955 Modernisation Plan (British Transport Commission, 1955) has been criticised for its lack of attention to costs and financial returns (Aldcroft, op cit, p156; Gourvish, 1986, Chapter 8).

Railway modernisation and reshaping

The Modernisation Plan resulted in electrification of the west and, eventually, east coast main lines; further suburban electrification, including extensions into outer south east England; the construction of British Railways' first substantial fleets of diesel locomotives and the widespread introduction of diesel multiple units; and the partial fulfilment of a programme of freight and marshalling yard updating and expansion. An improvement "of the order of £85 million a year", with "very few traffics that will not be covering at least the direct costs of their movement" (para. 134) was hoped for.

That the outcome was not as planned is made clear by the publication of the famous Beeching Report, *The Reshaping of British Railways*, (British Railways Board, 1963) and its less well known successor *The Development of the Major Railway Trunk Routes* (British Railways Board, 1965). The first report is best known for its proposals to discontinue many loss-making passenger and freight trains and to close many lines and stations. Some 270 passenger services were proposed for withdrawal and seventy others for modification, involving the closure of around 2,000 stations. 99% of BR's passenger miles was found to be carried on 67% of the route mileage and a similar proportion of freight tons were identified to be carried on two thirds of the freight-carrying network (British Railways Board, 1963, Appendix 1).

Train services in numerous urban areas were scheduled for withdrawal, principally in the provincial towns and cities, but including some London suburban links. Most of the programme of closures inspired by the report took place over the remainder of the 1960s, although some threatened lines were reprieved (for example London's North London and Kentish Town-Barking lines; Leeds and Bradford to Ilkley and Skipton; and Manchester-Bury (now part of the Metrolink tramway, which carried 13 million passengers, 18% over budget, in 1993). Others, not originally proposed for closure, were shut, such as the controversial closure between Oxford and Cambridge. Forming a north-east to westerly link around the north of London, between East Anglia and western England and South Wales, connecting areas of increasing population (including the new city of Milton Keynes), high car ownership, and inadequate roads, the line is a prime example of one whose closure was ill advised, and at the very least, whose route should have been safeguarded, in case of future need. The area through which the line passed is currently the subject of controversy as the route of a proposed east west road link from Felixtowe to Oxford, to form part of the Trans-European Road Network (Daily Telegraph, 21 October, 1993).

There were however positive elements to the Beeching report too, including improved inter city services and the "co-ordination of suburban train and bus services and charges, in collaboration with municipal authorities" (p59), together with the development of freight liner trains and more block trains, operating without re-marshalling from origin to destination. The second Beeching report, of 1965, emphasised the need to rationalise duplicatory routes and terminals, both passenger and freight. A 3,000 mile network of routes was identified, related to the country's main population centres, and proposed for upgrading by 1984. Although there are differences in the details, the Beeching concept of investing heavily in certain routes, to enable them to become the principal inter city corridors, has been put in place. Some former duplicatory lines have been closed (Great Central north of Aylesbury) or downgraded (London Waterloo-Exeter), though both the east and west coast routes to Scotland remain and competition may be revived as moves to privatize British Rail take place.

Local authority relationships, co-ordination and competition

Improved co-ordination between transport operators, with the involvement of local authorities, came with Barbara Castle's Transport Act 1968, of which the system of Passenger Transport Authorities in the provincial conurbations are a lasting and valued legacy. Throughout their existence, which both pre and post dates the shortlived metropolitan counties, the PTEs have retained a multimodal responsibility for public transport planning. Since bus deregulation under the Transport Act 1985, they have lost their bus operating role, together with the power to control fares and co-ordinate bus services. However, the PTEs retain responsibility for public transport infrastructure, such as bus and rail stations and for the unified marketing of public transport. As facilitators of public transport, the PTEs are the tendering authority for non commercial bus services and also fund local railways, including, for example in West Yorkshire, by paying for additional rolling stock.

Before 1986, the operation and co-ordination of bus services, in each conurbation the dominant form of public transport, assumed the greatest importance for the PTEs, although the Tyne and Wear Metro, Liverpool's Loop and Link and Birmingham's Cross City line date from this period. During the pre deregulation period, PTE policies for buses centred on keeping fares down, most notably in South Yorkshire, and in fleet investment, although infrastructure investment did also take place, for example construction of the Bradford Interchange. In the eight years since the depletion of their responsibilities for bus services, the PTEs' attention to rail matters has increased. New services, mainly using routes which had previously closed, have been introduced, for example in Strathclyde and West Yorkshire and many new stations have been opened.

The PTEs and, outside the Metropolitan conurbations, the county councils act as procurers of non commercial bus services, which nationally account for 19% of bus kilometres run (Department of Transport, 1993c). Before 1986, like the PTEs, the shire county councils had been responsible for the co-ordination of all local bus services, without the now universal distinction between commercial and non commercial services. Some counties play a more active role than others in public transport matters; for example by providing countywide timetables and maps, as in Lancashire and Berkshire, and by supporting higher levels of service, and Hertfordshire is beginning to consider policies to restrain the growth in car travel. Service levels are determined locally. There are no national policies or guidelines, although government spending limits have the effect of restraining councils from "excessive" expenditure on high levels of service.

Some counties are involved with rail projects, for example Leicestershire with the Ivanhoe line (Leicester-Burton) reopening and Nottinghamshire with reopening the Robin Hood line (Nottingham-Mansfield), each of which received expenditure approval in the government's Autumn 1993 budget (Department of Transport, 1993d). For privately owned, commercially oriented bus companies, the provision of new local rail services, heavily reliant on public finance, represent an irksome intrusion in the market place. Generally, counties are wary of taking over local rail service funding, because they fear this could encourage the wholesale transfer of responsibility for local trains from central to local government. If that did occur, there is a danger of the fragmentation of rail services, as most operate across county boundaries; the problem would be exacerbated by the creation of smaller unitary authorities to replace the present two tier county/district structure in England and Wales and Scotland's region/district structure.

Local and regional government influence on public transport provision is stronger in some continental countries than in Britain. In Germany, the State (Land) governments influence policies, and the largest cities and conurbations each have a combined transport authority (Verkehrsverbund), which plans and co-ordinate fares, services and investment. Regional authorities in France, the Departements, support local rail services, and in Switzerland, many local railways are owned by local authorities.

Ownership and regulation of the bus industry

Throughout Britain, including in London by means of competitive tendering, privatization has changed the face of ownership of the bus industry, with the good effects arguably outweighing the bad. Perhaps least lamented is the passing of the National Bus Company (NBC), which had been formed in 1969 and was sold company by company in accordance with the Transport Act 1985. Although paralleling deregulation, the effects of bus industry privatization are quite distinct, as has belatedly been recognised by the government in its decision to privatize London Buses without waiting for deregulation. Although privatization is as yet incomplete, with around half the municipal companies and most of London Buses' local bus operating subsidiaries still publicly owned, a clear pattern of ownership is emerging. Large groups, headed by Stagecoach and Badgerline, are evolving into national concerns, with subsidiaries throughout the country (and in the case of Stagecoach, also overseas, in Africa and New Zealand). Both companies are now quoted on the Stock Exchange. Expansion takes place both by the purchase of public sector firms when they first come on to the market and through the acquisition of other private companies or groups. Alongside the largest groups are smaller ones such as Grampian, Caldaire and Proudmutual, and freestanding companies, some of which were in existence before privatisation commenced (eg Grey Green), whilst others have been created as a result of management buyouts; for example the former municipal undertakings at Southampton and Fylde and former PTE companies such as Yorkshire Rider and Busways.

The pattern of ownership is expected to evolve gradually, as further public sector companies come on to the market and through additional sales of private companies, for example as their owners reach retirement age. Expansion, especially by the largest groups, will continue to be tempered by requirements of competition legislation. The Office of Fair Trading (OFT) and Monopolies and Mergers Commission (MMC) seek to restrain operators perceived to be creating or exploiting monopolies (see, for example, Office of Fair Trading, 1991 and Monopolies and Mergers Commission, 1990) and agreements between operators must be registered. The intervention of the competition watchdogs sits uncomfortably alongside a supposed policy of deregulation. Many in the bus industry perceive regulation by the OFT and MMC, by gradually creating precedents on a case by case basis and by hedging competitive freedoms about with detailed rules, as less satisfactory than a formal, legal structure in which operators know where they stand. This would run the risk, however, of cautious legislators throwing the baby out with the bath water; removing the benefits of competition in order to rid the system of its blemishes.

Deregulation of bus services outside London also took place under the Transport Act 1985; the government considered privatisation to be an essential accompaniment to deregulation. Separation of the impact of each of the two changes is difficult. Overall, there have been some positive and some negative outcomes. An undoubted gain has been the reduction in bus operating costs, which has lead directly to a reduced requirement for subsidies. 84% of bus services were provided commercially in 1992-93. Revenue support for public transport outside London, excluding payments to British Rail, fell by 41% in real terms between 1985-86 and 1991-92 (Department of Transport, 1993a, Table 1.18). The quantity of service supplied, as measured by local bus kilometres run, increased by 20%, partly as a result of the introduction of smaller buses running at more frequent intervals, but where competing services duplicate one another on routes which already have frequent buses, shadowing each other's timings, the advantage to passengers is reduced.

The impact of increased bus mileage may be observed in the stability of employment it has provided for platform staff. The number of drivers (who constitute the great majority) and conductors has risen slightly since deregulation, from 101,000 in 1984 to 103,000 in 1992-93, with a peak of 105,500 in 1989-90, before the onset of the recession. Bus driving is essentially a labour-intensive task, but in other areas of employment, significant staff reductions have occurred, as the deregulated and privatized, or about to be privatized, companies have sought to reduce costs. 44% less maintenance, managerial, clerical and administrative staff were employed in 1992-3 than in 1984 (Department of Transport, 1993c). Whilst in most respects, this signifies a welcome improvement in productivity and efficiency, there is concern that the industry has cut staff levels by too much, and is not paying sufficient attention to planning for the future. The industry's safety record has not been made worse by deregulation and privatization (White, Dennis & Tyler, 1992).

Adverse effects of the current legislative regime centre on the failure of deregulation to stem the loss of ridership, on the loss of service and fare co-ordination and on organizational and investment failures in parts of the industry. After omitting the period immediately following deregulation, during which ridership fell because of large fare increases induced by strengthened central government controls on local authority spending, bus ridership declined by 18%, an average of 3.6% per annum, between 1987-88 and 1992-93, compared to a constant level of patronage between 1982 and 1985-86 (Department of Transport, 1993c). The steepest decline has been in the metropolitan conurbations (20%), where populations fell by 2% (1981-1991), compared to a population increase of 4.7% in the English and Welsh shire counties (OPCS, 1993). In London, where population grew by

1% over the decade, bus use fell by only 7% between 1987-88 and 1992-93, an average rate of decline of 1.4% per annum. Many commentators have concluded that the regulatory system in force in London, whereby bus operators bid for the right to run a service in a protected environment and within a co-ordinated fares system, is more appropriate to the needs of a large urban area than on the road competition (Higginson, 1991). The relationship between deregulation and control is discussed in Berechman (1993), but no judgement is passed on the outcome in London.

Cuts in wages and holiday entitlements provide further evidence that the push to cut costs has been taken too far in some quarters ("pay cuts of almost 20%, a cut in holidays from 26 to 15 days a year" in Colchester in 1993: Bus and Coach Buyer, 12 November, 1993). Training and management development have also been reduced by some companies in order to achieve immediate cost reductions, but in the longer term, at the expense of service quality.

Planning for the future, rendered difficult by the ability of operators to compete at short notice, has regrettably often been sacrificed in the interests of trimming management costs. Lack of investment in new buses has been a much criticised feature of bus operation in Britain since the mid 1980s, as operators of commercial services have sought to minimise unit costs in the face of actual or feared competition, and as service tenders have been awarded to the cheapest bidder, sometimes with insufficient regard to operational quality or to the fitness for purpose of the vehicles. There are, however, signs of the privatized and restructured industry maturing, with investment in new vehicles, attention to service quality, concern to enhance the industry's image and awareness of the need for political support increasing. Some tendering authorities specify vehicle types and standards, for example with regard to step heights, door widths and to the presence of Department of Transport DiPTAC (Disabled Persons Transport Advisory Committee) features such as colour contrasted grab rails. Research, such as that commissioned by the Bus and Coach Council into the longer term role of the bus (Wootton Jeffreys Consultants Ltd, 1994) and the value of marketing to the bus industry (University of Central England, 1994), provides further evidence of the industry seeking to strengthen its position.

London

In London, public transport co-ordination has lived on, despite deregulation in the rest of Britain. Ostensibly, London's buses were not deregulated in 1986 because reorganization had only just taken place under the Transport (London) Act, 1984 (Department of Transport, 1985). Subsequently, as deregulation's worst performance has been in the metropolitan conurbations, warnings against its extension to London have come from many quarters, not least from the Conservative controlled House of Commons Transport Committee (1993b). A few days before the Queen's Speech outlining the government's 1993/94 legislative programme, and to the disappointment of the London Buses directors who had been appointed on a deregulation platform, the Secretary of State for Transport announced London deregulation's indefinite postponement (McGregor, 1993). Since patronage retention has been better than in the other conurbations and significant reductions in unit costs of operation have been achieved by the subsidiaries of London Buses Ltd and through competitive tendering (albeit less than some of the cost reductions outside London), many observers expect, and hope, that the postponement of London bus deregulation will become permanent.

Controversy still surrounds bus policy for London, as the announcement also made clear the government's intention that bus service tenders should henceforth be invited on a minimum subsidy basis, in place of the previous full cost method. The case for the change is that operators will be given more incentive to run reliable, well used services than are afforded by the prevailing regime of performance targets, penalties for failure, and the long term incentive of contract renewal every three years. Whilst it may be true that "innovation" has been slower in London than in some cities, a criticism of deregulation outside London has been the loss of stability.

It remains to be seen to what extent operators of London bus services will be given the freedom to plan and market services under the revised regime. The strong public and political support for the London Travelcard, on which the Minister for Transport in London has staked his future, suggests that, despite its weakness in matching revenue to costs, Travelcard will survive in the immediate future, even in its multi operator form, with whatever new structure of rail operators emerges to succeed British Rail's Network SouthEast in the era of rail privatization. In the longer term, economists, and perhaps financiers too, will encourage London Transport to capitalise on smartcard technology to remove the opportunity to travel at zero marginal cost; but this is a benefit which lies at the heart of Travelcard's popularity. Therefore, on transport and traffic planning and environmental grounds, such encouragements must be resisted.

Rail re-openings in London and the south east have been fewer, partly because London is already well served and few lines had closed, but due also, since the abolition of the Greater London Council, to the lack of a co-ordinating body equivalent to the PTEs. Although joint working parties including British Rail and other bodies examine wider issues, such as Crossrail and rail access to Heathrow Airport, London Transport's own rail planning responsibility is limited to the London Underground.

Bus operation on the continent

Bus operators in other European countries tend to regard British bus privatization and deregulation with suspicion. Typically, urban buses, metros and trams are operated by publicly owned organizations; municipalities, either directly or through wholly owned companies, through separately constituted public companies, or under contractual arrangements. In many French cities, public transport provision is under contract, for example in Lyon by Societe Lyonnaise des Transports en Commun (TCL) on contract to a joint city and Departement du Rhone passenger transport authority and under similar arrangements in Toulouse, Nantes and Lille (Bushell, 1993).

One of the largest transport co-ordination schemes is that of Germany's Rhein-Ruhr conurbation, which serves a population of 7.5 million. The Verkehrsverbund Rhein-Ruhr is responsible for the operation of a common tariff throughout the region, for marketing, public relations, planning, service integration and co-ordination in Dusseldorf, Duisburg, Muhlheim, Essen, Wuppertal, Dortmund, Krefeld and the surrounding area. Services are run by nineteen individual municipalities and by German Railways. Operators retain fare income, in a revised structure aimed at reducing the provision of unnecessary, duplicatory services (Bushell, op cit. p.263). The Rhein-Ruhr structure is thus not unlike that of London, where operational efficiency is encouraged by placing responsibility for running tube and bus services with numerous operating companies, each adhering to service patterns and a fare structure determined by London Transport.

Railway organization and ownership

British Railways has been in existence for nearly twice as long as the lifespan of the "Big Four" companies (1923-1947), which are nevertheless sometimes nostalgically looked upon as the legitimate owners of the railway network. Despite intermittent changes to regional boundaries, and Scotland being designated a railway "Region", a structure resembling that of the four companies has remained recognisable on British Rail almost to the present. Staff and user loyalties and perceptions even now relate to the Eastern or Western Regions, for example, despite their having been superseded for marketing purposes in the 1980s and operationally in the early 1990s by a functional organisation, with InterCity, Network SouthEast and Regional

Railways covering the passenger side.

Despite the availability of less funding than they would wish, the passenger sectors of the railway have largely been a success. Network SouthEast has created a unified grouping from what were formerly disparate services run by four of British Rail's five regions. Thameslink, NSE's only service linking areas north with those south of London, symbolises this union. Regional Railways operates local trains in the metropolitan conurbations on behalf of the PTEs, together with suburban services to and from cities such as Cardiff and Bristol, and interurban services such as trans-Pennine links. Of particular note is the wholesale fleet renewal achieved by Regional Railways over the past decade, enabling it to operate higher levels and standards of service at lower total costs.

A key element in the success of railway sectorisation has been the change from a production oriented to a market oriented philosophy. Although sometimes decried as too complex, BR's fare structure, which stratifies passengers according to time, day and season of travel, urgency of journey, personal circumstances and journey purpose, as well as by class of travel, is a model of market segmentation. Nevertheless, the highly peaked nature of commuter demand, especially in the south east, the availability of private and company supported motoring at less than its social cost, and the political sensitivity of rail fares make subsidies necessary for Regional Railways and Network SouthEast. InterCity, which has limited involvement in urban and commuter travel, is not subsidised (British Railways Board, 1993).

Whilst Network SouthEast is the principal operator of commuter services, its involvement in the intra-urban market is limited by the dominance of the Underground in central, north and west London. Since the introduction of a joint Travelcard (initially called Capitalcard) covering British Rail as well as London Transport services, in January 1985, inter operator distinctions have become less important. A remaining difference, however, is that Underground services usually run at more frequent intervals. This is a consequence of the Underground's structure, with individual lines operating across the centre of London, whereas most British Rail services fan out from termini around the edge of central London, to serve a multiplicity of destinations in and beyond London. BR also has to marry the competing demands on route capacity of long distance and suburban trains.

From 1994 onwards, the consequences of the Railways Act 1993, under which British Rail is to be privatized, will gradually make their mark. Train services are eventually to be run by a series of franchised operators, each responsible for individual lines or groups of routes, possibly supplemented by competing operators entering the market under "open access" rules. Track and infrastructure come into the ownership of Railtrack, a separate body, initially nationally owned, but intended for subsequent privatization.

The first public evidence of the outcome is fare and service competition between London and Gatwick Airport between three route operators, two of which were previously content to leave the airport market to the dedicated Gatwick Express and concentrate on the all-purpose suburban and inter-urban market. A less welcome outcome is the loss of distance based fare taper (reducing price per mile, as distance increases), when the services of more than one sectional BR operator are utilised.

Despite warnings to the contrary, including from its own supporters (House of Commons Transport Committee, 1993a), the government remains committed to its chosen form of rail privatization. Competition within rail operation is viewed as an essential ingredient, that between rail and other modes as not enough. Critics fear loss of network benefits, possibly including universally available railcards and discounted tickets; a breakdown of service co-ordination, reductions in train services, especially in the evenings and on Sundays; and a decline in rail safety. The retention of network benefits and service patterns and frequencies appears at present to be something the government is prepared to leave to market forces, although the May 1994 timetable (BR's last) is to be taken as "definitive" for service planning and support by the Franchising Authority, and some railcards have been safeguarded (for Pensioners and the Disabled, but not the Family Railcard). As when bus deregulation took place, additional resources are being dedicated to ensuring operators do not neglect safety. The issue of rail safety has been the subject of a thorough investigation by the Health and Safety Commission (Department of Transport/Health & Safety Commission, 1993) and the government is determined it should not decline.

The initial verdict on rail privatization must be that the government has taken a huge gamble with an industry whose role will have to grow as environmental considerations assume greater importance in transport policy. A major worry is that, as with bus deregulation, the government's greatest concerns are the twin ideologies of enhanced competition and reduced public spending. In the case of bus deregulation, they have never admitted that the continued and accelerated losses of bus patronage, notwithstanding the industry's improved financial performance and increased bus mileage offered, represents a fundamental failure of deregulation to meet the objective of increasing bus use.

Many observers, political, lay and professional alike, fear that, so long as the cost of rail subsidies to the Exchequer falls, operators make a little profit and some high profile changes to train services and ownership can be vaunted, levels of patronage, erstwhile social obligations and the level of investment in the railways will be of minimal concern to the government. Network fragmentation in the conurbations has been one of the most criticised outcomes of bus deregulation; yet only in the provincial conurbations, where the Passenger Transport Executives retain influence over rail services, does the Railways Act provide a safeguard against network fragmentation. It is too soon to say what the outcome will be. It must be hoped that the prophets of doom will be proved wrong; but there are some ominous omens.

Continental European railways

On the continent, some quite spectacular urban railway developments have taken place, although the combination of high levels of investment and lower fares means that the financial results of systems such as the German and French railways are less satisfactory than those of British Rail. Each of these administrations incurs a large annual loss and has a substantial capital debt. The newly re-unified German Rail network, Deutsche Bundesbahn AG, is undergoing a financial restructuring in preparation for privatization.

In France, north-south and east-west links have been created across Paris, linking previously separate suburban lines of French Railways (SNCF) to form the Reseau Express Regional (RER). Similar cross city and trans regional networks have been formed in several German cities (S-Bahnen). Many of these, for example in the Ruhr and around Cologne, are based on existing through lines, expanded and provided with more intensive services, but elsewhere, as in Munich, cross city tunnels were required.

The Dutch and Swiss railway networks are being upgraded to enable faster and more frequent train services to be run, as part of government initiatives to stem the growth in car use. Airport stations and rail links have been built, for example at Brussels, Dusseldorf, Zurich and Stuttgart. This is an area in which British performance compares reasonably with that on the continent, with London Heathrow's second line under construction, Manchester's airport railway opened in 1993 and Gatwick and Birmingham served by purpose-built stations on existing main lines. In an era when rapid inter-urban communication is highly valued by industry, commerce and governments, not least by the administrative machine of the multi-centred European Union, new and improved high speed rail links have usurped some of the former air travel market, such as that between Paris and Lyon. Further modal transfers will take place as the European high speed network expands, for example to link London and Paris to Brussels, Amsterdam and Germany. Increasingly, urban transport is coming to include inter-urban transits.

Preparing for the future

Every few years, policy watersheds are reached, after which things are never the same as they were before. Urban transport in Britain has experienced several watersheds since the 1940s. The first of these was the war itself, after which society opted, by electing a Labour Government in 1945, to set off in a new direction. This led to the attempt under the Transport Act 1947 to produce a publicly owned, unified and co-ordinated system of transport, of which British Railways became the principal lasting legacy. The 1950s saw the end of wartime strictures such as the rationing of food, petrol and consumer goods. The 1950s were the "you've never had it so good" decade of renewed personal wealth and consumption. By the end of the decade, the second watershed was reached as private motoring became the principal means of mechanised transport in Britain.

The 1960s brought the beginning of stricter controls on car use; vehicle testing, the breathalyser, parking meters and traffic management schemes; but also the deregulation of road goods transport. A more precisely focused attempt to plan and co-ordinate public transport, under the Transport Act 1968, saw the formation of the first Passenger Transport Authorities, the third urban transport watershed, which have survived even the fifteen years of Conservative government since 1979. The commercialisation, privatisation and deregulation of bus operation, including the "quiet revolution" at London Transport, and the commercialisation of British Rail, are the key public transport influences of the 1980s.

The National Road Traffic Forecast of 1989 was significant in making clear the impossibility of continuing indefinitely to cater for unrestrained road traffic growth and was described by Goodwin et al (1991, p166) as "the watershed", which together with the onset of concern about global warming "had a traumatic effect on the thinking of people involved in the planning and provision of transport services". The county councils in Hertfordshire and Hampshire, where car ownership levels are among the highest in the country, are some of the first authorities publicly to plan traffic restraint in the present era; although that is what the low fare policies of authorities such as South Yorkshire PTE and the Greater London Council in the 1970s and 1980s aimed (with not inconsiderable success) to achieve by a different, and now outlawed, means.

The 1990s is so far proving a decade of contradictions. A tidal backwash from some of the excesses of the 1980s is being experienced in the bus industry. The regulatory authorities are seeking to restrict competition at local level, in order to encourage it nationally, to stem the tide of mergers and takeovers and to prevent the industry from becoming monopolistic. In London, the government has postponed bus deregulation indefinitely, in effect conceding that it may never take place in the capital. While the bus industry becomes more controlled, remnants of the previous decade's free market zeal have survived to ensure the passage of the Railways Act 1993; but only time will tell whether it is the marketing expertise of the competing rail service operators, or the bureaucracies of track access charging, regulation and safety controls which are the real winners.

Motoring, too, will experience contradictory policies in the 1990s. Pressures from Europe and beyond, tinged with a little home grown conscience, will dictate more stringent emission and safety controls, increasing real prices for fuel, restrictions on traffic movement by means such as traffic calming, bus priorities and pedestrianisation; and possibly even road pricing. Further restriction on motoring may be anticipated in areas such as reductions in speed limits on local roads, a possible tightening of drink-driving limits and maybe ultimately speed limiters for cars. The package approach to local transport spending will increasingly see local authorities diverting monies from highway to public transport, walking and cycling projects.

Motor traffic is forecast to increase by between 16% and 26% by 2000, and by between 66% and 106% by 2025. Only bus traffic is expected to remain constant; every other category of mechanised road use would increase (Department of Transport, 1989). Although it will be impossible to increase road network capacity in line with these forecasts, the Department of Transport is still pushing ahead with its motorway widening and trunk road expansion programme, as if determined to achieve as much as it can, before the whistle is finally blown. Personal interests and aspirations, encouraged by government policies, continue to foster the greater use of cars, without really knowing how the problem will eventually be resolved. The march continues towards the inevitable time when demand must stop increasing.

For the present, traffic restraint still, for the majority of people, means other people reducing their use of scarce road and parking space, so that their own "necessary" trips can be undertaken more easily. The car commuter complaining in his local newspaper (Hampstead & Highgate Express, 1994) that he was incensed at a London Borough of Camden traffic calming scheme in Belsize Village, London, and berating the council's arrogance in dictating whether or not he should use his car for work, expresses a sentiment which is still typical; but all urban authorities will sooner or later have to make similar decisions to restrict car use.

Opinion is gradually moving towards a consensus, at least among transport specialists, that unrestrained car use must give way to increased and more attractive public transport (Goodwin et. al. 1991, Chartered Institute of Transport, 1993). Even motoring and road transport organizations such as the Automobile Association and the British Road Federation recognise that mass movement in urban areas may be better undertaken by public transport. Rather grudgingly, the government's Environmental Strategy states "public transport, where there is sufficient demand for it, will often be the most efficient transport choice" (Department of the Environment et al, 1990). "Choice" will soon have to be influenced more strongly than hitherto, by various forms of demand management, including physical restraint, pricing policy, and the improvement of alternatives to the car.

Environmental policies, which will assume increasing importance as issues such as air quality and global warming become better understood, may barely succeed in maintaining the status quo, unless fundamental policy changes are effected. Some of these will involve restrictions to what at present are cherished by many as personal freedoms, in particular concerning car use. Conflicts with the desire for mobility, associated for example with the choice of where to live, work, shop and educate ones children, will be inevitable, if authorities seek to restrict the personal behaviour of drivers, to place restrictions on modal choice, or to tighten land-use planning regulations; but such developments are becoming necessary. Environmental policies impacting adversely on business will face even greater obstacles, due to their potential implications for the economy, in areas such as employment, competitiveness, company profitability and the balance of payments. The balance between short term sacrifices by individual citizens and businesses and long term gains to society as a whole will be difficult to achieve.

Although not in itself an urban transport project, the Channel Tunnel is expected to have an important psychological effect on transport policies for British cities. Trains linking London to Paris and Brussels as quickly and as frequently as to Newcastle or Swansea will strengthen both our physical and our emotional ties with "Europe". Continental ideas and practices will become more accessible and seem more relevant to Britain; lower local public transport fares, extensive bus priorities, cross city rail links, light rail networks and pedestrianised town centres, for example.

Conclusion

This chapter shows the speed with which developments have taken place in urban transport over the past forty years. The car has come to predominate in all except the heaviest radial and city centre flows in the largest towns and cities. The car has delivered many freedoms; to live, work, shop and play in an unprecedentedly wide range of locations; to make a more diverse range of journeys more quickly than ever before; and to travel with a degree of privacy matching that of the home, accompanied only by chosen companions, and entertained by a personal choice of music or speech.

However, the car, especially in urban areas, has also taken away much freedom; noise and pollution pervade the atmosphere; thousands are killed, and hundreds of thousands injured in accidents; and journeys are delayed because there are now more cars than the present (or probably any future) road network can efficiently cope with.

Transition over the coming decades in Britain and continental Europe must lie in the re-organization of the transport market, to ensure that it reflects more accurately the varying degrees urgency and importance attaching to different elements of transport demand. Greater regard must be paid to safety from accidents and to ensuring that one person's freedom is not bought at the expense of another's loss, be that the freedom to live an active, healthy life; to regain a modicum of rural quietude; or to travel by a benign and inoffensive mode, unthreatened and uninterrupted by fast-moving and ill-disciplined traffic.

Towns and cities have spread to such an extent that some form of mechanised transport is essential. In the 1990s, demand must be shifted back from what has become an excessive reliance on a mode of transport which consumes too much space to be sustainable. The car must begin to concede some of the ground it has gained back to higher density modes, if cities as we know them, with their high densities of population, employment, commerce and entertainment are to survive. The cliche of the need for "improving public transport services and making them more attractive to passengers, and improving conditions for pedestrians and cyclists" (Department of Environment, 1993, paragraph 1.13) must be translated from policy objective into universal adoption and implementation in every urban area, in every country.

As one of the world's richest and most advanced regions, Europe owes it to less developed countries to demonstrate that the degree of motorisation with which Europe is seeking to come to terms is not the only way forward. This will not be easy. It must not be seen as the "haves" preaching to the "have nots", but as a genuine desire to help other nations learn from the transport policy mistakes of the richest countries. Nor will it be a simple matter to convince governments and industrialists, keen to increase employment opportunities, industrial output and profits that "an upturn in the car market" should not necessarily be viewed as a barometer of a successful economy.

Correct and far-sighted decisions in the construction of infrastructure will also be essential as, once built, infrastructure has a long life. Public transport alignments must be safeguarded, cherished road proposals abandoned in favour of more productive and sustainable alternatives, and priorities for the use of funds redirected away from projects designed to accommodate increased numbers of cars. Achieving the balance between professional judgement and popular or democratic demands may prove controversial, for example in respect of relationships between personal and collective or public gain, and between short and long term solutions.

This chapter has demonstrated that during the period under scrutiny there has been an inexorable increase in the demand for transport. People have become richer, they live, work, shop and seek their entertainment and recreation in more widely dispersed locations, and like to live in a low density, often quasi-rural environment, whilst losing none of the benefits of living in a city. The key challenge for policy makers is to maintain and improve living standards, but also to halt the parallel rise in the demand for transport. The solution is likely to lie in finding ways of enhancing wealth and meeting travel demand, which need less transport. Conceptually, thinking must move away from technical solutions based on "transport" and "mobility", to demand based concepts such as travel and accessibility. The idea is not new; it has been around since at least the 1970s. It now requires re-examination and adaptation to the more market orientated environment of the present decade.

To summarise, the achievement of revised policies to meet rising demands for travel and accessibility will depend on the combination and interaction of five factors.

The first of these is personal; public acceptance of transport and travel demand management will be an essential ingredient, without which anarchy along present lines is doomed to remain.

Secondly, political will must be present which, given the short lives of governments and the long lead time required to effect a fundamental change in the travel market, implies a need for consensus between the main political parties, between central and local government, between the governments of different nations, and with international organizations such as the European Union. The political factor is closely tied to the personal and collective demands of the electorate for action to improve the global and travel environments by cutting air and noise pollution and the rate of deaths and injuries from road accidents.

Thirdly, economic policies must change, to encourage more localised economies, requiring less personal travel, shorter distances for goods transport, and a pricing structure which charges "undesirable" transport its full social costs. The support and co-operation of business and industry is vital. It will be crucial for the changes in policy to be achieved without causing serious damage to company profitability and markets. Some extensive re-orientation of industrial production will be required, including changes in what is manufactured and how and where production takes place. The location and organization of commerce, administration and retailing will also be affected, with some re-orientation back to more localised structures.

The fourth component of the package is demography. A reversion to more localised communities, reducing the need to travel and facilitating the provision of more services within each area will be required. If travel demand is to be reduced, there will be a greater need for the provision of facilities such as shops, schools, health care and employment closer to where people live.

Fifthly, technical developments have a part to play. Improved public transport will be essential in urban areas, in order to increase their attractiveness in comparison with decentralised developments. Technical changes outside transport, in areas such as computing and telecommunications, facilitating more working from home and reducing the demand for travel to, from and in connection with business, will also make a contribution, although the commercial importance of personal interaction and man's social nature suggest that too much should not be expected from such developments.

It would be over optimistic to expect a complete re-orientation of living and employment patterns within a single decade; but looking back less than one lifetime, it may be seen how different lifestyles and expectations have become over a forty year period. The agenda suggested in this paper should therefore be considered, not as one to be achieved by the millennium, but perhaps only by the middle of the next century. It will be a worthy legacy for our children and grandchildren, if we can achieve a convincing re-orientation of policy firmly in the direction of that goal by the end of the 1990s.

References

Barker, T. & Robbins, M. (1974), *A History of London Transport, Volume II - The Twentieth Century*, George Allen & Unwin, London.

Berechman, J. (1993), *Public Transit Economics and Deregulation Policy*, North-Holland, Amsterdam.

Berkshire County Council (1993), *Transport Policies & Programmes 1994-95*

Bonavia, M. (1987), *The Nationalisation of British Transport*, Macmillan/LSE, London.

British Railways Board (1963), *The Reshaping of British Railways*, HMSO, London.

British Railways Board (1965), *The development of the major railway trunk routes*

British Railways Board (1993), *Annual Report & Accounts 1992-93*

British Road Federation (1993), *Basic Road Statistics 1993*

British Transport Commission (1955), *Modernisation and Re-equipment of British Railways*

Buchanan, C. (1963), *Traffic in Towns*, Reports of the Steering Group and Working Group appointed by the Minister of Transport, HMSO, London.

Bus & Coach Buyer (1993), "British Bus - Colchester bid", 12 November

Bus & Coach Council (1993), *Buses Mean Business*, Bulletin

Bushell, C. (1993), *Jane's Urban Transport Systems 1993-94*, Jane's Information Group Limited, London.

Chartered Institute of Transport (1993), *Bus Routes to Success*

Daily Telegraph (1993), "EC expressway threat to bypasses", 21 October

Environment, Department of, et al (1990), *This Common Inheritance*, HMSO, London, Cm1200

Environment, Department of/Welsh Office (1993), *Planning Policy Guidance: Transport* (PPG13, Draft)

European Conference of Ministers of Transport (1993), *Statistical Trends in Transport 1965-1989*, Paris.

Goodwin, P. et al (1991), *Transport: The New Realism*, Transport Studies Unit, University of Oxford for Rees Jeffreys Road Fund.

Gourvish, T (1986), *British Railways 1948-1973: A Business History*, Cambridge University Press, Cambridge.

Hall, P. & Carmen H. (1985), *Can Rail Save the City?* Gower, Aldershot.

Hampstead & Highgate Express (1994), 14 January

Hibbs, J. (1968), *A History of British Bus Services*, David & Charles, Newton Abbott.

Higginson, M. (1991), "Deregulate - Who Dares?", *Transportation Planning & Technology*, 15, 181-205

Higginson, M. (1993), *Tramway London: Background to the Abandonment of London's Trams 1931-1952*, Light Rail Transit Association/Birkbeck College, London.

House of Commons Transport Committee (First Report; 1993a), *The Future of the Railways in the Light of the Government's White Paper Proposals: Interim Report*, HMSO, HC375, London.

House of Commons Transport Committee (Fourth Report; 1993b), *The Government's Proposals for the Deregulation of Bus Services in London*, HMSO, HC623, London.

Irwin, C. (1990), *A Nostalgic Look at North East Trams Since the 1940s*, Silver Link, St. Michaels, Lancashire.

Jackson, A. (1973), *Semi-Detached London*, George Allen & Unwin, London.

James, L. (1980), *The Law of the Railway*, Barry Rose, London.

Joyce, J. (1987), *Operation Tramaway: The End of London's Trams 1950-1952*, Ian Allan, London.

London Transport (1994), *The London Low Floor Bus Project*
McLachlan, S. (1983), *The National Freight Buyout*, Macmillan, London.
Modern Railways (1991), 'Speedlink Axed', February
Monopolies & Mergers Commission (1990), *Stagecoach (Holdings) Ltd and Portsmouth Citybus Ltd*, HMSO, Cm1130, London.
Munby, D. (1978), *Inland Transport Statistics Great Britain 1900-1970*, Oxford University Press, Oxford.
Office of Fair Trading (1991), *Restrictive Trade Practices in the Bus Industry*
Office of Population Censuses & Surveys (OPCS) (1993), *Final mid-1993 population estimates for England & Wales*, OPCS Monitor PP1 93/1, 24 June.
Ratcliffe, J. (1981 edition), *An Introduction to Town and Country Planning*, Hutchinson, London.
Robertson, K. (1989), *The Great Western Railway Gas Turbines*, Alan Sutton, Gloucester.
Sommerfield, V. (1933), *London Buses: The Story of a Hundred Years*, St. Catherine Press, London.
Starkie, D. (1982), *The Motorway Age: Road and Traffic Policies in Post-War Britain*, Pergamon Press, Oxford.
Suffolk County Council (1993), *Transport Policies and Programmes 1994-95*
Sustrans (1992), *Annual Report 1991-1992*, Bristol
Transport, Department of, Scottish Office & Welsh Office (1984), *Buses*, Cmnd 9300, HMSO, London.
Transport, Department of (1989), *National Road Traffic Forecasts Great Britain 1989*, HMSO, London.
Transport, Department of (1993a), *Transport Statistics Great Britain 1993*, HMSO, London.
Transport, Department of (1993b), *National Travel Survey 1989-91*, HMSO, London.
Transport, Department of (1993c), *Bus & Coach Statistics Great Britain 1992-92*, HMSO, London.
Transport, Department of (1993d), *Funds for Local Authority Transport*, Press Notice 509, 15 December
Transport, Department of and Health & Safety Commission (1993), *Ensuring Safety on Britain's Railways*, London.
University of Central England (1994), *Marketing Strategies in the UK Bus Industry*, Report to the Bus & Coach Council
White, P. (1986), *Public Transport, its Planning, Management and Operation*, Hutchinson, London.
White, P., Dennis, N. & Tyler N. (1992), *Analysis of Recent Trends in Bus and Coach Safety in Britain*, Proceedings of First World Congress on

Safety of Transportation, Technical University, Delft.
Wootton Jeffreys Consultants Ltd (1994), *The Role of the Bus in the Community*, Report to the Bus & Coach Council
Yearsley, I. & Groves, P. (1988), *The Manchester Tramways*, Transport Publishing Company, Glossop.

8 Problems of market mechanisms in the development of EU combined transport networks

Mike Garratt

Introduction

It is relatively popular and widely held view that long distance road haulage imposes social and economic costs on the community at large which are not faced by the economic agents who actually make the decision to use road tracks. Policies are being introduced by the European Union to address this issue by introducing incentives for the extensive use of rail, barge and shipping services as an alternative. However, the initiative revives an old issue, that of "fair competition" between the rail and the maritime mode. The semi-monopolistic private sector railways which operated pre-1948 in Great Britain had an uneasy relationship with coastal shipping. The railways could "cross-subsidise" between inland and "coastal" traffics, an opportunity not available to coastal shipping. Railways in Europe are now almost universally in the public sector, and, privatisation notwithstanding, rail infrastructure is likely to remain publicly owned. The promotion of rail is therefore likely to involve public sector investment (or subsidy). On the other hand, shipping is almost universally in the private sector. The relevant directorates of the EU are implacably opposed to public sector subsidy of shipping routes. There is considerable suspicion of public sector subsidy in the ports industry, and the British ports in particular have drawn critical attention to such investment in Continental ports. This presents the maritime industries with an interesting dilemma. Opposition to subsidy may promote an efficient and internally competitive maritime industry, but could leave it ill-equipped to seize the commercial opportunity offered by EU policies to capture road traffic, as compared with rail traffic. This chapter explores some of these issues in more detail.

EU policies towards long distance road haulage

To date, the principal control measure introduced has been to impose limits on the maximum speed of trucks, which are now physically governed to a maximum speed of 90 kph. Energy taxes may, of course, follow later. However, it is clearly not in the philosophy of the EU to discourage long distance freight traffic. Indeed, the removal of tariff and other barriers to trade between Member States is designed to improve economic welfare by increased specialisation, exploiting economies of scale, and active competition across the EU. This requires that alternative modes of transport are available to replace and supplement road haulage.

The principal positive transport plank on which this policy is based is "combined transport", which is the intermodal technique of stowing goods in a freight unit which can be lifted or rolled onto different modes of surface transport; road, rail, ship or barge. This technique is well established. Railways used road to rail containers before World War II. The standard maritime container, developed during the 1950s, was well established by the end of the 1960s and approached saturation market shares by the end of the 1970s. However, the process did nothing to encourage a shift in modal shares away from road haulage. Indeed, it had the reverse effect in raising the economic size of ship and expanding port hinterlands so that the mean length of inland haul to the port actually rose. It did provide a new market opportunity for rail borne freight, however. The longer hauls required to service container ports provided lengths of haul for rail which allowed Freightliner in the UK, CNC in France, RENFE in Spain, Transfracht in Germany and Intercontainer across the Continent to develop new trades. These were, however, mainly transfers of freight from shipping to rail, and not from road haulage. It was a consequence of deep sea container ships concentrating services on just a handful of ports. Those serving Northern and Central Europe will typically call at only four or five ports per voyage, say Le Havre, Felixstowe, Rotterdam and Hamburg. Nevertheless, the rail borne transportation of maritime containers did at least demonstrate that rail could offer a competitive option to long distance road haulage.

Perhaps more encouragement for the future potential of rail can be derived from the performance of the UIRR (Union Internationale Rail Route) club of companies. There is generally one such company in each west European country (eg Novotrans in France, Kombiverkehr in Germany). These companies are joint ventures between a number of road hauliers and forwarders, and the relevant national railway (almost always a minority share holder). These companies either own or lease intermodal wagons, or rent them from the national railway, and hire track and traction services also from the national railway. The capacity offered by the scheduled trains they offer from terminal to terminal is then available to hauliers, either to use for the whole road vehicle ("rolling motorways"), semi-trailers (piggyback services), or swapbodies (non-stackable containers). Until recently, the

UIRR group have avoided the carriage of maritime containers, which have been the preserve of the national railways directly (eg CNC), or Intercontainer, who did not carry trailers or swapbodies. This implicit restraint on competition has been frowned upon by the EU, and now each of the different organizations are in competition. However, the market share which rail has so far won of all long distance freight in the EU is limited. Rail within the EC carries only some 4-5 million intermodal units per annum, of which less than half a million are trucks or trailers. This can be compared with 7 million units per annum in North America, of which haif are trailers. The UIRR group argue that only 8% of long distance (over 300 kms) unit load transport in Europe is by rail.

EU combined transport policies

It is important to appreciate that the overall philosophy of EU policy towards competition precludes an "administered" transfer of cargo from road to an alternative mode. Thus, for example, a straightforward subsidy to a railway authority together with an instruction to win more traffic, would be unacceptable because this opportunity is not available to other transport companies, and would discriminate against shipping or inland waterway transport. Furthermore, a "global" subsidy would inevitably be wasteful. It would subsidise traffic which would not move long distance by road in any case (eg oil, coal or aggregates). An important virtue of the combined transport definition is that it focuses on traffic which is mainly carried by road at the moment. Combined transport is also applicable to waterways and shortsea shipping, which adds a further dimension into the competitive framework.

Railways have generally acted as vertically integrated monopolies. A railway has acted as a "through transport operator", often owning containers, terminals, wagons, locomotives and track. This has normally been presented as a strength, but it is actually a barrier to entry; companies which forward cargo but are not existing railway undertakings cannot themselves offer rail services. The general effect has been for there to be a single monopolistic supplier of intermodal rail services in each country. EU policy has therefore been directed at providing a definition of combined transport which can be the basis of subsidy or privilege, and then insisting that the suppliers of combined transport services operate in a competitive environment. There have been a number of directives through which this policy has developed, of which the most recent are 91/440 and 92/106. These established the following:

* That "combined transport" should include all swapbodies, container, semi-trailers and powered road vehicles. Rail, inland waterway and shortsea shipping should all be included, providing the "feeder" road-haul is no more than 150 kms (in a straight line). All shipping services of above 100 kms length are eligible.

* That any railway undertaking be entitled to operate combined transport trains across any part of the EU rail network without discrimination in terms of track access and charges. This, in principle, allows a railway undertaking to operate its own locomotives across the whole community. This approach has given rise to dispute as to the definition of a railway undertaking. The UK interpretation suggested any company which wished to operate trains was entitled to do so. The French view was that only existing national railway authorities could be considered to be railway undertakings. The French view has prevailed in an amending directive, but the UK Government's rail privatization programme will effectively result in any UK based railway undertaking being in the 'private sector', and apparently, entitled to operate over any EU tracks.

The definition of "combined transport" actually confers only one automatic right; that of equal access to a rail network. It does not provide automatic subsidy or any other advantage. Further privileges remain, to date, in the gift of the individual Member States. In fact, most of the EU economy is covered (through its member states) by systems of privileges which allow road vehicles to carry excess cargo weight (in the road feeder leg), which provides a valuable incentive to use rail or, particularly in the Low Countries and Germany, inland waterways. In France and Germany, that privilege adds about four tonnes to the weight of cargo which can be carried per unit. In the UK, there are government proposals to allow for six tonnes, but for rail only, and not for ferries or coastal shipping. This will discriminate against the maritime mode. There are also extensive proposals to improve the available loading gauge along various rail corridors across the EU to provide a common "GB+" gauge. This offers the prospect of grants of matching funds from the EU. The gauge is designed around the existing UIC gauges and allows for maximum height containers to be carried on standard height flat wagons, and four metre high semi-trailers with air suspension to be carried on recess or "pocket" wagons. "Rolling motorway" trains (where the whole truck "rolls" onto a train), require a more generous gauge. They currently only exist in parts of the "German" system (and the Channel Tunnel), but are proposed for France. In the UK, the maximum gauge defined by British Rail is over 60 cms lower at the "top corners" of an intermodal unit. This allows almost all containers and swapbodies to move on "multi-fret" wagons, but does not allow continental piggyback rail wagons to be used because of their wider design below station platform level. A study which is 50% EU funded is currently investigating the practicability of using narrower wagons and air-suspension trailers, and raising some overline structures to carry standard size body semi-trailers in the UK. The wider wagons are not feasible in the UK because of the high platform edges adopted in Britain.

The framework which is being both encouraged and imposed by the EU on the railway industry is very different from that which has existed before. Railways generally developed as vertically integrated organizations, whether public or private, offering a door-to-door or terminal to terminal service. Prior to the development of long distance road haulage, they were natural monopolies and were generally regulated on price and required to act as common carriers. In North America, and in the UK prior to nationalization in 1948, these vertically integrated organisations exchanged running rights over their different networks, charging each other for that privilege. There are few examples of independent train operators running over separately owned networks (in the passenger field, Amtrack in the USA does play this role). However, the combination of EU competition policy and UK privatization policies will effectively impose a structure which allows an independent train operating company to operate over rail networks which are separately owned. The implications are most interesting. The network itself will remain under state ownership. To avoid any accusation of bias in offering access to the network (EC 91/440), it will be impossible to subsidise any specific organization offering intermodal (combined transport) services. That is, where the national railway (eg BR, SNCF, DB etc) operates its own trains, it will have to be able to show that long run direct train operating costs are being covered. Track charges could be set at a low level, or even at zero (this is allowed for under the Railways Bill in the UK to facilitate the development of traffic under privatization). The Railways Act allows for grant of up to 100% of track charges on environmental grounds. However, free track access for one route may tend to lead to free access on other routes. For example, free access based on an environmental case between Birmingham and Felixstowe must surely allow free access to a competitor who loads his ship at Southampton. A train operator who runs from Manchester via Birmingham to Southampton will clearly have an environmental case for low track charges if he carries containers between the two inland centres. It is difficult to see how the Rail Regulator appointed under the Act will not find that he has to require free access on many intermodal rail routes.

At this stage, we can only speculate on how the European intermodal rail industry will develop. However, the steps which have already been taken in planning for Channel Tunnel rail services provide an insight into how the railway authorities have responded to the EU's directive. The established railway industry has attempted to retain a general control despite EU policy by establishing two separate train operating companies, Combined Transport Ltd (CTL) and Allied Continental Intermodal (ACI), who will own or lease wagons and purchase track and traction, both from the nationalised railways companies at common (monopolistic) rates. ACI and CTL will then sell space on their trains to international freight forwarders, and will not compete door-to-door so as to avoid conflicts of interests with their clients. The only technical excuses that the railways might have for retaining a monopoly on traction for these terminal to terminal services is that the Intergovernmental Channel Tunnel Safety Commission has established rigid conditions on the type of traction allowed through the Tunnel and that only the public sector railways have yet to strike a deal with Eurotunnel for access to the Tunnel. The privatization of traction in the UK is likely to put this arrangement under severe pressure, and it is quite foreseeable that ACI and CTL will find it suits them to purchase track access (which could be free) and traction separately. In that event, these two companies will play a role which is remarkably similar to that of a third party shipping line. The "ship" (wagons/locomotives) will be owned or chartered. Passage across the "sea" (rail tracks) may be more or less free. Payments will be made for "port" services (intermodal rail terminals). The clients will be identical, international forwarders, who may often be involved in shipping services in their own right. It is now appropriate to consider the advantages and opportunities of the two different modes.

Rail versus sea under combined transport

Within Europe, ownership and control of the two modes has had a very different history. This is not the case in the USA, of course, where, for example, the huge CSX corporation is a railroad operator which owns a global container shipping line (Sealand). The vertically integrated, publicly owned, European intermodal services have not needed to seriously examine the relative importance of the different factor costs they face and have cross-subsidised between routes. That those privileges will now disappear allows us to make useful comparisons on a cost basis. This is not an idle exercise. There will be several routes, especially from the UK, where rail and sea will be in active competition. A container delivered into Seaforth Dock in Liverpool could move by rail or sea to Spain depending on the costs and level of service on offer. To date, the rates offered by the railways have not reflected their own costs, but the costs of competing private sector road and shipping modes. At best, the railways have been able to identify a margin they have earned between direct traction and wagon costs and revenue which is a return to infrastructure and overhead costs. For international traffics, this calculation has been more or less impossible given the nature of the bilateral tariffs agreed between the railways on a wagon load basis. These tariff agreements actually allow one railway authority to offer discounts for an entire journey using the track and traction of the different authorities the wagon passes over. The implication of the EU policies described above suggest that the different national Governments may have to be prepared to offer track capacity at a relatively low tariff, but will not easily be able to subsidise long-run operating costs.

Rail is likely to be viable for containers or trailers for hauls of over 800 kms. This breakeven distance is much reduced if local road haulage distances are shorter or an intervening ferry faces the road haulier. Costs by shortsea shipping are not significantly greater than for rail, and where shipping is more direct, could be cheaper. Where road haulage would face an intermediate ferry crossing (short crossings between the UK and the Continent and charged at least $175 per trailer), then rail is competitive for the shortest of hauls, *if rail infrastructure costs are insignificant.* Rail can offer rates as low as can shipping, and in some circumstances, longer distance "short sea" shipping can be remarkably successful. For example, over 90% of intermodal traffic between Denmark and the UK moves directly from a Danish port and does not use inland transportation to reach the "shortest" crossings between Kent and Belgium. There are also already isolated cases where rail also captures a large market share; over 80% of containers moving between the UK and Northern Italy use rail, not road, from the Benelux coast to the Milan area.

Policy issues and the efficient allocation of resources

What then, are the important features of EU policy towards combined transport?

The definition of combined transport is, in itself, academic. The privileges which most countries offer it in terms of weight allowances succeed in cutting rates per tonne for "heavy" goods, but not for "bulky" goods (cargoes which "cube-out"). This concession may cut rates across the board by about 5% for rail, waterway or road. This may make a significant contribution to a modal shift, but is unlikely to be crucial. Insofar as rail is concerned, EU policies offer the prospect of driving down the contribution which intermodal traffic makes to infrastructure costs, and by introducing competitive pressures, will reduce rates charged for rail traction to a level which approximates to long-run average costs. Those costs may be remarkably low. It will generally lead to an end to rail pricing based on the long-run average costs of other modes, a remarkably unreliable market signal if the object is the efficient allocation of transport resources. Just as no oil company would consider using road haulage for the long distance movement of petroleum, so there is the prospect of the same logic being applied to intermodal traffic; long distance road haulage will simply become commercially irrational.

If we can look forward to a competitive environment for train operation, similar to the market mechanisms which apply in shipping where ships are bought, sold and chartered on an international market, then the focus of our attention should turn to infrastructure. It has already seen that port infrastructure charges play a significant role in the maritime mode. If rail infrastructure charges are indeed reduced to a very low level, then there will be little commercial incentive for new investment in new or improved track. In those circumstances, it will be the 'government' which will find itself funding new or improved rail infrastructure if rail is to succeed in terms of "combined transport". EU subsidy is likely to be available.

It has been argued that EU policies will lead to the rail industry replicating the commercial mechanisms of the shipping industry. Unfortunately, that industry has also failed to fulfil its potential where it is faced with expensive ports. Where ports are in open competition, rates are forced down. Even so they are still substantially higher than rail terminal rates. However, effective total port charges for handling containers in the Iberian peninsula can reach $150 per unit, and have been approximately $100 per unit in Dublin. As a result, only some 40% of unit load traffic between the UK and Spain moves directly by sea; there is more or less no roro traffic, and the remaining 60% moves by road through France.

It has been shown that if infrastructure costs are set to one side, rail and maritime intermodal costs are similar and significantly lower than for road haulage. While in the short run, opening up the rail market to competitive pressure may work against some maritime interests, in the longer run we need not be that concerned about equity in the transport market because any company will be entitled to operate in any mode it chooses. The shipping line may acquire rail interests.

What is crucial, however, is that charges levied for infrastructure do not distort routeing. It would, for example, be unfortunate if low terminal handling costs in the railway system led to circuitous rail routeing (eg UK to Portugal), when a direct sea passage should be both quicker and cheaper. Similarly, it will be most important that different countries do not charge radically different rates for the use of rail infrastructure. While the EU has established the principle of non-discrimination, it may not be sufficient if it allows, for example, some countries to offer low rates to any operator serving a national port instead of ports or overland routes into other countries. Insofar as port terminals are concerned, there is a good case for cargo handling in a port to cost more than in a rail terminal, largely because of the high cost of building a wharf as compared with laying down tracks beneath a crane, and of providing ship access channels and navigation aids. For intensively utilized terminals, however, that is unlikely to explain a difference of more than $15 per container handled. It is clear that the principle of open access must apply in practice to the ports industry if the maritime mode is to thrive. There would be a good case for the EC considering a formula for encouraging competition within the ports, so that charges reflected the cost of providing services, to parallel the steps which have been made in the railway industry.

One further handicap inhibits the maritime industry from fulfilling its potential. It has been argued that the rail industry has suffered by not operating along open market principles. However, in one respect, its monopolistic structure has allowed it to develop an important feature of integration which assists its performance; train sorting or "marshalling". There are few region-to-region flows which justify a whole daily train. This is solved through the division and re-assembly of part trains at marshalling areas. It is therefore not necessary for there to be, say, 30-40 containers per day to move from Leeds to Bordeaux; it is sufficient that there is a trainload from Leeds to the whole Continent, and a trainload of goods from the whole of the UK to Bordeaux.

This facility has not been developed within the shortsea intermodal industry. Some deep sea lines practice "transshipment", but there is much less such activity in the shortsea sector. There is potential for transhipment on shortsea routes between the Iberian peninsula and the UK and Benelux countries, and from Ireland. The obvious point of transhipment; the Western Approaches to the English Channel, do not correspond to major cargo generators in their own right, so that the necessary port handling facilities are not in place. Furthermore, the different shipping lines are not generally in the habit of carrying cargo for each other. It follows that to foster new and busier shipping routes that the "government" will have to assist in the provision of transhipment facilities to allow region-to-region flows of traffic to have access to frequent shipping services. Not only will it be important for "government" to encourage shipping lines to "exchange" cargoes (ie carry for each other), but to ensure that any fragmentation of a hitherto "monolithic" railway industry does not discourage rail transhipment. Perhaps more important, it is vital that the cost of cargo handling is kept to a minimum, and that handling charges are not levied to fulfill social programmes (eg docker redundancy packages), but simply reflect the cost of providing a port service. The very essence of combined transport is that it allows cargo to be switched readily from mode to mode. That switch must therefore be at a minimum cost.

Conclusion

The EU combined transport programme would appear to have taken the first steps towards the development of an effective alternative to long distance road haulage. However, if it is to fulfill its potential, then a pro-active approach will have to be adopted towards an infrastructure network. Except in the case of such "natural monopolies" as the Channel Tunnel, it will be difficult to charge sufficient infrastructure charges to justify new rail investments; the most that can be expected is a charge to contribute to maintenance. The "government" will therefore almost certainly have to define a policy for new or upgraded rail network, marshalling yards and maritime transhipment depots. It may also have to consider imposing rules on open access to ports to minimise rates charged, perhaps as a quid pro quo for assistance in port infrastructure investment. Insofar as the efficient allocation of resources are concerned, EU policy initiatives to promote competition within the rail industry are encouraging, but it is important to ensure that shipping can also play an appropriate role. The combination of a competitive railway operating industry running on subsidised track may itself tend to divert traffic better suited to the maritime sector.

References

EC directive 91/440 (July 1991) and 92/106 (December 1992)

Railways Act 1993

UIRR Annual reports (1993 and earlier)

9 The development of road freight distribution depots

Frank Worsford

Introduction

This chapter queries the rationale behind the business policy of motorway distribution centre location and poses some fundamental questions for the year 2000 and beyond. It maintains that in many respects, economically and environmentally, the best location for distribution centres and heavy goods vehicles is the motorways. To what extent this will continue to be so in the future, in the light of various obstacles that may threaten present day strategic locations, will be a key industry issue to be addressed. The solution may be in operators making more effective load utilisation from their vehicles, improved fuel conservation, and where feasible the use of combined transport.

Today in the UK over 80% of internal freight is lifted by road transport. The distribution warehousing infrastructure, powerhouses of modern logistics, required to facilitate this industry has gone through a revolutionary process during recent years. Whereas, at one time most distribution centres were usually small, located within urban areas using small type vehicles, the situation has now dramatically changed.

The 1980s and 1990s experience of company consolidation and centralisation, coupled with increasing usage of computer technology and new logistics concepts resulted in a road distribution industry requiring warehousing to be

* larger and better designed
* purpose built to customer specifications
* hi-tech sophisticated
* strategically located near motorways

For a large segment of the distribution industry the shift in the pattern of warehousing location continues unabated. Companies will seek to take advantage of locations enabling speedy, efficient, cost-effective vehicle and core customer access. The trend is evident with the movement from older and smaller urban based warehouses to large new builds, strategically located on the motorway spine routes. This has been especially true for the major retailers and blue-chip companies who have established their national and regional distributions centres in such places. The increasing competitive market of the 1990s, bringing about mergers and acquisitions throughout the industry will reinforce this trend. As a consequence the process will also generate spare warehouse capacity in parts of the country and in some industry sectors.

This chapter considers the strategic developments of this process, within the context of other freight modes. Looking beyond 2000, in the light of global problems and rapid changes on the domestic scene, concern is expressed at the inherent risk in putting too much reliance on a single freight mode presently dependent on diesel fuel, and with hugh volumes of inventory located in motorway based warehousing - with the only means of freight access being via road.

With the opening of the Channel Tunnel and growth in pan-European markets there is a possibility that rail freight may be a beneficiary, but only for a suitable and limited section of the freight market, despite government initiatives and encouragement towards modal-shift in the usage of 44 tonne trucks. Distribution centres which offer additional modal access, such as rail sidings or port, may find themselves more in demand beyond 2000. However, for the foreseeable future there is no alternative to road and road will continue to remain the dominant distribution mode. In overall terms, strategic and environmental considerations, will strengthen motorway location for the majority of companies in the industry.

These developments raise a number of important questions, which may have implications for the future location of some distribution centres. Industry decision makers will need to ask themselves the following:

* what will be key factors influencing the industry's location decisions?
* where and how will they impact on the industry?
* what measures can and should the industry now be taking?

In just over two centuries of freight transport history the U.K. has experienced, the rise and partial demise of its canal and railway systems. During each decade of this century road transport has steadily gained in strength, especially during the post-war years. However, it is now arguable that road transport has reached a stage of peaking and is about to enter a down-turn period. Naturally, within the industry some elements would claim such a suggestion is far-fetched, flying in the face of conventional wisdom. However, those having an open mind and vision may think otherwise. Indeed, a prudent move may be in viewing distant and ominous clouds gathering on the horizon. There is a message questioning in general road transport's future role in freight movement and the location viability of the large distribution warehouse centres - which are at the epicentre of the industry.

The type of warehouses concerned are those that have been built close to the main motorway network, to high quality standards and occupying space up to 500,000 sq ft. Such warehouse developments cost many millions in construction and internal equipment, and usually require servicing by large fleets of commercial vehicles on a 24 hour/7 days per week basis. In essence these warehouses are the powerhouses of modern logistics, providing the essential storage and transhipment facilities of the industry. Indeed, nothing stands out more prominently as an accolade to the road transport industry's success as does the 1980s monster distribution centres. They bear testimony to the present development, growth and achievements made in the art of modern logistics methods. The majority of large distribution centres that sprang up during the last decade, located close to major motorway junctions, tend to have no alternative modal links in place - rail or water - being mainly dedicated to road movement. Such goods can only be delivered and collected from these centres by a single mode - a mode moreover currently dependent on a finite fossil fuel with quantifiable limited reserves. As a consequence, and taking a long term strategic perspective, there may be embryonic developments in progress that may in time make other modes relatively competitive and attractive to freight users. If this is so, the implications for the so-called "outdated" or "unfashionable" modes, such as rail and water, the possibility of change offers a glimmer of light towards future revival, but limited both in market share and range of freight products. On this basis it is anticipated that the immediate years ahead will bring into sharp focus a crucial issue for road transport viz. the past and current policy of locating so much of their warehousing on the motorway system.

Perhaps, the situation is best appreciated if viewed from an historical perspective in terms of road supply and demand. Beginning with the post-war period, these were years of full-employment, continuing economic growth and rising prosperity for the majority of people - in contrast to the experience of Britain in the early 1990s. From a supply side, in response to Britain's increasing traffic population, mainly privates cars, governments committed themselves to a lengthening and improvement of the total road network. Between 1952 and 1992 the overall length of all roads increased from 297,466 kilometres to 362,327 kilometres; an increase of almost 22%. Motorways in particular were greatly expanded, from a mere 219 kilometres in 1962 to over 3,147 kilometres by 1992; in sharp contrast an increase of 1337% - see Table 1.

Table 1
British road lengths - kilometres

Year	All Roads	Motorways
1952	297,466	-
1962	315,649	219
1972	327,717	1,669
1982	343,942	2,692
1992	362,327	3,147

Source: *Transport Statistics GB.*
Department of Transport, 1993 HMSO.

From the demand side, impressive as road length figures may seem, they soon pale into insignificance when judged against the phenomenal post-war growth in road vehicles numbers. As illustrated in Table 2. there has been a progressive growth in total vehicle population. In the early 1950s there were approximately 4 million registered vehicles using the Britain's road network. Forty years on this figure had increased sixfold to over 24.5 million - excluding large numbers of foreign vehicles now regularly using UK roads.

As indicated by the figures, it is interesting to note that heavy goods vehicles (hgvs) as a segment (defined in transport legislation as commercial vehicles with a gross weight of 3.5 tonnes) have declined in number, presently represent less than 2% of the total vehicle.

Table 2
Vehicles on Britain's roads 1951 - 1991(000s)

Vehicle Type	1951	1961	1971	1981	1991
Private Cars	2,095	5,296	10,443	14,867	19,737
Light goods	457	944	1,452	1,641	2,215
Heavy goods	451	508	542	486	449
Public Transport	123	82	96	110	109
Agriculture	250	400	380	365	346
Motor Cycles	725	1,577	899	1,371	75
Other	26	76	92	95	65
Exempt	63	106	126	42	860
Total	4,190	8,989	14,030	19,347	24,511

Source: *Transport Statistics.*
Department of Transport 1992 HMSO.

The Department of Transport (DoT) has plans in the pipeline to complete the unfinished links in the motorway system. However, in the light of the currently huge £50 billion Public Sector Borrowing Requirement (PSBR) it is doubtful if present or future governments will retain the same level of commitment to public funded road expansion programmes. For example, in the early stages of the M25 widening scheme criticism was directed at the DoT in regard to estimated costs over-running by 100%. Furthermore, a British Roads Federation report estimated that over 20% of roads, under local authority control, were in a state of poor repair through lack of funding.

There are strong indications that economic necessity will force future governments to sharply trim back expenditure on road building. For example, in the 1993 November Budget, 7% cutbacks were announced in road building and the introduction of toll roads is now envisaged *as soon as the appropriate technology becomes available.* Furthermore, increasing vociferous environmental opposition is being mounted from many quarters, including green campaigners and local authorities against more roads. The latter group in particular, especially in the south-east, are becoming alarmed at the impact new motorway widening schemes, such as the M25, and new link roads will have on their areas. Concern focuses on the greater volumes of traffic being attracted to wider motorways, landtake and associated environmental deterioration in general - and who pays for these external impacts resulting from more road traffic.

The most recent DoT statistics indicate that the UK's road system carries eight times as much traffic today as it did in the early 1950s. Furthermore, over the same period road length has only increased by just over 20%. The latest DoT statistics reveal:-

> The length of public roads in Great Britain increased by about 5% between 1982 and 1992. There were considerable differences in the growth rates of the different road classes. Motorway length increased by about 17% while the length of other minor roads by about 6%. For minor roads, the fastest growth in length was seen in unclassified roads which increased by 8% over the decade (Transport Statistics Great Britain. DoT HMSO. 1993).

It is obvious from the statistics that a position of disequilibrium exists between road lengths and adequate capacity required to cater at a private, commercial and safety level for the UK's inexorable traffic growth. Current and future road building programmes, especially when reduced by budgetary pressure, will severely put to the test the government's ability to bring about a position of equilibrium.

The development of the motorway network in particular and resulting traffic attracted has resulted in the following

* a substantial change in traffic flow patterns

* growing congestion costs

* higher levels of environmental pollution

A substantial change in traffic flow patterns

Cars and taxis account for about 80% of all traffic. The building of motorways in particular has changed traffic flow patterns substantially, these now being the most heavily used part of the road network. Latest Department of Transport figures reveal that traffic has grown much more rapidly on motorways than on other roads. Statistics indicate that this traffic has more than doubled over the last ten years compared with an increase of only 17% in motorway length - see Table 3.

Table 3
Traffic by vehicle type and road class 1992
Billions vehicle kilometres

	Cars and Taxis	Buses and Coaches	Light Vans	Goods vehicles
Motorways	46.9	0.5	5.0	8.4
Built-up major roads				
Trunk roads	7.8	0.1	0.9	0.7
Principal	57.2	1.2	6.0	3.3
Non-built up major roads				
Trunk	47.0	0.4	5.3	6.6
Principal	48.7	0.5	5.4	4.0
All minor roads	127.3	1.9	14.1	5.4
All roads	334.8	4.6	36.5	28.4

Source: Adapted - *Road Traffic Statistics GB*
Department of Transport 1993 HMSO.

From a supply perspective, while all motorways in the UK account for less than 1% of the total length of roads they in fact carry 15% of all traffic. In addition motorways attract over 30% of goods traffic - mainly heavy goods vehicles (hgvs). In the early 1950s about 35% of goods moved (tonne kilometres) were carried by road. In 1991 the share had risen to 61%. The trend has been towards the use of larger, heavier vehicles (usually articulated vehicles) for long hauls and smaller, two axle rigid vehicles for local deliveries. It is obvious motorways, hgvs and large distribution centres have gone hand in hand during the 1980s.

Growing congestion costs

The rapid growth in total vehicle numbers coupled with their greater usage has contributed to increasing congestion. From a demand perspective, there are currently over nine times as many private cars as there were in 1952. On the passenger front the greater use of private cars has hastened the decline in public transport, especially rail. In terms of freight the larger and more powerful lorries, coupled with increasing flexibility and vehicle utilisation afforded by an expanding motorway network, also hastened the decline of other freight modes - again rail being the main victim.

Currently, a growing level of concern is being expressed by industry, government and environmentalists at the costs and problems being generated by unprecedented traffic growth. In 1989 the Confederation of British Industry (CBI) estimated that congestion was costing Britain over £15 billion per year - probably a much higher figure today. Matters will not be improved if future traffic forecasts turn out to be correct. In 1989 the national road traffic forecasts estimated that all traffic will increase by between 83% - 142% by the year 2025 - Table 4. There are increasing complaints that business is hampered by poor road and rail infrastructure and difficulties in getting products to the market. In the circumstances, and given high road building costs, it is no surprise current government policy is encouraging the private sector to bridge the gap in new road capital expenditure. Or why British motorways will be electronically tolled before the year 2000.

Table 4
Road traffic forecasts 1989 - 2025
traffic growth (%)

Vehicle Type	Low forecast	High forecast
Cars and Taxis	82%	134%
Light goods vehicles	101%	215%
Heavy goods vehicles	67%	141%
Public service	0%	0%
All traffic	83%	142%

Source: *National Road Traffic Forecasts*
Department of Transport 1989 HMSO

Higher levels of environmental pollution

For some years environmental pollution from vehicle traffic has been a source of growing concern to many people and organizations. This situation is likely to increase in the future in line with the inexorable growth in traffic and resulting pollutants. From an historical perspective, in 1991 road transport emissions accounted for 51% of nitrogen oxides, 89% of carbon monoxides, 18% of carbon dioxide and over 35% of volatile compounds.

Between 1981 and 1991 road transport emissions grew faster than those from other sources. According to the 1992 review of the government's White Paper, *This Common Inheritance*, road transport has been identified as the fastest growing source of CO2 emissions. The review singles out the diesel engine as taking over from domestic fires as the main source of smoke.

There are other wider environmental pollution issues in terms of vehicle noise and intrusion, which can be especially acute when impacting on a residential area. Viewed from this perspective, a strong environmental argument can be put forward in support of distribution centres being located adjacent to motorways. Both is terms of warehouse build and generating large movements of vehicles motorways may be the most suitable location.

In parallel with the developments outlined above road transport has under gone fundamental structural changes during this period. Predominately the industry is made up of relatively small operators, typically having fleets of less than five vehicles. While this type of operator is prevalent within the industry they control a minority of vehicles and correspondingly also less of the large distribution centres. Medium and major size companies generally tend to have in excess of 100 vehicles, serving large type distribution centres. In the late 1980s and early 1990s, due to competitive and recessionary forces, the industry went through a process of mergers and acquisitions. The result has been an industry shakeout with fewer number of companies, but larger in size, remaining in control of a greater share of the total market.

According to a recent study by Reed Business research 80% of companies within road freight operate hgv vehicle fleets in the 1-4 range; representing 22% of the total vehicle base figure in 1992. The remaining 20% of companies control almost 80% of vehicles. In essence we can view the relationship between road freight companies and hgv ownership in a number of ways. For example:-

    20% of companies operate 78% of hgvs
or
    9% of companies operate 65% of hgvs
or
    3% of companies operate 49% of hgvs

During the last decade other trends have emerged, which at first glance may present a contradictory picture. For example, while the actual number of hgv operator licences (O-licences) have increased the number of hgvs registered on those licences has decreased. In 1986 there were 129,396 hgv O-licences in issue, increasing to 133,960 by 1992. Over the same period the number of hgvs fluctuated between 431,700 to 446,412 - with a marked decrease in recent years. More interestingly, there has been a sharp decline in the number of companies holding O-licences and operating hgvs.

While the volume of freight moved has greatly expanded, the number of vehicles required has remained almost static. Greater carrying capacity vehicles, consolidation of loads into larger type vehicles and improved operational efficiency account for this. Over the past two decades lorry characteristics have greatly changed in terms of size - length and weight.

For example, as a result of the 1980 Armitage Report recommendations hgvs had a permitted maximum weight limit of 38 tonnes for articulated lorries (on 5 or 6 axles). Today, an articulated lorry has a length of 16.5 metres. The trend has been to use larger type vehicles (artics) for long distance hauls (trucking) and smaller vehicles (rigids) for shorter journeys. In August 1993 the Government announced an increase in total permitted weight from 38 to 44 tonnes, but only for vehicles engaged on the road leg of a combined transport operation, ie. hgvs taking freight between ports and rail terminals. Additionally, because of just-in-time concepts and optimal operational utilisation, hgvs are on average doing longer trunk hauls. In short, hgv traffic has grown faster than their actual numbers. While representing less than 2% of the total vehicles population these factors account for the public perception that there are actually more hgvs on the road. However, the hgv parc has remained fairly static, but there has been a decline in the number of companies within the industry. In 1987 there were 91,900 companies; falling to 86,200 in 1990 and 72,400 by 1992 respectively. The trend reflects the effects of the recession, driving out smaller companies and generating more mergers and acquisitions in the medium sized sector. The result is a greater segment of the road freight industry - vehicles, warehouses and market share - being controlled by a smaller number of larger sized companies. These companies commonly hold multiple O-licences, operating in most Traffic Areas.

Such companies, by the very nature of their size, power and market share, will have a large degree of influence in determining where future distribution centres are located, what size, and level of activity generated. In addition there has been a knock-on effect from the process of company mergers and acquisitions in the amount of spare warehouse capacity currently available. Even more warehousing will come on to the market in the foreseeable future. These are important factors to consider in appreciating changes and developments taking place within the industry.

Other developments were taking place during the period also having significance for the industry. In the main these were the following:-

*   a substantial rise in freight movements.

* a shift in preferred freight mode.

* a change in warehouse location.

A rise in freight movements

The substantial rise in the transport business of total freight movements following in line with a growing general economic prosperity. In the early 1950s just over 1000 million tonnes of goods were lifted. By the 1990s this figures had more than doubled to almost 2000 million tonnes. Over the same period goods moved increased from 88 (billion tonne kms) to over 208 by 1992.

A shift in preferred mode

In terms of choice there was a shift in preferred freight mode to road, mainly at the expense of rail. Traditionally, modes such as canal, coastal shipping and rail carried a large proportion of internal freight. Over the years they gradually lost their hold on bulk markets, coal, cement, aggregates, grain, and others such as newspapers, postal and parcels. In the 1950s rail accounted for over 40% of goods moved. Today, it stagnates at around a 7%. share of the market. Given uncertainty generated by rail privatization and competition this situation is likely to remain for some time. However, there is some optimism on the horizon for rail enthusiasts. As rail tends to be more suitable for long distance freight movements the 1994 opening of the Channel tunnel presents the possibility of new markets and customers. But, a word of caution. Assumptions are made that the Channel Tunnel becomes fully functional, within an acceptable business time-frame, offers a competitive package to potential users and that the rail infrastructure on the British side soon comes up to an equivalent European standard.

Turning to coastal shipping, this still commands a small percentage market share, covering a limited range of traditional freight. It will require investment in new type cargo ships, breaking into markets where road dominates, or opening up new markets to make headway, coupled with investment in port infrastructure and improved road/rail access. Furthermore, there is the inhibiting factor of market resistance to these "outdated" transport modes. The fact that the freight industry has been dominated for so long by road partially reinforces a strong road culture among a whole generation of distribution managers and companies. This may explain a reluctance by the industry to try out "new" or "alternative" modes.

The fact is that road clearly dominates the freight market. In percentage terms the other modes all combined represent less than 20% of goods lifted. Obviously, the U.K. is heavily committed to a road freight culture, and this situation will remain for some time.

A change in warehouse location

Within the road freight industry, as an integral development and part of continual productivity efficiency, there has occurred a dramatic change in distribution warehouses in terms of their size, function and geographical location. Responding to growing markets, new customers and just-in-time (JIT) opportunities, made possible by an expanding motorway network, has resulted in a distribution centre warehouse revolution. The consequences of these changing trends has now emerged. Whereas at one time most road freight warehouses were small and attracted small vehicle fleets based in urban areas, the situation has dramatically changed, especially among major retailers and national brand companies. In recent years the large multiple retailers, Tesco, Sainsbury, Safeway etc, and third party road freight contractors opened high stock volume, high value, large purpose built distribution warehousing. Warehouse developments such as these attract daily high volumes of hgv fleets. Most have been located in close proximity to major motorway junctions. Warehousing infrastructure of this variety usually involves management in long term marketing and strategic planning. These warehouses usually cost millions of pounds in investment. The value of stock contained in these massive warehouses and JIT throughput usually costs many more millions of pounds.

Distribution warehousing of this variety is the powerhouse of modern logistics, being essential for the continual smooth functioning, profitability and implementation of JIT techniques. There are numerous concentrations of these warehouses near the spine of Britain's motorway network. They have become a familiar sight on the landscape with their company logos clearly visible on building frontage. There is a particularly heavy cluster around the M1/M6/M69 *golden triangle* catering for major industrial companies, food distributors and parcel carriers. The process towards clustering has gathered momentum as the industry has gone through various stages of rationalisation and centralisation into larger business groups during the past decade. The new concept distribution parks have also had a tendency to follow similar location preferences. An analysis of 124 distribution parks, either built or being built, indicates most are located a short distance from motorway junctions - Table 5. Again, locational evidence indicates a heavy clustering in the Midlands area.

Table 5
Distribution parks in Britain - 1993

Area	Number
South East and East Anglia	28
The South West	14
The Midlands	52
The North West	18
The North, North East and Scotland	12
Total	124

Source: *The Distribution Business Guide to UK Distribution Parks 1993*

Given existing knowledge, best information, customer JIT requirements and quick market access the warehouse proliferation in close proximity to motorways made good business and strategic sense. However, the equation factors upon which past judgements were made, making motorway location attractive, may no longer hold true beyond 2000. Such thinking may be entering a stage of redundancy, especially for those located north of the *golden triangle*, whose core customer market base is pan-European and/or in the South-East. There are a number of reasons accounting for this. Today, various variables are slowly coming together that may form a lethal cocktail for the industry, bringing into question most of the assumptions upon which it was built. In the main these are the following:-

* Continuing motorway congestion reducing the advantage of speed

* Introduction and impact of 56mph speed limit in 1994

* Difficulty of relocating to scarce, available and suitable sites in the South East

* Possibility of road charging measures being introduced especially in areas of high density

* Possibility of premium priced fuel - diesel

Motorway congestion

The combined effect of greater vehicle numbers and usage has resulted in ever growing road congestion. Each day more sections of the arterial road network are blocked with traffic cones, adding to driver's frustration, environmental pollution and congestion levels. Some roads experience extreme congestion levels at different times of the day. Such conditions are especially acute in main urban areas and heavily utilized motorways such as the M1, M4, M6 and M25. Parts of the road network are so overloaded at times that the smallest accident, vehicle breakdown or road maintenance results in severe and rapid congestion growth, overspilling onto side roads. At such times the fastest moving thing is the rate of congestion, as it fans out onto side roads. For seasoned road travellers it is no surprise to discover that average speeds of 10mph in some of the UK's major cities has not improved much since the days of horse drawn transport - indeed got worse. Statistics suggest that the decline in urban speeds is not just confined to cities, but also to outer zones, indicating that congestion is spreading both in terms of time and geographical area. From another perspective the UK is a country on the periphery of Europe. According to the British Roads Federation (BRF) the effectiveness and efficiency of UK ports is being undermined by inadequate road links. The BRF points outs that:-

* Traffic congestion adds to industry's costs and harms the competitiveness of ports.

* The majority of Britain's ports are not connected to the motorway network by high standard roads.

* Much port traffic has to pass through towns and villages.

* Heavy goods vehicles in residential areas degrade the local environment.

Despite the government's current road building programme there is widespread consensus that congestion will be an increasing problem for Britain's road users. If the UK is to keep its lead in the distribution marketplace this problem will have to be solved. With growth in the private car market coupled with road works and a slowing down in the roads building programme it is likely that congestion will be particularly acute, especially near sections of heavily used motorways - removing the advantage of speed in the years ahead. For those distribution companies, with their core customer market dependent on delivery service by motorway or time sensitive deliveries, the question of speed will be a significant consideration in determining optimal site location.

56mph speed limits

An EC Directive coming into force by 1994 will restrict hgv speeds to 56 mph. Companies, based north of the *golden triangle*, serving the southern markets or wishing to reach Channel ports, might experience difficulties doing this in single journeys. Given the current geographic pattern of distribution warehousing there are suggestions that the warehouse centre of gravity may shift south or eastward in order to be able to meet customer requirements and core market. It is worth expanding on the aspect of speed limitation and potential impact.

The 56mph limit could effectively reduce the radius distance travelled during a single journey. A simple example, illustrates the point. Assume a perfect world with no road congestion, no vehicle breakdowns, no accidents, no adverse weather and a constant speed of 60 mph. Given these conditions a total distance of 540 miles could be travelled within the maximum permitted driving time of 9 hours. Accepting the same assumptions, but reducing the speed to the new 56mph, a total distance travelled is now 504 miles. In a 4.5 hour period, after which the driver must take a break, the distance travelled is 252 miles. In short, depending on point of origin, the radius able to be covered in a single journey is reduced by 18 miles or 36 miles respectively on the basis of a 4.5/9 hour trip. If the distribution centre is based in the north of the *golden triangle* and core customers are southern based an 18 or 36 mile radius band effectively removes a huge population slice out of this high density area. There are obvious implications for those companies with significant market segments within this radius.

This simple analysis, of course, ignores the real world of congestion, breakdowns etc, which could in practice extend the radius ever wider, thereby posing an even greater threat for operators. Some leading distribution companies are already well aware of the limitations speed restrictions may impose on their operations. Major companies like TNT, Transport Development Group, Exel Logistics, BOC Distribution, have taken steps in advance of the introduction of 56 mph speed limit in gearing up their vehicle fleet specifications. This approach ensures they are able to adequately serve existing or new customers. The vehicle fleets of these companies are equipped with engines, giving sufficient power and torque to maintain constant average speeds, irrespective of road gradients.

Locating in the South East

If such scenarios as described develop then distribution companies may seek warehousing premises further south and eastward. This means being near the major motorway intersections; the M25, the M4, M3, M1 and all this involves - in regions where land values are at a premium and planning regulations are tight. These are also high population density regions. For example, the South East while representing less than 10% of Britain's land mass contains over 17 million people - almost 30% of the population. Though the new river crossing at Dartford was opened in 1991 and the M20 missing link is completed, counties like Kent have geared up their road infrastructure as a result of the Channel Tunnel opening and the anticipated traffic growth. Concern is being expressed about excessive demand expected to impose extra pressure on an already over burdened region. Additionally, within the context of the hgv O-licence system there has been a remarkably consistent level of objections registered each year. There are, however, also noticeable regional variations. Traffic Areas in the southern part of the U.K. have tended to register above average levels of environmental objections in percentage terms. Continuing traffic growth and the Channel Tunnel opening may generate resistance among local authorities and residents against "lorry generators" such as warehouse developments. A reversal in environmental objections in these regions seems unlikely. Not a pleasant prospect for those distribution companies perhaps seeking new warehouse sites that require servicing by large vehicle fleets.

Road charging

As each day passes there are increasing signs that government policy is turning towards road charging, in the form of motorway toll roads and urban road pricing. In the November 1993 Budget, Chancellor Kenneth Clarke, announced that toll roads would be introduced when the technology became vailable - probably within a few years. A few days previously, Alastair Morton, Channel Tunnel chairman and government appointee on seeking private funds for transport infrastructure, pointed out, "I see no way forward unless there is tolling of some of our roads. Some form of payment is inevitable" (BBC2 Money Programme 28/11/93). It is very likely that the southern urban areas will be among the first to be subjected to government road pricing initiatives within the foreseeable future. Of particular interest to road distribution companies will be the actual technical mechanism, price level and how the policy will impact in terms of financial and operational costs.

In broad terms road charging measures are designed to ease congestion. However, the overall impact will be difficult to assess because road users are not a homogeneous group. Any resulting impact from a system of road charging will not be uniformly spread. Two main road categories are identified - private cars and commercial vehicles. Each will respond differently to road charging. For example, car users may have the option of alternative transport or be able to delay their journey until after peak rate periods. However, road distribution companies will have a limited range of options available to them. Frequently companies have to use roads during peak morning periods because of customer time-slot demands and due to lack of viable alternative freight modes. Furthermore, the road freight market is segmented into perishable and non-perishable products. A high percentage of present day road freight is highly time-sensitive; newspapers, fresh food, chilled foods, market garden and dairy produce. Off-peak delivery times are not a practical proposition for companies engaged in these commercial activities. Therefore, road charging is a factor distribution companies will have to take more into account in future cost equations. With more local authorities imposing route and time restrictions, together with traffic calming methods the option of avoiding motorway tolls or urban road pricing schemes by back street rat-running will not be a practical proposition for hgv drivers.

Premium priced fuel

An even bigger and more threatening time-bomb is ticking away. It is one the industry would prefer not to have to think about - higher priced fossil fuel. Research findings strongly predict future fuel shortages. If so, supply and demand laws will most likely bring about price increases. For good or bad a large section of Britain's freight industry are committed to diesel driven road transport. Furthermore, by locating major sections of their logistics warehouse system along-side motorways, having no access for alternative modes, they create extra risk for themselves. Because of road distribution's inelastic ability to change or respond to fuel shortages in the short term Government and oil companies will have leverage in squeezing more revenue and higher prices from the commodity. According to the 1992 EC White Paper on transport - *The Future Development of the Common Transport Policy - a global approach to the construction of a Community framework for sustainable mobility* - fuel consumption could rise by 25% by the year 2000. On present estimates, more than two thirds of fossil fuel burned world wide is burned by European countries and the USA. Indeed, the USA is believed to have only 10 years oil reserves left, being increasingly dependent on imports.

A comprehensive and important report published in late 1993 by the World Energy Council, *Energy For Tomorrow's World*, confirms a depletion of oil supplies. The report reveals that because of current squandering of finite resources, future world population expansion and its demands, fossil fuels will be depleted in the next century. Based upon possible scenarios experts warn that there is about 40 years of oil supplies left. Even more worrying is the finding that most of the world's oil reserves are in some of the most politically volatile countries. If developments turn out as predicted, combined with environmental aspects, and the road industry's current inelastic demand for diesel fuel will future governments have any qualms about raising revenue through higher fuel prices? Perhaps, it is no coincidence that the Department of the Environment's own current consultation document, *UK Strategy For Sustainable Development*, points out the need to, "Look at the range of measures which could contribute to reduced impacts from the (road) sector, including fiscal and market measures to increase the price of transport and reflect wider costs; regulations, such as additional vehicle standards or better speed enforcement".

How the road transport industry responds to these possibilities and impacts will be an issue increasingly becoming more topical - but with no clear answer at the moment. To paraphrase a familiar saying distribution managers may be asking themselves the following question i.e. are we in the right place and using the right mode to get to the right customer. At best modern warehouses have a life span of about 30 years. In view of pending premium priced fuel, a road network severely subjected to congestion, environmental pressures, speed restrictions, road charging and other factors, what criteria will determine suitable distribution warehouse centre location in the years ahead? This is the key industry issue to be addressed.

As a new century approaches it may be that road distribution companies in seeking practical and viable solutions may respond by devoting more serious consideration and assessment of the following:-

* greater vehicle energy conservation - lean burn engines

* greater vehicle energy efficiency - aerodynamic vehicles, defensive driving

* greater use of alternative and environmentally cleaner fuels

* greater use of alternative modes and inter-modal transport

- greater use of trailer load space technology - double decker trailers

- greater use of cabotage freedom

- greater attention to full vehicle load utilisation

- greater re-evaluation of JIT methods as they become less economically and environmentally acceptable

- greater agreements with competitors on backloading

- greater use of night time motorway usage

- greater thought as to ideal future warehouse location

The above developments may offer some solutions to future and growing challenges. Many of these are already happening, some being very advanced. For example, truck manufacturers have made tremendous improvements in body and aerodynamic design, cleaner, lean burn, quieter, more fuel efficient engines and are experimenting with alternative fuelled vehicles. For example, Exel Logistics has for a number of years been doing advanced work on fuel saving improvements with aerodynamic designed trailers and traction units. BOC Distribution are currently conducting trials with an ERF rigid/British Gas powered lorry. TNT Express has an even more exciting project with a Gas Turbine/Electric Hybrid Truck, the idea being to use gas power to cover stem milage from the distribution centre to the outer limits of an urban zone, then switch over to electric power for urban deliveries. While in the early stages of development these ideas indicate the degree of forward thinking in some quarters of the industry.

However, in time further re-appraisal, perhaps radical thought, may be required, in particular the use of alternative modes or intermodal methods. For example, greater utilization may be sought from rail or coastal/inland shipping after 2000 although expectations of a revival in rail freight must be tempered by the reality of the market. Even if rail were to double its market share, in overall terms this would not make a significant dent in the number of hgvs required. In any case the freight market will continue to grow, especially pan-European. This growth will probably be soaked up by road transport given rail's unfortunate image problem in terms of delays, cancellations and overall reliability, generally being held in low esteem by the market as an effective and efficient distribution mode. As one senior distribution manager critically remarked to me "Rail has neither the right management, attitude, skills, equipment, professionalism or discipline to offer a viable and reliable freight mode at present. They are reasonably good at getting mobile freight (passengers) from A to B. When it comes to real freight, especially at marshalling yards or rail heads, they fall down." This may sound harsh, but represents a widely held view by the road industry towards rail. However, giving the many developments that will impact on road freight in the coming years, coupled with a growing pan-European market and the Channel Tunnel opening then long distance rail freight may become:-

* a more cost effective mode

* a more efficient mode

* a more competitive mode

* a more attractive mode

* a more sustainable mode

* a more environmentally friendly mode

As diesel become more expensive those companies with distribution centres having access to rail sidings or within a short distance from a rail link may find themselves on prime locations - providing the product is suitable for rail and the cost margins are right. It is possible that some companies may attempt to make use of railheads as a result of government initiatives in regard the use of 44 tonne trucks. For example, in August 1993 the DoT announced measures to encourage industry to switch freight off roads on to rails. Lorries taking freight to a railhead are to be allowed to carry heavier payloads, providing they use six axle vehicles with road friendly suspension. This type of movement would be suitable for articulated vehicles and drawbar combinations carrying containers or swap-bodies. Operators may attempt to reduce some long-distance domestic trucking, doing stem milage from the distribution centre to a railhead, as a method of saving on increasingly expensive diesel.

On another level, those companies also having excess warehouse capacity, now or in the future, may benefit by holding on to their southern based sites. The same may apply to locations with good access to port facilities, especially inland, as coastal shipping is also considered as an alternative mode. As in the case of rail, a change in attitude will be required, in addition to major investment in facilities, ship design, technology and appropriate market identification. However, coastal shipping and inland modal use is already widespread in Europe. In Japan, an island economy not unlike the U.K. in 1991 coastal shipping was responsible for 8.3% of domestic freight movements. Also, like the U.K., road transport is the dominant mode, responsible for 90% of domestic freight movements. But equally important, the Japanese acknowledge their transport infrastructure is suffering from similar problems to the UK.

> The trucking industry which accounts for the largest share of domestic cargo traffic, is being increasingly beset by problems such as a shortage of labour, road congestion, and restrictions on CO_2 emissions. It is against this background that a proportion of domestic cargo is now being switched from land to sea transport because of coastal shipping's greater efficiency and lower pollution, a phenomenon known in Japan as "modal-shift".
> (Japanese Shipping 1993 - The Japanese Shipowners' Association).

The Japanese are responding by stepping up investment in vessels compatible with this modal-shift, such as RoRo ships and container vessels, as well as upgrading its information handling infrastructure at an industry level. There is no reason why the UK cannot benefit from similar transference of such methods and technology in the next century. For example, make better use of inland waterways and estuaries that allow passage to coastal shipping and good access to concentrations of distribution centres, such as the Manchester Ship Canal and the Trafford Park complex.

In many respects Europe may hold the answer to many questions. Currently the European Commission is encouraging industry to adopt an intermodal approach. The 1992 EC White paper *The Future Development of the Common Transport Policy* for example recommends that each mode of transport is developed and improved so that it meshes better with all other modes. According to the White Paper the development of the trans-European networks would be underpinned by measures involving:-

* Better use of existing networks by modernizing equipment and an improved flow of information between the different systems using electronic data communications and telecommunications.

* greater coordination of research and development work on the interfaces between the various modes of transport (intermodal

transfer points) and on the new technologies with a view to enhancing the quality of service.

* network users meetings all the costs, particular the external ones (due to pollution, noise, etc) in order to achieve a fairer balance between the various modes and foster the use of the most suitable modes or combinations.

* diversification of the financial resources by resorting more to private capital; the Community's contribution will focus on stimulating projects of Europe-wide interest by helping to integrate regional and national projects and connect isolated regions to the network.

As a possible indicator toward future thinking on these lines in October 1993 the European Parliament Transport Committee organized a hearing on *The Problem of Environment and Transport.* This was a follow-up to the EC's 1992 White Paper on transport. The EC Transport Commissioner, Abel Matutes, emphasised his determination at this hearing to reduce intermodal disparities which create distortion of competition.

Conclusion

While road distribution is presently considered flexible, efficient and competitive in comparison to other modes this situation may be called more into question in the future. First, there is the consideration that if congestion increases and road deliveries become less reliable, less productive and more expensive the market will force change, especially in warehouse location. How much diesel price is raised and other forces exert pressure before motorway based warehousing becomes less attractive, in comparison to those locations able to be serviced additionally by rail and or port, is a question that will increasingly become more topical.

Second, there is the issue that a great deal of money has been invested by the industry in motorway distribution centres, on the assumption they will continue to play a mayor role in distribution beyond the year 2000. In economic terms motorway location will continue, probably expanding, if road transport responds to future challenges with better use of their vehicles, operational procedures, fuel saving measures and more use of combined transport - where appropriate. In environmental terms, especially for the large type distribution centres, attracting high volumes of vehicles, motorway location is probably the most suitable.

Finally, there is a possible wider inherent risk facing the industry; a lack of available suitable sites and local resistance in the southern part of Britain. This might force UK based companies to relocate their distribution centres to northern France - especially if encouraged by financial incentives and other inducements. Southern UK markets could easily be serviced from here within acceptable trip times. If this were to happen it would not only mean that the UK is seen to be geographically on the periphery of Europe, but treated as such in economic terms.

One thing is now certain, the road transport industry is entering a new era, imposing extra levels of risk and uncertainty. Now may be the right time for decision makers to take stock and review their options for 2000 and beyond, thereby manage coming changes rather than have changes managing them.

10 Ownership and productive efficiency: The experience of British ports

Zinan Liu

Introduction

Generally speaking, ports throughout the world are owned and controlled publicly, though the extent of the involvement of public port authorities concerned in port operations varies. The UK was no exception to this before 1980, with the dominance of public ports of various forms in the industry. Port privatization has dramatically changed the ownership structure of the industry, and nearly 70% of the UK's port capacity in terms of tonnage handled is now controlled by private enterprise. And more is to come. Many eyes are cast in the direction of the UK with the complete withdrawal of government from the ownership of the port sector. At the heart of the debate about port privatization is the question of the optimal form of industrial organization for ports. While the arguments against privatization pointed to particular characteristics of the port industry which made it unlikely that a market solution would be economically efficient, the arguments for privatization rested on the generally assumed superiority of private enterprise over public enterprise in terms of productive efficiency. In what follows we shall consider the issues raised in the arguments of both sides and assess privatization in the port industry in terms of economic efficiency.

The chapter is organized as follows. Section 2 describes the different types of port ownership and the events of port privatization in the U.K., which gives useful background. Section 3 is concerned with the main ways in which, and the underlying causes by which, market failure manifests itself, and also considers whether government intervention in the form of public ownership is necessary in the port sector. Section 4 examines the implications of alternative forms of port ownership for managerial incentive structures, together with empirical evidence on whether the transfer of port ownership from the public sector to the private sector will bring about significant efficiency gains. The final section provides a Conclusion.

The port industry in the UK

There are well over 300 ports and harbours in the UK ranging in size and complexity from small river wharves and fishing harbours to more than 100 commercially significant port authorities.[1] Among them, only about a dozen deserve the adjective 'major', dealing as they do with nine-tenths of the total foreign trade by value.[2] Ports and harbours facilitate the import and export each year of more than 470 million tonnes of freight traffic - including raw materials for manufacturing, the bulk of consumer and industrial products and fuels. In addition, over 24.5 million passenger journeys are made by sea, with 4.6 million passenger-accompanied cars travelling on roll-on/roll-off ferries.

Different forms of port ownership

Port ownership is best defined in terms of who provides port facilities and services. A port basically functions as a meeting point for various transport modes, including maritime shipping, inland navigation, highway and railway transport. A bundle of facilities and services, which have to be provided in order to fulfil the basic function of a port, can be broadly classified as follows. First, there is the *infrastructure*. This includes land, water area, docks, locks, breakwaters, channels, navigational aids, physical links to inland transport, etc. Secondly, there is the *superstructure*. This includes quay cranes, gantries, forklifts, warehouses, sheds and so on. Thirdly there are the *services* provided by the port. The basic service is cargo loading and unloading, but a number of complementary services are also necessary, such as storage, pilotage, towage and so on. Since any party, including national government, local authorities, independent public bodies and private undertakings, may be involved in providing port facilities and services, port ownership is not simply a dichotomy between private and public ownership. The allocation of the provision rights, and hence the property rights for the infrastructure, superstructure and services among various parties gives rise to different patterns of port ownership.

Normally public ports refer to those in which at least the infrastructure is owned by the public. The legal status of "the public" can be national government, or local authorities or public autonomy. Hence there are what are known as *nationalized ports*, *municipal ports* and *autonomous ports*. It is usually the case that a separate administrative service, namely a public port authority, is created to act on behalf of the public owner in question. The port authority may or may not involve in other port operations than the provision of the infrastructure. At one extreme there are so-called *landlord*

ports in which the port authority concerned restricts its duties to the provision of the infrastructure, while the provision of superstructure and services is leased out to private-sector companies. At the other, there are *service ports* in which the public authority is responsible for everything and runs ports as a total organization. Between these two extremes, one can find *tool ports*, in which the port authority provides the infrastructure and superstructure, while cargo handling operations are carried out by private lessees. In addition, a port authority also has a number of other essential non-operational functions, including planning and coordinating developments, safety and pollution control. When the public port authorities withdraw entirely from its ownership of the port, one has the case of *private ports*.
Therefore port ownership can be characterised in terms of the *status* and the *jurisdiction* of a port authority. In the status dimension, port ownership represents the degree of devolution from the case of centralized administration to the case of comprehensive privatisation. In the jurisdiction dimension, port ownership represents the extent of public control from the case of a pure public port to the case of a pure private port. Indeed port ownership can be viewed as a range of public policy options from public control to *laissez faire*.

Port ownership in the UK

Nearly all kinds of port ownership can be find in the UK. Before privatization, a majority of ports was trust ports, which are in character autonomous ports. Among 13 major ports, 8 of them were trust ports before port privatization, including Clyde, Dover, Forth, London, Medway, Milford Haven, Tees and Hartlepool and Tyne. The system of trust ports grew up in the 19th century and provided a means of ensuring that harbour facilities in a given area were properly maintained for the benefit of the local shipping and fishing communities. Trust ports are set up by individual acts of Parliament or statutory orders. The boards of trustees which govern trust ports are drawn from representatives of port users, trade unions and other local interests. The Secretary of State for Transport may appoint some board members including the chief executive of the port. Although the constitution and duties of trust ports are laid down by an act of Parliament, they are not directly responsible to Parliament. They are however legally bound to submit an annual statement of accounts to the Secretary of State. The remit of trust ports is typically, to provide a service for the import and export of goods by sea; to provide navigational conservancy; and to make the best use of their assets. Trust ports are not profit-making and were not permitted to engage in non-port activities before Transport and Works Act

1992.[3] However, they are required to earn enough revenue to cover depreciation on assets at replacement cost, to pay interest on loans, and to provide for loan redemption. In years when they realise surplus revenue they must devote such a surplus to the furtherance of their statutory objectives, not the least of which, from the user's point of view, is a reduction in port dues and charges levied on ships and cargoes.

The second type of port ownership involves nationalised ports, which were the product of the nationalization programme when the Labour Government was in power during 1945-1951. Following the nationalization of the Bank of England, the coal industry and the Air Corporation, several transport sectors including railways and their ports were nationalized. Under the Transport Act 1947 all properties owned by railway ports and docks were transferred to the British Transport Commission (BTC). Later, under the Transport Act 1962, the BTC was dissolved and separate public corporations in the form of various boards were established, each with its own power and jurisdiction and each responsible to the Minister of Transport. Most of the ex-railway ports (19 of them) were put under the control of British Transport Docks Board (BTDB), and 4 small docks linking with the inland waterway system were put under the control of British Waterways Board (BWB). Two factors led to the passing of the 1962 Act (Thomas, 1981). One was the huge deficit of the BTC from its railway undertakings. The other was the inability of BTC to manage its vast undertakings, including railways, the ex-railway ports, long distance road haulage, road passenger transport, inland waterway transport and London passenger transport.

The third type of port ownership involves those which are in effect owned by the citizens of the municipality in which they are located and are administered by the town council, or a committee of the council. Although municipal ports were the earliest form of port ownership, being the approach to port administration under the British monarchy as early as the 10th century, this form of ownership is not widely practised in this country and the most significant example is Bristol, though there are other such as Boston and also Ramsgate.

It is common in industrialised countries that cargo handling operations are carried out carried out by private undertakings. Furthermore there is also a tendency of increasing private investment in the infrastructure and superstructure and accordingly of decreasing public provision of these port facilities. But ports entirely owned and controlled by the private sector are rarely seen in the world, a phenomenon observed in the UK even before the advent of port privatization. The best known private ports were Felixstowe, Liverpool and Manchester. The ownership structure of private ports varies. Some are subsidiaries of larger companies, some are public limited companies in their own right, and some of the recent privatized trust ports have been taken over and run by their own management and workforce. British port ownership in the jurisdiction dimension is also characterized by a complex and fragmented structure. The structure was, until the early 1960s, very similar to that currently prevailing in Continental European countries with the existence of non-operational port authorities while cargo-handling and other services were provided by private operators. As a result of the rationalization policy carried out by the National Ports Council in line with recommendations of the Rochdale Committee *(Rochdale Report, 1962)* the number of licensed private operators fell significantly and port authorities assumed an increasingly important roles. The rationalization policy had the support of law with the introduction of a more rigid and effective licensing procedure under the Harbour Act 1966 and the requirement for the licensed employers to prohibit the continuing practice of casual employment under the amended National Dock Labour Scheme 1967. Since then port authorities have collectively controlled no less than 50% of port operations in terms of employment size in scheme ports, though the proportion in non-scheme ports has been smaller. However, the recent restructuring of port operations following the abolition of the dock labour scheme in 1989 has reversed the industry back to its fragmented structure before 1960 (Turnbull and Weston, 1991, 2, pp.3-8). The deregulation of employment has led to the expansion of the private sector, which was discouraged by the job-for-life status accorded to any new recruit under the scheme. While cargo handling is now undertaken predominantly by small private operators, many port authorities no longer own and operate stevedoring companies.

Privatization in the port industry

The port industry was one of the earliest sectors involved in the UK Government's privatization programme. The Transport Act 1981 empowered the Government to transfer the ownership of the BTDB from the nationalized sector to the private sector and renamed the former BTDB ports as Associated British Ports (ABP). Unlike most cases of privatization where the Government retained important ownership rights, no restriction on the amount of individual shareholdings, the reservation of golden share and the prohibition of foreign ownership was applied to ABP. The thorough withdrawal of ownership rights in ABP reflects the attitude of the Government to treat the ports as normal commercial undertakings. The powers of ABP were expanded as compared with that of BTDB, including the right to acquire and develop land and engage in any business in connection with its ports and harbours. Much of the growth ABP (valued at £60 millions in 1983 but valued at £490 millions in 1990), has been attributable to property development. The privatization of BTDB was merely the first wave of port privatization. In January 1990, Boston, was privatized, which can be considered as the starting point of a second stage of privatization in the industry. Boston was followed in 1991 by Bristol -the largest municipal port, which was sold by Bristol Council to First Corporate Shipping. In August 1990 the Prime Minister, in answering a Parliamentary question, said that the Government was looking into the possibility of an enabling bill aimed at the privatization of the trust ports. In the mean time trust ports wishing to become limited companies have been encouraged by the Government to submit Private Bills to Parliament. In the Government's view, the conversion of "old fashioned" port constitutions into companies would remove the rigidity which hampered the operation of market forces, because the benefits from privatization, as expressed by the then Transport Secretary Macolm Rifkind, would include:

* enhanced prospects of port development as a result of (trust) ports having greater access to share capital.
* the redevelopment of surplus land through the removal of statutory restrictions.
* diversification of port business.
* clearer accountability and a greater emphasis on profits
(*Transport* March/April 1991).

Under the Ports Act 1991, Tees and Hartlepool were taken over by a private company, which beat off a staff buy-out and led the way in the campaign to privatize the trust ports. The sale embroiled the Government in controversy with Labour after it refused to overturn the offer by the private company. In March 1992 Clyde, Forth, Medway, and Tilbury (a division of the Port of London Authority) were taken over by their management and employees in deals totalling about £90 million as the Government moved swiftly to offload ownership before the general election intervened to prevent sales. This time the Government avoided further damaging rows by agreeing to sell to local managements in regions where any other decisions could have had political repercussions.

The privatization policy was not unanimously endorsed in the industry. Some ports questioned whether the substitution of responsibility to shareholders for responsibility to "the public" would improve commercial performance or enhance competition. Meanwhile the substitution of responsibility was believed to endanger the interests of port users, given qualified local monopoly powers of ports. In addition, privatization was also opposed by many small ports which rely on specialist trades, or one or two major customers. They would it was claimed be susceptible to the market and predatory takeover by the private sector (Turnbull, 1, 1991). The reluctant trust ports were warned in 1991 to provide strong reasons why such a move is impossible, or they would face compulsory sale if they failed to come up with privatization proposals. Three ports, Milford Haven, Harwich and Lerwick, are believed to have convinced the Government that they should be allowed to remain in the trust sector. Ports like Dover, Tyne, Aberdeen, Ipswich, Poole and Dundee are currently forced into a new wave of sell-offs that could raise £200 million for the Treasury.

The limitations of the market solution [4]

The UK's approach to port administration has traditionally been less interventionist than many industrialized nations (for instance, most of Continental Europe). Receiving neither financial assistance nor intervention from the state, public ports in UK operate in much the same way as private ports. The view which underlies the port policy of successive UK Governments, whether Conservative or Labour, is that ports should be treated as commercial undertakings whenever appropriate and public control in the port sector should be kept to the minimum. The present Conservative Government went even further and completely withdrew from its ownership of the port sector. It firmly believed that the efficient provision of port facilities and services would be best left to the working of market forces. But the traditional wisdom which still underlies port policies of many industrialised countries is that the port sector is not like other industries and that it requires special and different treatment in financial management and policy. We are now in a stage to consider what are the arguments for government intervention in the form of public ownership in the port sector and whether these arguments are still well-founded.

The scope for port competition

It is argued by many industry analysts that the scope for port competition is limited. Ports enjoy monopoly power over their exclusive hinterland and competition only appears feasible in boundary areas along the borders between neighbouring ports. Clearly, the larger the number of individual competing ports, the greater is the scope of this type of boundary competition. However, modern port technology is highly capital intensive and exhibits substantial economies of scale. More importantly, modern ships are large in size and expensive in terms of opportunity costs of waiting time at ports. Thus both port and ship operators' interests require traffic to be concentrated at bigger and fewer ports than they once were. However, the degree of spacial competition between ports is a function of the geographical separation of the ports, the configuration of the inland transport system and the nature of the trade. Its long coast line endows the UK with a large number of seaports and they are connected with their hinterland by a well developed inland transport system. Thus the local monopoly power enjoyed by UK ports is probably limited.

The extent of economies of scale provided by modern port and shipping technologies were questioned by Gilman (1980), who argued that economies of scale in terminal operation is weak. For deep-sea trades where container dwell times are typically long, it is found that a wide spread container exchange of 3000 to 6000 TEUs are indigestible in many terminals, and the increase of potential terminal throughput and the reduction of costs are difficult. The economies of scale of ship size are also not so powerful as expected. Concentration of deep-sea ship itineraries is associated with a much higher cost of secondary distribution. Earlier Bennathan and Walters (1979, pp.43-50) argued that traffic concentration in a smaller number of ports increases inland transport costs, and after a certain level of concentration locational disadvantages may more than offset economies of scale derived from the concentration of port traffic. Thus there is a trade-off between economies of scale in operation and diseconomies in location. Empirical evidence in UK seems to support the view that economies of scale exhibited in the modern port and maritime technologies are not so substantial as expected (Liu, 1992). Surprisingly there has not been a tendency of increase in port market concentration for various cargoes. Particularly the concentration ratio of the fifth biggest port for container and Ro-Ro traffic has been fairly stable within the range from 45 per cent to 50 per cent over the last 25 years. Thus, although technological developments in the maritime sector may reduce the scope for inter-port competition, port markets continue to be reasonably competitive. The general consensus among economists is that private ownership works best in a competitive environment. According to this presumption, privatization in the port industry is appropriate. However, four counter-arguments can be made in this respect. The first is that there are other important instances of market failure that make Adam Smith's "invisible hand" incompetent in a port economy. These will be discussed shortly. Second, public ownership need not be incompatible with competition. Competition sharpens the managerial incentives of not only private ports but also public ports. In fact the port industry is an example of "mixed markets" - i.e. markets where private and public firms compete. The existence of competition is likely to limit the efficiency difference between private and public ports if any. Third, the dominance of public ownership in the industry was probably an important barrier to unfavourable market concentration. Without their public ownership status, many ports would be very vulnerable to acquisitions and take-overs in the private sector, especially those small ports which tend to rely on specialist trades or a few major customers. Given that merger and acquisition is a major route of firm growth in the private sector, there is a real danger that privatization may reduce the scope for inter-port competition. The government showed little interest in policies designed to increase competition in privatizing the port industry. BTDB ports accounted for almost 25% of total port traffic of this country, which amounts to significant market power. But when BTDB ports were privatised, no attempt was made to break up the port group to promote competition. In the recent proposed sell-offs of trust ports, (e.g. Dover, Tyne, Aberdeen), a number of private ports are among the prospective purchasers, including Felixstowe, Liverpool and two recently privatized ports, viz Forth and Tees and Hartlepool. Obviously if some ports are in common ownership with others, then inter-port competition will be largely reduced.

Last but not least, public ownership can create potential competition. As mentioned earlier, public ownership does not necessarily imply complete public control of port activities. Rather a variety of arrangements are available in terms of the jurisdiction of port authorities. One arrangement would involve restricting port authorities to landlord functions as in Continental European countries, Canada, USA and Japan. This will potentially enable the port authorities in question to create competition - in the form of auction - for monopoly, with several firms competing to be the one that actually provides cargo handling services, although few port authorities take advantage of this position. The terminals built by the port authority would be leased out for a period of time to the competitor offering to supply port services at the lowest prices or in general the best price-quality package. It is competition *for* rather than *in* markets, and hence particularly valuable in the port sector where demand permits room for very few terminal operators in a port, given economies of scale provided by modern port technology (Goss, 1987, pp.31-9). The potential competition would ensure port charges to be in line with the cost level and hence allocative efficiency. Moveover, when there is no opportunity of overcharging customers or reducing quality of port services provided, the only way to maintain profitability is to make sure that what is done is done at minimum costs and hence productive efficiency. The increasing importance of private sector companies in providing port services in the UK further necessitates the role of the public port authorities as a franchise regulator. But the wholesale privatization missed the opportunity to create potential competition.

The need for planning

Government intervention is often justified by the need for planning port development for both individual ports and the port system of a whole country (Goss, 1983 and Goss, 1990, pp.260-61). To decide on the location and form of a port is rather similar to determining the layout of streets and public services for a new city in the sense that conscious planning should be carried out by a unifying public authority in the best interests of the local community. Port construction must be in right sequence. For example a hydraulic regime needs to be considered in relation to tides, currents, littoral drift, erosion and silting before dredging a channel or constructing a breakwater or a jetty. Moreover, schemes of port development are interrelated and hence constructing one will frequently exert external effects, either beneficial or detrimental, on others. An example of the former is the removal of a limestone barrier or a dredging programme which may enable the whole of an inner port to be created or attract larger ships into the port and hence increase trade to the great advantage of locality. An example of the latter is the construction of a jetty at one place may slow down a current to a channel which will catch silt. In both cases public initiative and involvement is necessary whereas private provision of these facilities tends to be either insufficient if the external effects are beneficial or excess if the external effects are detrimental as compared with the social optimum. True, these external effects will be internalized when a rather large-scale monopoly is involved. But this will certainly permit the seeking of economic rents of valuable port sites. The argument of the need for planning may be extended from the local level to the national level. Since ports are sub-systems of the total transport systems of the country, the public sector becomes the more appropriate agency to ensure integrated and co-ordinated planning of all transport services in the country. The claimed benefits of co-ordinated investments and national planning would be avoidance of duplication of port facilities and more efficient use of scarce capital resource for conscious and integrated port development for the best interests of the whole nation.

In the UK there has been an unsuccessful attempt at national planning and coordination of port development. The Rochdale Committee (1962) envisaged, among other things, the establishment of a national port authority, which would be non-operational but would be given necessary statutory powers to accomplish a responsibility for the overall development of UK ports. The Conservatives then in power rejected the idea of a national ports authority, and established in its place, a National Ports Council (NPC). It was established by the Harbours Act 1964 and given the responsibility, subject to the Secretary of State's approval, for "formulating and keeping under review the improvement and development plans of port authorities in the UK and encouraging and promoting more efficient management of port facilities and services". However, the NPC was an advisory body which did not possess the power to enforce national port policies. In 1981 the NPC was dissolved because it was regarded by the industry too expensive in relation to its usefulness. Today it would be even more difficult to accept the call for port planning at national level. It is argued that this will almost certainly be in conflict with the work of market mechanism and hence the incentive to efficiency provided by inter-port competition (Goss, 1990, 2, pp.230). However, national co-ordination and planning need not apply comprehensively. Rather it can be confined to the infrastructure of major ports of the country, while investments on other facilities than the infrastructure as well as port operations remain the business of private-sector companies. National planning machinery of this kind has advantages of controlled port development in a desirable direction without restraining the work of the competition mechanism. A further argument against co-ordination and planning is that the claimed benefits may not actually be realised. There may be disagreement in forecasts of traffic flows, planning processes carried out by bureaucratic organization may take too much time, and conflicts between different interest groups (e.g. the central government and local authorities). All of these will cause delay and hence failure to respond to market situations adequately and promptly. While these drawbacks cannot be overcome entirely, they can certainly be reduced to some extent. The forecasting and planning work can be contracted out to independent and professional consultative agencies. The decision process can be made simpler and more efficient.

The significance of public goods

Some port facilities can be said to fall under the concept of public goods, which involve non-rivalry and non-excludable consumption, and hence a case for public provision, which implies public ownership, of these facilities. Examples cited by Goss (1990, pp.261-262) include dredged channels, beacons, buoys and other fixed or floating navigational aids. It should be argued that dredged channels, although they may share some same characteristics as those with public goods (we shall return to this point shortly), are private goods rather than public goods. By definition an increase in one individual's consumption of a public good does not reduce the amount available to any other individual. One cannot say that an empty railway compartment is a public good, because the consumption of the railway journey by one individual potentially although not actually reduces that of anyone else. The same is true of dredged channels.

Navigational aids are public goods, but they do not necessarily justify the case for public provision. The implications of public goods for efficiency are two folds. First, since many public goods are non-excludable, firms will find it difficult to collect revenue from consumers to cover the cost of producing the public good. If any consumers free ride because they cannot be excluded, the price that firms charge will not be an adequate measure of the marginal benefit for the good and there will be a less than efficient supply of the good. However, the costs of navigational aids are covered by port dues and there are actually little difficulties in collecting dues from ships and cargoes. There is a second and more fundamental reason why the market may fail to provide an efficient amount of public goods even when they are excludable, arising from the defining characteristic of public goods i.e. non-rivalry. Because navigational aids are public, an additional unit consumed by one individual ship does not reduce the amount available to other ships. This means that the marginal cost of the additional unit is zero. From welfare point of view the appropriate price should be zero. But except public owners no one will be willing to offer free service of navigational aids. The same can be said about dredged channels although it should not be regarded as public goods by definition. Up to the point where they are congested, the opportunity cost of using any of these is zero. But the free provision of navigational aids and dredged channels must imply financial deficit, and the public authority has to raise money somewhere. It is possible to argue that financing such facilities through taxation will create distortion in resource allocation and involve administrative costs. An alternative method to finance public goods, which will not distort resource allocation and in the meantime can be justified on the ground that one who benefits more pays more, is to charge what traffic can bear. Practically port dues should be levied on the basis of cargo values or net tonnage of vessels. These physical measures relate closely to the corresponding consumer surplus of cargo owners and ship operators. However, such a price discrimination policy will naturally be pursued by private-sector companies to maximise profits without deterring customers. Although intentions are different and implications for income distribution are different, the welfare effects remain the same regardless of whether the use of navigational aids and dredged channels are charged on what traffic can bear by the public or private owner. Therefore, the case provided by public goods characteristics of some port facilities for public ownership of these facilities is a weak one.

Externalities of port production

Externalities of port production are significant in many ways (Goss, 1990, pp.262-64). The arrival of ships and cargo handling frequently cause pollution of air, water and land, whether noise, bacterial, chemical, radiological and etc. Other examples include the congestion of port approaches and safety of people and property within the physical boundary of the port. This line of argument justifies the need for public control but not necessarily the need for public ownership, because a non-operational public port authority without owning any port assets can deal with the externalities mentioned. However, the ownership of some key port assets (e.g. the infrastructure) will enable the port authority to be in a stronger position to control external effects.

The relevance of wider benefits

In continental European countries, it is widely believed that the national and regional economy can derive considerable benefits from the existence and development of ports such as accessing foreign markets, increased international trade or trans-shipment trade, reduced transport costs, and attracting and stimulating industries which in turn creates jobs, as well as personal and business income. Ports are thus viewed not as discrete commercial entities, but as components of the regional infrastructure acting as catalysts for regional development. The benefits derived from the provision of port facilities and services are dispersed throughout the population and are not fully reflected in the accounts of private-sector companies or commercialised public ports. This idea has provoked numerous 'port impact studies' in the USA, using input-output analysis to compute multiple effects of port investment through the backward and forward linkages on the local economy.

While the argument of wider benefits may have substance in developing countries, where port and other transport infrastructure has frequently been a bottleneck to economic development, it is less persuasive in developed nations where there are is often excess capacity. The multiple effects can be generated by any sector, and there is no reason for believing why the magnitude of the benefits created by the port sector should be particularly larger. Moreover, port cities no longer enjoy the greater employment opportunities that ship calls used to generate.

The performance of public ports in the UK

There are clearly instances of market failure in the port sector. But this fact alone does not necessarily justify public control. Market failures should be weighed against government failures. The preference of private over public ownership stems largely from the conviction that public ownership is perforce synonymous with inefficiency. The consensus among economists is that public monitoring systems are generally less effective than their private counterparts. However, much analysis about public monitoring systems were concerned with public ownership at national level, little thought was devoted to other types of public ownership. This point is particularly relevant to the port sector where public ports are held in the trust sector, the local authority sector as well as the nationalized sector. In what follows the managerial incentive structures in the context of British ports will be considered. We shall also examine evidence on whether public ownership has led to poor port performance in the industry.

Port ownership and incentive structure

The incentive problems associated with the control of nationalized firms are well-known (Vickers and Yarrow, 1989, pp.7-44). Viewed from the perspective of the principal-agent theory, the most evident feature of public ownership is that the principals (the general voting public as the ultimate principal and the ministers as the intermediate principal) do not typically seek to maximise profits and the agents (the management) are not typically threatened by take-over and bankruptcy. Moreover, while the principal-agent relationship in the case of private enterprises (between the shareholders and the management) is fairly direct, the public monitoring hierarchy involve multiple levels of the principal-agent relationship, including voters and elected politicians, elected politicians and civil servants, civil servants and the management. Since imperfections are exhibited at each level, the public monitoring system is vulnerable to goal displacement, excessive government intervention, and bureaucratic inefficiency.

The line of argument is not entirely relevant to municipal ports and trust ports. While the ownership of nationalized firms is in principle dispersed over the whole country, the ownership of municipal ports is basically restricted to the local community. Clearly the local community is likely to have greater control via the local authority over the management of municipal ports. The delegation of administrative power from the national government to local authorities may also alleviate the problem of information asymmetry. In general local authorities tend to know more about the circumstances and performance of port management. This make it easier for local authorities to design and enforce incentive schemes to ensure that ports be run in the interest of the community. The monitoring of municipal ports may involve fewer levels of bureaucratic hierarchy. In some ports, management is exercised directly by a department of the local authority. In others managing directors are members of local councils. Thus the gap between local government and port management is narrower. In consequence port management is likely to suffer less from the inefficiency of red tape and respond to market conditions more promptly and adequately.

In contrast to nationalized ports, trust ports are independent and free from political pressure. No one is entitled to intervene as long as trust ports act properly in accordance with statutory objectives laid down by Parliament. As a result, trust ports enjoy almost the same degree of managerial freedom as private ports, and suffer little from government intervention and the inefficiency of bureaucracy. Another feature of trust ports are their financial independence, which provides valuable managerial incentives to cost efficiency. Thus the deficiencies of public monitoring systems can be largely reduced in the case of trust ports and municipal ports. On the other hand, the capital market for corporate control is also imperfect. Both theoretical analysis and empirical evidence suggest the significant weakness of shareholders' control and the threat of take-over. Managements of private ports may well have a great deal of discretion to pursue non-profit objectives. On balance, it is not clear why monitoring systems for trust ports and municipal ports should be less effective than those for private ports. The managerial incentive structures are determined by a complex set of factors that include not only the types of ownership, but also the nature of product market, and so on (Vickers and Yarrow, 1989, p.44). It is well accepted that competition is more important than ownership for both allocative and productive efficiency. However, inter-port competition existed before the advent of privatization. As argued above, the act of port privatization has not enhanced, and may have even reduced, the prospect of competition.

The relative performance of public and private ports

Table 1 reports productive efficiency scores of 13 major British ports. The efficiency scores are measured relative to a frontier production function.[5] The relative efficiency scores indicate which port obtain the highest level of output from a given set of inputs. [6] Two different approaches are used to compute the efficiency scores. One uses mathematical programming techniques, the other employs econometric techniques. The advantage of the first approach is that no explicit functional form needs to be imposed on the data. However, it will over- or under-estimate the true extent of inefficiency when the data are contaminated with measurement errors and random shocks. The second approach can distinguish between inefficiency and exogenous influences beyond the control of firms, but it imposes explicit, and possibly overly restrictive, assumptions on technology and inefficiency distribution. Since the empirical analysis has important policy implications, it is appropriate that both approaches be used. In Table 1, the efficiency scores shown in the third column are annual averages of 1985 to 1990, with parametric measures in the first sub-column and non-parametric measures in the second sub-column. The 13 ports are ranked in terms of the parametric measure. The ownership status of each port in this period is indicated in the second column.

Table 1
Productive efficiency of major British ports 1985-90

Ports	Ownership	Parametric Measure[a]	Non-parametric Measure[b]
ABP	Private	0.94	0.85
Forth	Trust	0.91	0.92
Tees	Trust	0.91	0.88
Dover	Trust	0.90	0.90
London	Trust	0.90	0.97
Tyne	Trust	0.88	0.76
Milford Haven	Trust	0.88	0.65
Medway	Trust	0.88	0.65
Clyde	Trust	0.87	0.71
Felixstowe	Private	0.87	0.85
Liverpool	Private	0.86	0.83
Bristol	Municipal	0.75	0.55
Manchester	Private	0.72	0.59

Notes:
[a] Parametric estimates are calculated using the econometric technique.
[b] Non-parametric estimates are calculated using the mathematical programming technique.

The picture emerging from the Table reveals no clear-cut pattern of relative efficiency of public and private ports. By the parametric measure, ABP was the most efficient one, but all other private ports ranked behind trust ports. The non-parametric measure suggests wider efficiency differentials across ports and a different efficiency ranking, but again there is no evidence that public ports tended to be less efficient than private ports. It seems that the inter-port efficiency can be explained by locational differences rather than the diversity in the forms of port ownership. Among those at the bottom of the efficiency league table are mainly ports located on the West Coast of this country. This correlates to the changing pattern of the UK's international trade. Since the mid 1960s, the relative importance of short sea trade with EU countries has increased whereas the significance of links with the UK's traditional partners has declined. Unlike other industries, ports are unable to relocate to meet the geographical change of markets. In consequence, port business has become prosperous on the South and East Coasts but diminished on the West Coast. A possible explanation why ports like Bristol, Liverpool and Manchester appear less efficient is then that they are on "the wrong side" of this country.

Conclusion

Privatization in the UK port industry is perceived as a means of sharpening managerial incentives, increasing the ability of trust ports to diversify activities and widening access to sources of capital investment. However, port privatization offers little prospect for efficiency improvement. Public ports were already commercialized and they need not have had less emphasis on profits than their private counterparts. The UK port industry was a clear example that public ports need not be less efficient than private ports. There are a number of institutional arrangements that can be made to improve port performance whilst preserving the public ownership of the ports concerned. The feasible options to alleviate incentive problems associated with public monitoring systems include decentralising port administration, setting up autonomous port authorities and, most importantly, exposing port management to competition in the market place.

Competition is an overriding efficiency determinant. But port privatization had virtually nothing to do with competition. The opportunity to promote competition in the industry at the time of privatizing BTDB ports by dividing the largest port group into potentially competing parts was missed. No public policy measures were taken to guard against the real danger of anti-competitive port mergers and take-overs in privatising trust ports. The attitude of the UK Government to port privatization has not been in keeping with its declared pro-competitive intentions.

Other benefits from privatization may also be overstated. Under the Transport and Works Act 1992, the restriction on trust ports to diversify activities has been removed. It is then unnecessary to privatize ports for this purpose. Company status may facilitate a wider access to sources of capital for investment than is currently available to trust ports. However, according to a recent study (Turnbull and Weston, 1991, 2, p.10), only less than 2% of port operators considered port status as a constraint on their future investment plans. Therefore, it is hard to avoid the impression that privatization in the industry was about the transfer to private hands of valuable port assets - terminals, cargo handling equipment, warehouses, and so on.

Privatization in the port industry would probably be more advantageous if the provision of cargo-handling and other services and perhaps the superstructure was left to the private sector through contractual arrangements while the provision of the infrastructure is retained under the control of a public port authority. In other words privatization would implement the landlord concept rather than take the comprehensive form currently adopted. The case for such an option of port privatization is considerable. Cargo handling and other related services are normal commercial activities and presumably best carried out by private undertakings. Meanwhile one cannot deny some port activities clearly concern public interests (e.g. control of pollution, safety of people and property, coordinating and planning development for individual ports if not for the port system of the whole country) and is best performed by impartial service which can only be expected from public bodies. Such an arrangement would divide the domain of the private and the public sector in a sensible way and enable the benefits from the working of market forces to be maximized at no expense to the public interest.

More importantly, it has been emphasized that a particularly important role that such a public port authority with landlord functions can play is to promote port competition and hence efficiency. The existence of public ownership cannot only prevent unfavourable industrial concentration and hence maintain competition *between* ports, but also can promote competition *within* port. One of the immediate effects of the abolition of the dock labour scheme is the increased competition within port. But given that technology is the long run determinant of market structure and economies of scale provided by modern port technology, intra-port competition will probably diminish in the long run. When the number of stevedoring companies is not sufficient to ensure effective competition, a public port authority as a regulator is then necessary to prevent anti-competitive behaviour (e.g. price fixing agreement). Moreover a public port authority performing landlord functions can potentially act as a franchise regulator to create potential competition.

Notes

1. There are 112 British ports recognized by Her Majesty's Customs for statistical purposes.
2. Whatever method is used to choose the major seaports of the UK, based on whatever lower limit is chosen, some large ports will fall just below a line rigidly drawn. See Bird (1963, p.21).

3. Under the Transport and Works Act 1993 restrictions on the right of trust ports to diversify their activities was removed.
4. Some arguments advanced in this section draw heavily on Goss (1983 and 1990).
5. Farrell (1957) proposed a computational framework to measure productive efficiency relative to a frontier production function. The textbook definition of a production function holds that it gives the maximum possible output that can be produced from a given quantity of a set of inputs. The word "frontier" may meaningfully be applied in this case because the function sets limit to the range of possible observations. One may observe points below the production frontier but no points can lie above it. A one-sided departure from the frontier is an evidence of inefficiency for a firm concerned. Following Farrell, a number of frontier models and efficiency estimating techniques have been developed by frontier researchers and have gained increasingly wide application for private and public policy analysis purposes. See Forsund, Lovell and Schmidt (1980) and Bauer (1990) for reviews of developments of frontier techniques.
6. The data were gathered from annual reports and financial accounts of selected British ports. Given the data available one output and two input (labour and capital) variables are identified. Output is measured by turnover, labour by total staff costs and capital by netbook-value of fixed capital assets.

References

Bauer, P.(1990), "Recent developments in the econometric estimation of frontiers", *Journal of Econometrics*, Vol.46.

Bennathan, E. & Walters, A. (1979) *Port Pricing and Investment Policy for Developing Countries*, published for World Bank, Oxford University Press, Oxford.

Bird, J. (1963), *The Major Seaports of the United Kingdom*, Hutchinson, London.

Farrell, M. (1957), 'The measurement of productive efficiency', *Journal of the Royal Statistical Society,* 120, Part III.

Forsund, F., Lovell, C. & Schmidt P.(1980), "A survey of frontier production functions and their relationship to efficiency measurement", *Journal of Econometrics*, Vol.13.

Gilman, S. (1980), "Editorial: A critique for the super-port idea", *Maritime Policy and Management*, Vol.7, No.2.

Goss, R. (1983), "Policies for seaports", Lecture given to the Chartered

Institute of Transport, London, 10 November.

Goss, R. (1987), "Port authorities in Australia", Occasional paper 84, Federal Bureau of Transport Economics, Australian Government Publishing Service.

Goss, R. (1990), "Economic policies and seaports: 3, Are port authorities necessary?", *Maritime Policy and Management*, Vol.17, No.3.

Liu, Z. (1992), *Port Ownership and Productive Efficiency*, Unpublished PhD dissertation, Queen Mary and Westfield College, University of London.

Thomas, B. (1981), "The changing structure of the UK port industry and its impact on stevedoring costs", *Maritime Policy and Management*, vol.13, No.3.

Turnbull, P.(1991), "The docks after deregulation", *Maritime Policy and Management*, vol.18, No.1.

Turnbull, P. and Weston (1991), "Continuity and change in the British port transport industry: a study of the ports since the national dock labour scheme", Working Paper, Cardiff Business School, University of Wales.

Rochdale Report (1962), *Report of the committee of Enquiry into the Major Ports of Great Britain*, Cmnd 1824, HMSO; London.

Vickers, J. and Yarrow G. (1989), *Privatization: An Economic Analysis*, MIT Press, Massachusetts.

Zhuang, J. (1988), "A study of ownership and management of British ports", Working Paper, Humberside College of Higher Education.

Index

A.U.C. (Air Transport Users' Council)   50, 51, 57, 58
Aberdeen   169, 171
Adam Smith Institute, The   78, 79, 80, 81, 82
Addison, P.   17, 23
Aeritalia   30
Africa   113
Air Corporation, The   166
Air France   32
Aitchison, C.   36, 37
Alitalia   30
Allied Continental Intermodal (ACI)   135
America   26
American Airlines   43
Amsterdam   120
Amtrack   134
"Anarchy, State and Utopia"   28
Arab-Israeli War, 1973   20
Armitage Report 1980, The   149
Ashfield, Lord   18
Asia, South East   26
Associated British Ports (ABP)   35, 167, 178
Astrop, A.   89
Austrian   100
  School of Economics   5
Automobile Association, The (AA)   122
Avon   104
Aylesbury   97, 111

BBC2   155
Bacon   27, 37
Badgerline   94, 113
Bagwell, P.   18, 19, 20, 23
Baker   98
Balcombe, R.   89
Balfour   15
Balladur, Edouard   32
Bank of England, The   166

Barking Line 110
Barvarian Christian Social Union, The 34
Beeching 111
Beeching Report, The 110
Beesley 80
Belgium 100, 107, 136
Bell, P. 8, 10
Benelux 106, 138
Bennathan, E. 170
Berechman, J. 115
Berkshire 112
Berkshire County Council 104, 105
Berlin 102
Bianchi, P. 30, 31, 37
Biffen, John 22
Birch, A. 37
Birmingham 14, 15, 100, 105
Bishop's Stortford Ticketholders' Association, The 55
Blackpool 100
Broom, P. 42, 43, 58
Board of Trade 14, 15
BOC Distribution 154, 158
Bonavia 97
Booth, A. 23
Bordeaux 138
Boston 166, 168
Boucek, F. 32, 37
Bradford 100, 110
Bradford Interchange, the 112
Bristol 166, 168, 171
Bristol Council 168
"Britain's Transport at Britain's Service" (1938) 18
British Airways 18, 35
British Electric Traction 109
Bristol Overseas Airway Corporation, The 18
British Rail (B.R.) 134
British Rail Passengers' Charter, The 44
British Road Federation, The (BRF) 55, 107, 122, 144, 153
British Transport Act 1947 19
British Transport Commission, The (BTC) 19, 109, 110, 166
British Transport Docks Board (BTDB) 166, 167, 168, 171, 179
British Waterways Board (BWB) 166

Brown, R. 12, 23
Brussels 100, 102
Buchanan, C. (Sir) 80, 101
Buchanan Report 3
"Bundling" Practices 93
"Bureaucracy : Servant or Master?" 83
"Bureacracy and Representative Government"(1971) 83
Burke, Edmund 29
Burton 112
Bury 110
Bus and Coach Buyer, The 115
Bus and Coach Council, The 115
"Bus Industry Monitor 1992" 91
"Bus Strategy for London, A" 54
"Bus Wars" 94
Buses - Technical Evolution 97
Bushell, C. 117, 127
Butcher, H. 65
"Butskellism" 20
- Conservatism 22
Byrne, T. 13, 23, 69

CNC 131, 132
CSX 135
Callaghan 20
Caldaire 113
Cambridge 103, 110
Canada 171
Capitalcard 118
"Care in the Air" 51
Cars 106
Carter, S. 33, 38, 42
Cartledge, J. 44, 49, 58
Cassese S. and Della Sala 30, 37
Castle, Barbara 111
"Cease and Desist" Order 1, 9
Central Electricity Board 16
Central Policy Review Staff, The 78
Central Transport Committee, The 18
Central Transport Consultative Committee, The (CTCC) 52, 53, 54, 58
Centre for Policy Studies, The 78
Chadwick, E. 13

"The Challenge of Socialism" (1975) 20
Chamberlain, N. 14, 15, 18
Channel Tunnel, The 35, 102, 123, 134, 135, 139, 141, 150, 155, 159
Chartered Institute of Transport, The 122
Cheek, C. 90
Chicargo School 29
- Economics 29
Chirac, J. 32
"Choice and Competition in National and International Transport" 6
Christian Democrats 30, 32
Christie 32, 39
Ciampi, C.A. 31
Citizen's Charter, The 44
City of London, The 105
City Police, London, The 105
Civil Aeronautics Board, The 42
Civil Aviation Authority, The (C.A.A.) 50
Clarke, K. 155
Cliff, J. 18
Cloke, P. 8, 10
Clyde 165, 168
Clydeside 67
Colchester 115
Colgan, F. 45, 58
Collectivism 12, 15
Collectivist Tendencies 11
Colonial Secretary 15
Cologne 100, 105, 120
Combined Transport Ltd. (C.T.L.) 135
Combined Transport Policies 132
Confederation of British Industry, The (CBI) 147
Conservative Election Manifesto, The 53
Conservative Government, The 8, 9, 18
Conservative Manifesto 1992, The 44
Conservative Party 17
Conservative Party's Economic Reconstruction Group 22
Conservatism - "New Right" 78
"Constitutuion of Liberty, The" 29
Consumer Bill of Rights, The President's 42
Consumer Movement, The 40
Consumer Policy Review, The 43, 58
Consumers' Association, The 43, 48

Consumers 44
- Problems 44
- Charters 44
Consumerism - Political Agenda 44
Contestable Market Theory 6
Contractualization 11
Conventional Tramways 99
Costs and Scale of Bus Services 80
County Based Travel Concession Schemes 93
Coventry 105
Crawley 106
Cross City, Birmingham 112
Crossrail, London 102, 117,
Crowther, G. 3
CTCC - Annual Report 1993 53
Cumulative Nationalism 17
Cycling 102

Daily Telegraph, The 111
Dartford 155
"Darwinist" Competition 94
Decay of Collectivism, The 19
Delors, J. 32
Dempsey, P. 6, 10
Denmark 107, 136
Dennis 114
Deptford 15
Department of Environment D.O.E. 104, 123, 124, 157
Department of Transport (D.O.T.) 54, 58, 90, 96, 103-4, 106, 108, 112, 114, 116, 122, 143-7
Department Du Rhone Passenger Transport Authority 117
De-Nationalization 8, 9
Deregulation 9, 11, 36
Deregulation Act 1978, The 42
Deregulation - U.S. Airline 43
De Gaulle 32
- Political Party 31
- Liberation Government 32
Deutsch Bundesbahn A.G. 120, 134
Devon 87
"Dirigism" 32
Disabled Persons Transport Advisory Committee DOT 115

"Distribution Business Guide to U.K. Distribution Parks 1993, The" 152
Docklands Light Railway 54
Dorthund 117
Dover 165, 169, 171
Dublin 137
Duisburg 117
Dundee 98, 169
Dunleay, P. 84
Durham Road 98
Dusseldorf 117
Dutch
 - Tramways 100

Eastern Europe 100
Edinburgh 105
Edwardian Era, The 100
Electric Lighting Act, 1888 15
Eltham 99
Eltis 27, 37
ENASA 30
"Energy for Tomorrow's World" 157
English Channel, The 138
Enis, B. 45, 58

Ensor, R. 15, 23
Equal Opportunities Commission
 - Staff 48
ESOPs 90
Essen 117
Esser, J. 35, 38
Essex 97
European Commission, The 6, 36, 50
European Community Transport Commissioner, The 161
European Conference of Ministers of Transport, The (ECMT) 107
European Market, The 25
European Parliament Transport Committee, The 161
European Union, The 25, 37
Evans, A. 77, 87, 94
Excel Logistics 154, 158
Exeter 111

"Fabian Essays" 15

Fabian Society 15
"Fair Competition" Initiative 130
Fairhead, R. 89, 94
Family Railcard, The 119
"Fares Fair" Policy, The 69
Farrington J. 77, 78
Federal Intervention 42
Felixstowe 111, 131, 166, 171
Financial Supporter Role 67
First Corporate Shipping 168
Ford (President) 41, 42
Forsyth, M. 78
Forth 165, 168, 171
Foulkes, D. 61
Fourastie J. 38
France 107
Franchising Authority, The 119
"Free Enterprise Urban Transportation" 79
Freeman, C. 26, 38
Free Market System, A. 43
Freiburg 102
Freight 107
Freightliner 131
"G.B. Transport Statistics 1985-6" 90
Garratt M. vi
Gateshead 104
General Motors 30
Germany 102
German Democratic Republic, The 100
German Rail Network, The 120
German Railways 117
German Towns 120
General Policy Co-Ordinator 71
Gialloreto L. 42, 43, 58
Gilman, S. 170
Gladstone 14
Glaister, S. 62, 80
Glasgow 99, 100
"Golden Triangle" 152, 154, 157
Goodwin, P. 121, 122
Goss, R. 171, 172, 173, 174
Gourvish, T. 109, 110

Grampian 113
Great Central Line 111
Great Depression, The 41
Greater London Council, The 68, 69, 71, 73, 116
Great Western 97
Greenleaf W.H. 11, 23
Grenoble 100
Grey Green 113
Gwilliam 80

Hall, P. 100
Haly 107
Hamburg 131
Hamilton, K. 45, 58
Hampton, W. 70
Hannover 100
Hansard 80, 84
Harbours Act, 1964, The 172
Harbours Act, 1966, The 167
Harlow 106
Hartlepool 165, 168, 171
Harwich 169
Hass-Klau 100
Hayek, F. 20, 23, 28, 29, 38
  "Spontaneous Order" Influence 81
Health and Safety Executive, The 53
Health of Towns Association 13
Heath 20, 22
Heathrow Airport 117, 120
Hepworth, N. 61, 68
Hereford and Worcester 87, 88
Hertfordshire 104, 112
Hey, K. v
Hibbs, J. 16, 62, 63, 79, 80, 81, 82, 83, 90, 109
Hibbs Report, The 78
Higginson, M. v, 100, 115, 127
Hirsch, J. 27, 38
Hobart Papers 80
Holland, S. 20, 23
Holmes, M. 22
House of Commons 84
House of Commons Transport Committee, The 54, 55, 58

Hoverspeed 35
Huddersfield Corporation, The 65
Hume, David 29
Ibanez, M. 85, 86, 90
Iberian Peninsular, The 138
Imperial Airways 18
Industrial Freedom League 16
Institute for Economic Affairs, The (IEA) 78, 79, 80, 81, 83
Institute for Transport Studies, The 80
Intercity 118
Intercontainer 131, 132
Intergovernmental Channel Tunnel Safety Commission, The 135
International Monetary Fund (IMF) 9
Internationalization 24
- of Capital 24
- of Markets 24
Ipswich 104, 105, 169
Irish Home Rule 15
Irwin, C. 98, 127
Ivanhoe Line, The 112

Jackson, A. 98, 127
James, L. 108, 127
Japan 171, 160
Japanese Shipping, 1993 160
Japanese Shipowners' Association, The 160
Jay, R. 15, 23
Jenkins, L. 45, 58
Joint Omnibus Committee, The (JOC) 64
Joint Select Committee on Municipal Trading 16
Joint Transport Committee, The (JTC) 64
Joseph, K. (Sir) 22
Joyce, J. 100
Jubilee Line, London Underground 102
"Just-in-Time" Opportunity Requirements 151, 152, 157

Kay, J. 9, 10
Keith-Lucas, B. 66
Kennedy, J.F. 42
Kent 136, 155
Kentish Town Line, London 110
Keynes, J.M. 29

Keynesian Consensus, The 20
- Demand Management Technique 26
- Welfarist Consensus 28
King, A. 27, 38
King's Cross Station, London 107
Kingsway, London 100
Klapper, C. 66
Kohl, H. 32
Kombiverkehr 131
Kondratieff Style 26
Kotler, P. 41, 57, 58
Krefeld 117

Labour Government 8, 9, 17
Labour Party, The 16, 17, 18
"Laender" 34
Laker 42, 43
Lancashire 112
Lancaster 88
Lancaster, G. 58
Law, I.G. 65
Lawson, N. 80
Le Havre 131
Leach, A. 46, 65
Ledwith, S. 45, 58
Leeds 65, 99, 100, 101, 105, 110, 138
Leicester 112
Lerwick 169
"Let Us Face the Future" 18
Leyland National 98
Liberal Party 15
Liberalization 9
Libertarian Tendencies 11
Libertarian Values 12
Liberty and Property League 16
Light Railways Act 1896, The 65, 73
Lijphart, A. 33, 38
Lille 117
Liu, Z. vi, 182
Liverpool 98, 100, 111, 136, 166, 171, 179
Liverpool Loop and Link, Liverpool 112
Liverpool Street Station, London 97 97

Locomotives 97
- Experimental Diesel 97
- Gas Turbine 97
Local Government 60
Local Government Act 1972, The 63, 68, 71
Local Government Act 1974, The 68
Local Government Act 1985, The 69
Local Government Board 14
Local Government (Scotland) Act 1973 72
London, Port of 165
London and Home Counties Advisory Committee, The (LHCAC) 73
London Buses 54
London Buses Ltd. 116
London County Council (LCC) 15, 16, 66
London Dial-a-Bus Users Association, The 55
London Gatwick Airport 119
London Guildhall University 1
London Midland Railway 97
London Passenger Transport Act 1933, The 17, 63, 73
London Passenger Transport Board, The (LPTB) 17, 18, 63, 68
London Regional Passengers Committee, The (LRPC) 54, 55, 58, 73
London Regional Transport (LRT) 69, 73
London Regional Transport Act 1984, The 69, 73
London Traffic Act 1924, The 73
London Transport - Unit for Disabled Passengers 98
London Transport 54, 55
London Transport Board (LTB) 68, 73
London Transport Executive, The (LTE) 68, 69, 71, 73
London Travelcard, The 116
London Underground 54
"Long Boom", The 25
Lothian 65
"Lotizazzione" 30
Loughlin, M. 61, 69, 76
Lufthansa, The 35
Maastricht, Treaty of 31
MacDonald, R. 18
Mackie, P. 72, 80
Maher, M. 38
Maidstone Transport 89
Maloney, W. 36, 38
Manchester 99, 110, 166, 179

- Metro Link, The 52
- Ship Canal, The 160

Mansfield 112
Marshall, A. 2, 10
Martin, J. 38
Marx 20
Massingham, L. 58
Mather, G. 71
Matutes, A. 161
McConville, J. v
McDonagh, O. 13, 23
McGregor 116
McLachlan, S. 109, 127
Medieval Alchemy 17
Medway 165, 168
"Megaearners" 43
Metro Action Committee on Public Violence Against Women and Children, The. (METRAC) 46, 47, 48
Metrolink Tramway 110
Metropolitan Board of Works 16
Metrolpolitan Council, The 46
Metropolitan County Council, The 68
Metropolitan County Councils 70, 71
- South Yorkshire 69
- West Midlands 69
- Merseyside 69

Metropolitan County Passenger Transport Authorities (MCPTA) 70
Metropolitan Police, The 62
Milan 136
Milan "Borsa", The 31
Milford Haven 165, 169
Milton Keynes 106, 110
Mill, J.S. 13, 14, 23
Minister of Transport, The 17, 68, 109
Ministry of War Transport, The 18
Mitchell, David 84
Modern Railways 108
Modernisation Plan, The 110
Money Programme 28.11.93 155
Monopolies and Mergers Commission, The (MMC) 113
Morris, B. 43, 58
Morrison, H. 16, 17, 18, 23

Morton, A. 155
M1, The 15, 153, 155
M20, The 155
M25, The 97, 144, 145, 153, 155
M3, The 155
M4, The 153, 155
M6, The 151, 153
M69, The 151
Motorway Congestion 153
Mueller, D. 82
Muhlheim 117
Mullard, M. 65
Muller, W. 30, 31, 38
Mulley, C. 62, 75
Munby 100
Munich 105
Municipal Corporations Act 1835 13
Municipal Socialism 16
"Municipal Year Book", The 10
NBC Companies 89, 113
Nader, R. 41, 42
Nantes 117
Nash 80
National Dock Labour Scheme 1967, The 167
National Federation of Bus Users, The 55
National Freight Corporation 109
National Government 18
National Health Service, The 44
"National Planning of Transport, The" (1932) 18
National Ports Council (UPC) 167, 172, 173
National Road Traffic Forecast, The 121
National Road Traffic Forecasts 147
National Travel Survey 1989-91, The 103
Nationalization Programme 17
National Socio-Political Bargain 33
Netherlands, The 104, 107
Network Southeast 54, 118
  - Commuters 43
Newcastle 98
New Bus Grant 99
"New Right", The 28
New Zealand 113

"Next Steps" Initiatives 78
Niskanen, W. 38, 83, 84
Non-Stackable Containers 131
Norfolk 87
North London Line, London, The 55, 110
Nottingham 65, 112
Novotrans 131
Nozick, R. 28
National Freight Corporation, The 35
Nixon, R. President 42
Neo-Conservatism 5
Nicoletti, G. 38
Neo-Liberal "New Right" 24
Nozick, R. 38
Nott, J. 22
O'Conner, J. 27, 38
OECD 2
Office of Fair Trading (OFT) 7, 113
Old Corruption 12
O-Licences 147, 148, 155
OPCS 115
OFGAS 36
OFTEL 36
OFWAT 36
Oldcroft 109, 110
"Open Skies" Regime, The 42
Operator - Local Public Road Passenger Transport 65
Ouse, River, The 103
"Own Account" Operations 109
Oxford 97, 103, 110, 111
Oxford Reference Dictionary 40
Oxley, H. 35, 38
Pacific Rim, The 25
Pack, M. 23
Paddington Station, London 107
Paris 97, 102
"Passengers' Guide to Planning and Using Air Travel" 51
Passenger Transport Authorities 68, 71, 111
Passenger Transport Company, A. (PTC) 64, 67, 70
Passenger Transport Executive, A. (PTE) 63, 111, 112, 117, 118, 120
People Express 42, 43
Pepino, J. 46

Perez, C. 26, 38
Pick, F. 18
Pickrell 43
Pierre, J. 34, 38
Piggy Back Services 131
Pirie, M. 24, 30, 35, 38
"Planning Policy Guidance for Transport" 104
Plymouth 105
Ponsonby, G. 79, 80
Poole 169
Port Authority
 - Status 165
Port Infrastructure 164
Port Ownership 164
Port Services 164
Port Superstructure 164
Ports Act 1991 168
Ports
 - nationalised 164
 - municipal 164
 - autonomous 164
 - landlord 165
 - service 165
 - tool 165
Port of London Authority 16
Portugal 100
Post Office, The 44
Practical Monopolies 14
Premium Priced Fuel 156
Preston, L. 43, 58, 88
Preston 88
"Principles of Political Economy" 13
Private Enterprise 13
Privatisation 9, 11
"Problem of Environment and Transport, The" 161
Progressive Cause 16
Protected Expenditure Level, The (PEL) 69
Proudmutual 113
"Public Choice 2" 82
Public Choice Theory, The 82, 83, 84, 88, 89, 92, 94
Public Health 13
Public Health Act, 1875, The 62

"Public Operation of Transport, The" 18
Public Sector Borrowing Requirement, The PSBR 144
Rail Regulator, The 53, 134
Railtrack 53
Rail Users' Consultative Committees (RUCCs) 52
Railway Development Society, The 55
Railway Rates Tribunal, The 73
Railways Act 1993, 118, 122
Railways Bill 1933, The 52
Ramsgate 166
Ratcliffe 106
Reagan, R. 29
RER, The 120
RENFE 131
Reed Business 148
Regent Street, London 105
"Regulation, Subsidy and Cross Subsidy - A Critique" 80
Regulator, Public Passenger Transport 61
Request Stop Programme, A. 48
Reregulaion 36
Reseau Express Regional 97
"Reservicing Britain" 78
Rhein-Ruhr Structure 117
Richards 116
Richardson, J. 36, 38
Renault 32
Richardson, S. 42, 49, 58
Ridley, N. 78, 80, 83, 84, 85, 91
Rifkind, M. 168
"Right Approach to the Economy, The" (1979) 22
Rise of Collectivism, The 12
"Road to Serfdom, The" 20, 29
Road Traffic Act, 1930, The 62, 66, 73
"Road Traffic Statistics GB" 146
Robbins 98
Robertson 97
Robin Hood Line 112
Robson, W. 62, 65
Rochdale Committee, The 167, 172
Rochdale Report, The 167
"Rolling Motorways" 131
Rose, R. 27, 38

Roth, G. 79, 81, 82, 90
Rotterdam 131
Ruhr, The 120
Rutherford, B. 45, 58
S.Bahnen, The 120
SNCF, the 120, 134
Safe Routes for Schools Campaign, The 103
Safety and Security Dept., The 48
Safeway 151
Sainsbury 151
Salisbury, Lord 15
Salisbury 97
Salzburg 105
"Sanitary Report" 1842 13
Shaw, S.
Savage, C. 7, 8, 10
Scandinavia 100
Scarborough 46, 48
 - Women's Centre 48
 - Women's Action Network 48
Scotland 67
Scottish and Southern Railways 97
SEAT 30
Sealand 135
Sealink ferries 35
Seaforth Dock 135-6
Secretary of State for Transport, The 74, 165
Settle and Carlisle Line, The 55
Shaw, S. 35, 37-8, 51, 55-56, 59
Sheffield 99, 100
Sheldrake, J. v, 13, 18, 23
Shenfield 97
Shepherd, A. 79
Skinner, A. 13, 23
Skipton 110
Skytrain 42
Smith, Adam 12, 170
Socialism, Establishment of 15
"Socialization and Transport" 16
"Societal and Political Motivation" - Public Choice 82
Societe Lyonnaise des Transports en Commun (TCL) 117
Sommerfield, V. 98

Southampton Institute of Higher Education, The (SIHE) 86, 90, 92, 93
Southend Rail Travellers Association, The 55
Soviet Union 12
Spain 107
Speed Limits 154
Speedlink 108
Stagecoach 94, 113
Stanley, P. 77, 92
Starkie, D. 106
Stephens, J. 34, 38
Stevenage 106
Stock Exchange, The 113
Stockholm 102
Stockton 88
Strathclyde 112
Stuttgart 100, 105
Suffolk - County Council 104, 105
Sunderland 99
Sustrans 104
Switzerland 100, 122

Taff-Ely 89
"Tangentopoli" 31
Taylor, H. 14
Tees 165, 168, 171
Tesco 151
Thameslink 118
Thatcher, M. 3, 11, 12, 22, 24, 29, 34, 78, 80
"Think Tanks" 78
"This Common Inheritance" 148
Thomas, B. 166
Thompson, G. 36, 39
Thomson, J. 4, 10
Tilbury 168
TNT Express 154, 158
Town Police Clauses Acts, The
 - 1847 and 1889 - 62
Toronto
 - Police Force, The 46
 - Transit Commission, The 45-49, 59
Toulouse 117
Trades Union Congress (TUC) 17, 18

Transport Act, The
- 1947 64, 73, 108, 109, 121, 166
- 1953 109
- 1962 68, 73, 108, 166
- 1968 63, 64, 68, 71, 111, 121
- 1978 72
- 1980 73
- 1981 167
- 1983 69
- 1985 64, 67, 70, 72, 77, 78, 79, 91, 92, 94, 111, 112, 114

Transport and Works Act 1992, The 74, 166, 179
Transport (London) Act, The
- 1969 68, 71
- 1984 116

Transport 2000 55
Transport Advisory Service, The 91
Transport Development Group 154
"Transport for Passengers" 79
"Transport Policy" 79
"Transport Reviews" 80
"Transport Statistics" 144
"Transport Statistics G.B." 143, 145
Transport Supplementary Grant, The 35
Transport Tribunal, The 73
Transport Users' Consultative Committees (TUCCs) 51-4
"Transport without Politics?" 79
Trade Barriers 25
Traffic Commissioners, The 66, 73
"Traffic in Towns" 101
Trafford Park 160
Tramways Act 1870, The 62, 64, 65, 72
Tramway
- Electrification 63
- Schemes 62
- Ownership 16

Trans-European Road Network, The 111
Transfracht 131
Travel "Hotlines" 93
Treasury, H.M. 35, 38
Treaty of Rome, The 37
"Treuhandanstalt", The 32
Tsoukalis, L. 36, 37, 39

Turnbull, P. 169, 167, 179
Turnpike Trusts 13
Tyler, N. 114
Tyne 165, 169, 171
Tyneside 98
Tyne and Wear Metro, The 52
U.K., The 107
"U.K. Strategy for Sustainable Development" 157
U.S. Institute for Environmental Action, The 79
User Bodies 49
User Campaigns 45
Underground Combine, The 18
Union International Rail Route, The 131
United Vehicle Workers' Union 18
United States
 - Airlines 6
 - Privatization 9
 - Port Authorities 171
University of Central England 115
University of Leeds 80
Utrecht 105

Verkehrsverbund 112
Vickers, J. 29, 30, 176-7
Victoria Coach Station 54
Vietnam - Disabled War Veterans 45
Vipond, P. 36, 39
"Voice for the Passenger, A" 53
Volkswagen 30
Waller, P. 13, 23
Walking 104
Walters, A.A. 80
Walters, A. (and Bennatham) 170
Waterloo, London (and Exeter Line) 111
Waterloo Bridge, London 103
"The Wealth of Nations" 12
Webb, P. v, 31, 35, 38, 39
Webb, S. 15, 16
Webster, P. 32, 39
Wekerle, G. 45, 46, 58
West Germany 107
West Yorkshire 112

West Yorkshire PTE 65
Westland Helicopter Corpn., The 34
Westminster City Council 105
Weston 167, 179
Westway Motorway, London 101
"Wheels Within Cities" 79
"Which?" Magazine 43
White, P. 106, 114
White Paper (1992) "New Opportunities for the Railways" 53
White Paper (1992) - EC (Transport) 156, 160, 161
White Paper "This Common Inheritance" 148
White Paper, Buses 80-84, 87, 90
Whitehall 17
Wilson, H. 21
"Winter of Discontent", The 22
Wright, V. 29, 30, 39
Women - Personal Safety - Transport 45
"Women in Organisations" 45
Wootton Jeffereys Consultants Ltd. 115
World War I 16, 62
World War II 17, 68, 96, 101, 105-6
World Bank, The 80
World Energy Council, The 157
Wuppertal 117

Yarrow 176, 177
Yarwood, D. 45, 58
York 103
York University 46
Yearsley, I. 100

West Yorkshire PTE, 85
Westland Helicopter Group, The, 27
Westminster City Council, 105
Weston, 167, 179
Westway Motorway, London, 108
Wheels Within Cities, 79
Which?, Magazine, 42
Whitelaw, P., 170, 184
White Paper (1994) "New Opportunities for the Railways", 53
White Paper (1997) "PTE Transport", 146, 160, 181
White Paper "The Common Inheritance", 125
White Paper, Roads, 80-84, 89, 90
Whitford, 17
Wilson, H., 21
Windsor, Dieppe, car ferry, 72
Wirral, 7
Women – Passenger Safety – Transport, 48
Women in Organisation, 48
Women in Scottish Transport Ltd, 115
World War I, 61-62
World War II, 17, 66, 98, 101, 143-6
World Bank, The, 90
Wind Energy Council, 179, 187
Wuppertal, 112

Yarrow Ltd, 171
Yarwood, D., 18-19
York, 163
York University, 46
Yorkley, T., 110